Religion and the Making o

M000314819

Religious ideas and actors have shaped Asian cultural practices for millennia and have played a decisive role in charting the course of its history. In this engaging and informative book, Thomas David DuBois sets out to explain how religion has influenced the political, social, and economic transformation of Asia from the fourteenth century to the present. Crossing a broad terrain from Tokyo to Tibet, the book highlights long-term trends and key moments, such as the expulsion of Catholic missionaries from Japan, or the Taiping Rebellion in China, when religion dramatically transformed the political fate of a nation. Contemporary chapters reflect on the wartime deification of the Japanese emperor, Marxism as religion, the persecution of the Dalai Lama, and the fate of Asian religion in a globalized world.

THOMAS DAVID DUBOIS is Associate Professor of History at the National University of Singapore. He is the author of *Sacred Village: Social Change and Religious Life in Rural North China* (2005) and the editor of *Casting Faiths: Imperialism and the Transformation of Religion in East and Southeast Asia* (2009).

New Approaches to Asian History

This dynamic new series will publish books on the milestones in Asian history, those that have come to define particular periods or mark turning points in the political, cultural, and social evolution of the region. The books in this series are intended as introductions for students to be used in the classroom. They are written by scholars whose credentials are well established in their particular fields and who have, in many cases, taught the subject across a number of years.

Books in the Series

Judith M. Brown, *Global South Asians: Introducing the Modern Diaspora* (2006)

Diana Lary, *China's Republic* (2007)

Peter A. Lorge, *The Asian Military Revolution: From Gunpowder to the Bomb* (2008)

Ian Talbot and Gurharpal Singh, *The Partition of India* (2009)

Stephen F. Dale, *The Muslim Empires of the Ottomans, Safavids, and Mughals* (2010)

Diana Lary, *The Chinese People at War: Human Suffering and Social Transformation, 1937–1945* (2010)

Sunil Amrith, *Migration and Diaspora in Modern Asia* (2011)

Religion and the Making of Modern East Asia

Thomas David DuBois

National University of Singapore

CAMBRIDGE
UNIVERSITY PRESS

CAMBRIDGE UNIVERSITY PRESS
Cambridge, New York, Melbourne, Madrid, Cape Town,
Singapore, São Paulo, Delhi, Mexico City

Cambridge University Press
32 Avenue of the Americas, New York, NY 10013-2473, USA

www.cambridge.org
Information on this title: www.cambridge.org/9781107400405

First published 2011
Reprinted 2012

A catalog record for this publication is available from the British Library.

Library of Congress Cataloging in Publication Data

DuBois, Thomas David, 1969–
  Religion and the making of modern east Asia / Thomas David DuBois.
    p. cm. – (New approaches to Asian history ; 8)
  Includes bibliographical references and index.
  ISBN 978-1-107-00809-0 (hardback) – ISBN 978-1-107-40040-5 (paperback)
  1. Japan – Religion. 2. Buddhism – Japan – History. 3. China – Religion.
  4. Confucianism – China – History. I. Title.
  BL2202.3.D83 2011
  200.951–dc22   2010040091

ISBN 978-1-107-00809-0 Hardback
ISBN 978-1-107-40040-5 Paperback

Contents

List of Boxes, Figures, and Maps   *page* ix
Preface   xi

1 **In the beginning: Religion and history**   1

2 **Ming China: The fourteenth century's
   new world order**   15
   I.   Religious foundations of late imperial China   15
   II. The emperor monk: Zhu Yuanzhang and the
        new Confucian state   36

3 **The Buddha and the shōgun in
   sixteenth-century Japan**   53
   I.   Religious foundations of medieval Japan   53
   II. Burning monks: The assault on Buddhism   66

4 **Opportunities lost: The failure of
   Christianity, 1550–1750**   72
   I.   The Society of Jesus comes to Asia   72
   II. The roots of conflict and the long road home   84

5 **Buddhism: Incarnations and reincarnations**   94
   I.   Bodhisattvas and barbarians: Buddhism in
        Ming and Qing China   94
   II. The gilded cage: Funerary Buddhism during
        the Tokugawa   105
   III. Samurai and nothingness: Zen and the Japanese
        warrior elite   113

6 **Apocalypse now**   123
   I.   Why the world keeps ending   123
   II. The White Lotus: Six centuries of Chinese
        heresy, 1360–1860   131

7 **Out of the twilight: Religion and the late
   nineteenth century**   142
   I.   Fists of Justice and Harmony: Christian mission
        and the last stand of Chinese traditionalism   142
   II. Kill the Buddha! Shintō and the new
        traditionalism of Meiji Japan   151

8 **Into the abyss: Religion and the road to disaster
   during the early twentieth century**   161
   I.   Toward Confucian fascism: China searches for
        direction   161
   II. Spirit of the rising sun: Japanese religious
        militarism   179

9 **Brave new world: Religion in the reinvention of
   postwar Asia**   194
   I.   Opiate of the masses: Why Marxism opposes
        religion   194
   II. The people's faith: How religion survived
        China's socialist paradise   202
   III. The peace paradigm and search for meaning in
        Japan   215

10 **The globalization of Asian religion**   224

Glossary   231
Timeline of dynasties and major events   237
Suggestions for further reading   239
Index   245

Boxes, Figures, and Maps

Boxes

2.a. Confucian familial relations   *page* 20
2.b. Cosmic correlation   28
2.c. Ming mourning regulations   45
2.d. *Twenty Four Filial Examples*   48
4.a. *Deus Destroyed*   88
4.b. *Ex quo singulari*   91
5.a. Temples at Chengde   104
7.a. Two views of the Boxer siege   149
7.b. The imperial Rescript on Education   157
7.c. The Great Promulgation Campaign   158
8.a. Old and new deities in the Temple of the Empress of
      Heaven   174
8.b. The Fengtian shrine   186
8.c. Japanese shrines and temples in Manchuria   187
8.d. *Plane compertum*   192
9.a. Materialism and religion in the People's Republic   208
9.b. *Nakaya Yasuko v. Yasukuni Shrine*   222

Figures

1.1 Two views of the Virgin and Child   10
1.2 The transformation of Guanyin   12
2.1 *Taiji* and eight trigrams   27
2.2 Zhu Yuanzhang at middle age   42
2.3 Tears make the bamboo sprout   49
3.1 Shintō shrine in Kyoto   55
3.2 Great Buddha of Tōdaiji   60
3.3 Depiction of *honji suijaku*   62
3.4 Enryakuji, Mount Hiei   69

4.1	Statue of Francis Xavier	76
4.2	Jesuit scholar-missionaries	82
5.1	Buddhist cultural heritage	96
5.2	Qianlong as bodhisattva Manjušri	103
5.3	Puto Zongcheng temple, Chengde	104
5.4	Ten Oxherding Pictures	117
6.1	"Proletarians of the World Unite to Overthrow American Imperialism!"	129
6.2	The Heaven and Earth Teaching	134
6.3	Scenes of Chinese famine	137
7.1	Boxers in Tianjin	148
7.2	Foreign occupation of Beijing	150
8.1	Ah Q	171
8.2	Martial values in fascist propaganda	177
8.3	Sacred sites in Japanese Manchuria	188
9.1	"Pope with cross and pistol in his hands"	199
9.2	Propaganda cartoon from campaign against Yiguandao	206
9.3	The Japanese Shōwa emperor and General Douglas MacArthur	217
10.1	Chinese shrine to Malay datuk spirit	226

Maps

2.1	Chinese kingdoms circa 350 BC	19
3.1	Korea and Japan circa 525 AD	56
3.2	Feudal domains in late sixteenth-century Japan	67
4.1	New Catholic dioceses in Asia, sixteenth–seventeenth centuries	75
4.2	Southern Japan at the height of Christian influence	85
5.1	China and Central Asia during the Ming and Qing dynasties	102
6.1	Route of Taiping advance	140

Preface

Looking back over the incredible transformation of Asia during the past few centuries, it is easy to see only the big themes of political, military, and technological change and assume that religion was either a historical footnote, or else a relic that the modern world left behind. This book will show the many ways that religious organizations and conflicts, not to mention individual beliefs and convictions, shaped many of the big and small transformations of history, and how they continue to influence policy and society today.

I first taught the content of this book as an undergraduate course at the National University of Singapore, and I should begin by thanking my students for helping me to make connections between places and events that I would not have seen on my own. More than that, they helped me always to keep sight of how interesting this history is, not to mention how relevant it is to problems and events that continue to surface in the news.

I have many people to thank for bringing this book into the world. Marigold Acland at Cambridge University Press read the first proposal (and many subsequent ones) and encouraged me to discover the potential in my as-yet half-cooked ideas. A number of libraries, museums, and temples provided me with the pictures used in this book, often for free. I am especially grateful to Mr. Nitta Ichirō, of the Hōzenji temple in Nara, for providing me with the image of the Kasuga mandala that appears on the book's cover. Other friends came through with photos when I realized too late that most of my thousands of digital pictures of places mentioned in this book looked great on a computer screen but were not of sufficiently high resolution to use in print. A good many people have gone through the text, correcting mistakes, adding information, and making connections. I am very happy to acknowledge the kind assistance of Tim Amos, Ned Davis, David Ownby, and Judith Snodgrass, in addition to the anonymous readers arranged by Cambridge University Press. For a hundred other small kindnesses, I would like to thank Sheila Birch, Jack Meng-Tat Chia, Jack Fairey, Hu Wen, Ryoko

Nakano, Normah Osman, and Wang Luman. My sister Jennifer, who is a scientist rather than a historian, made herself wonderfully helpful by reading chapters from an outside perspective and purging my writing of the horrible jargon that helps academics like me disguise the fact that they don't always know what they are talking about. My other sister, Alicia, and my father, David, did absolutely nothing for this book but merit a mention for their residual awesomeness.

As always, Misako Suzuki is loveliest of all.

Note on names and transliterations

Most places and names are Romanized in standard form, with diacritics included. An exception is made for those that are known better in an older or dialect spelling, such as the city of Canton or the Chinese leader Chiang Kai-shek.

1 In the beginning: Religion and history

One morning early in 1551, a Spanish priest with Portuguese sponsors gazed out upon the great and ancient city of Kyoto. He had traveled from India to Japan to spread the Catholic faith, and to the capital in hope of receiving an audience with the emperor. We may never know why the priest was not granted his interview: was it the ridiculous cape that people said made him look like a flying bat, his ignorance of court protocol, or possibly just his horrible smell? But others were certainly happy to talk to him: access to the priests also meant access to lucrative trade routes, Western science, and, most importantly, European fire-arms. Before long, the missionaries had proven such a disruption that Japan would eventually ban Christianity and "seal the country," closing its door to nearly all foreigners for over two centuries.

Three centuries later, a few thousand people calling themselves God Worshippers gathered in a remote village in China's misty southern mountains to witness a solemn ceremony. That morning, Hong Xiuquan, a thirty-seven-year-old failed scholar who claimed to be the younger brother of Jesus Christ, was to be crowned monarch of the Heavenly Kingdom of Great Peace. Within four years, his kingdom covered nearly half of China. The financial cost of crushing its long-haired army dealt a deathblow to the mighty Qing Empire. The human cost was twenty million lives: more than twice the number killed on both sides of the First World War.

Nobody would think to write a history of the Western world without including religion. Even the most casual observer of Western history will know that the rise of Christianity radically transformed the Roman Empire, that the Protestant Reformation divided Europe for centuries, and that many of those who migrated to the American colonies came seeking religious freedom. For hundreds of years, Western art was de-voted largely to depicting religious themes. Many of the great political and social debates, including ones that remain current today, have their roots in religious ideals.

But is the same true outside the West? If someone wanted to convince you of the unchanging, essential nature of Asia, and in particular of the unbridgeable cultural gap between Asian and Western societies, religion might seem to be a good place to start. Images of Asian religion lay at the root of some of our more embarrassing racist stereotypes, but also of the seemingly endless stream of books about applying "ancient Asian wisdom" to our everyday lives. Back in the early 1990s, when Japan seemed economically unstoppable, popular authors wrote with great confidence about how the "way of the samurai" had entered the Japanese boardroom. In an earlier era, the argument went, samurai spirit had sent kamikaze fighter pilots on hopeless suicide runs against American warships. Now that same warrior ethos motivates mid-level businessmen to sacrifice their own personal comfort and independence in the name of the collective good. In either case, the view was that these were fundamentally unchanging values – as inextricably Japanese as sushi. Now in an era of Chinese ascendancy, we are likely to hear about the Dao of marketing, or how Sunzi's *Art of War* can help you overcome your fear of public speaking. Yet the basic assumption of these books remains the same – when Asian societies are boiled down to their essential elements, what remain are religion and religious ideas, and those ideas are fundamentally different from our own.

I disagree.

Religion is more than just ideas: it is ideas in action. Religion lives and breathes in human society. It gives people a way to structure their world, mark time, and express their deepest fears and desires. Even if the ideas are different, much about how religion behaves in society is universal. Without oversimplifying matters too much, it is safe to say that you can visit a small town religious festival almost anywhere in the world and find much that feels at least familiar: community leaders will sit in a place of honor, the publicly pious will raise their eyebrows at their neighbors, and, it seems, the main ritual will always be followed by a big banquet.

Keeping this in mind, it is perhaps no surprise that religion was as important to the history of Asia as it was in the West. In some cases, Western and Asian history even seem to run parallel to each other. Just as Christian clergy alternately advised and manipulated the crowned heads of Europe, so too did emperors in China and Japan contend with the intrigues of resident monks and priests. And just as England's Richard II longed to be rid of his "troublesome cleric," and Henry VIII had his momentous row with the papacy, so too did these monks and priests sometimes overestimate their welcome in the halls of power. In the second century BC, a full seventeen centuries before Henry began cutting off heads, Qin Shi Huang (259–210 BC), the first Chinese emperor (he of the terra cotta army), expressed his displeasure with the Confucian scholars in his court in a particularly direct and dramatic fashion. Famously, he had a large pit dug, asked the scholars to enter, and filled in the hole, thereby (or so he thought) ridding China of Confucianism forever. Governments both in the West and in Asia profoundly feared religious dissent among the common people. Just as many European states persecuted or denied rights to atheists, heretics, and religious nonconformists (not to mention Jews and Muslims), so too did Chinese law outlaw certain religious teachings, executing their leaders and banishing ordinary followers to the farthest borderlands. In the early 1600s, the government of Tokugawa Japan began scouring the countryside for Christians. It continued its search for nearly two centuries, ordering villages to turn over any they discovered hiding in their midst immediately.

These anecdotes are pieces in a much larger puzzle. There is, of course, a great deal more. Yet most of the big sweeping histories of Asia relegate religion to a small stage, focusing instead on themes such as modernization, political change, or the "clash of civilizations" between Asia and the West. When they mention religion at all, it is often as a footnote to particular events: the rise of a rebel leader who claimed to foresee the end of the world or a diplomatic crisis over the mistreatment of Christian missionaries. Yet religion is more than just a symptom or vehicle of other historical processes. Religious beliefs and aspirations shaped countless millions of ordinary lives over thousands of years. If for no other reason than this, it is worth taking the time to understand them. What this book will show is how religion also shaped the *big* themes of history – the economic, political, and military transformation of modern East Asia.

Our focus will primarily be on China and Japan. Other countries will necessarily find their way into the story – one can hardly understand why Christian missionaries came to Asia without first knowing what was happening in Europe – but the main story will focus on these two ancient and enduring cultures. You may wish to know why other regional actors, such as Korea and Vietnam, are not given the same attention. It is certainly not because they were unimportant. Korea was more than just a bridge between China and Japan; it also exerted a vital political and cultural influence of its own. And while no one who has visited the temples of Hanoi could mistake the cultural impact that China had on its southern neighbor, it is equally obvious that Vietnam adapted this influence into something uniquely its own. Of course, all of these perceptions are relative. For long periods of its history, Japan considered itself to be a cultural rival of China, but this rivalry was very one-sided. Until just over a century ago (very recent history, in Asian terms), China's cultural elites took little notice of their island neighbor and, if anything, thought of it as more like an irritating younger brother than a true competitor.

So why focus particularly on these two countries, and why view them together? Even if China was by far the larger and older civilization, Japan was also large, powerful, and distinct enough to be a cultural, military, and economic force in its own right, even before it began its spectacular rise in the late nineteenth century. China and Japan not only influenced each other, they also underwent many of the same processes and changes, albeit at different times. This is why the book begins with the fourteenth century in China and the sixteenth century in Japan, because these are the moments at which each country founded the long-lasting political dynasty that would fundamentally transform its political, social, and economic institutions. Similarly, although Catholic missionaries were active and influential in both countries, they arrived in Japan half a century before they first reached China and experienced very different challenges in each place. Often it is the differences that are the most interesting. Cultural elites in both China and Japan were drawn to Buddhism, but in China, these elites were Confucian scholars, while in Japan they were a hereditary warrior class, the samurai. During the mid-nineteenth century the two countries began to interact with each other more closely. By its end, both were striving for economic, military, and cultural dominance of East Asia. Religion became an important component of how these two competing poles saw themselves, and an important weapon in their struggle for influence. It still is.

But before we go any further, let us step back and consider just what we mean when we talk about "religion."

The modern concept of religion is Western in origin. If you look up the word *religion* in a Chinese dictionary, you will find it translated as *zongjiao*, which comes from the Japanese *shūkyō*.[1] But neither term is native to Asia: the Japanese word was actually translated from the German *Religionsübung*.[2] Of course, both Chinese and Japanese

---

[1] It may be helpful to know something about these languages. Although Chinese and Japanese are grammatically very different, they do share a significant amount of vocabulary, rather like the relationship between English and French. Shared words are written in identical Chinese characters, which are used by both languages (and formerly by Korean and Vietnamese, as well) but pronounced differently by each. The line that appears over *o* and *u* in some Japanese words means simply that the vowel is held for a slightly longer time.

[2] The Chinese term *zongjiao* did exist previously, but it had a more narrow meaning. Anthony C. Yu, *State and Religion in China* (Chicago: Open Court, 2005), 5–25.

already had words resembling religion before they decided to copy a German one, but the fact that someone felt that a new word was required suggests that the transformation of the idea was fairly fundamental. This is not simply a problem of terminology: some have argued that the Western concept of religion (for example, as scholars, governments, and human rights campaigners employ it) refers not merely to Christianity, but a particular *kind* of Christianity, the post-Enlightenment interpretation of faith as a personal dialogue with God. Thus when scholars try to compare religions (for example, by teaching a course in world religions), they are implicitly comparing other religions against a Christian standard, one that would consequently make non-Western religions look either incomplete or primitive.[3] Whatever we may think of these criticisms, they should at least provide a warning: before we attempt to examine the influence of religion on history, our first task should be to establish a more precise idea of just what we are to be talking about.

For most readers, the word *religion* instinctively calls to mind an ecclesiastic institution – a church. To avoid being unduly influenced by the Christian experience, we can define a church simply as any community that organizes around religion. By this definition, any church is both sacred and worldly. As a sacred institution, it will generally have a class of priests to serve as experts on matters of doctrine and ritual, but there are no set rules for what other roles they might play. In some traditions, these priests will also have a pastoral call to serve a community of lay faithful. In others, they will not. Sometimes holymen embark on a completely private quest for salvation, sharing a tradition of beliefs and practices with other specialists, but no other relationship to them. In others, they will be arranged into a formal hierarchy of authority. A religion with a strong hierarchy will often have a clear and unified theology, a doctrine, from which springs not only the existence of heresy, but also the possibility of religious schism on theological grounds. As a worldly institution, a church might have significant political and economic interests. Its representatives might find their way into government and exert considerable influence. Churches will

---

[3] See, for example, Talal Asad, *Genealogies of Religion: Discipline and Reasons of Power in Christianity and Islam* (Baltimore: Johns Hopkins University Press, 1993), and Tomoko Masuzawa, *The Invention of World Religions, or, How European Universalism Was Preserved in the Language of Pluralism* (Chicago: University of Chicago Press, 2005). For a variety of perspectives on the idea of religion in Asia, see the essays in Thomas David DuBois, ed., *Casting Faiths: Imperialism and the Transformation of Religion in East and Southeast Asia* (Basingstoke, England: Palgrave Macmillan, 2009).

often hold property, sometimes quite a lot of it, and their leadership will have to make decisions on how that wealth is disposed.[4]

Religion is also an intellectual tradition of teachings and beliefs, but what sort of ideas should a "real" religion include? If you approach the question from a Judeo-Christian perspective, you might expect that any religion is by definition theistic: that it has a concept of deities, angels, and other divine actors. If so, you would be disappointed. The distinction between religion and *philosophy*, somewhat arbitrary even in Western thought, makes even less sense in Asia. As we shall see (each of the major Chinese and Japanese religions are discussed in more detail in later chapters), many Asian religions are either agnostic or even atheistic, at least in their orthodox, scriptural form. The original texts of what would become Daoism say nothing about who lives in the spirit realm. When someone asked Confucius whether spirits exist, he responded that he had no idea, but that it is just as well to assume that they do.

The intellectual legacy of religion is larger and more expansive than scripture – but how *much* larger depends on the degree of authority wielded by its ecclesiastic institution. A religion that is highly decentralized may have no single authority responsible for deciding the fine points of theology. It may have a sacred text, but no mechanism for controlling how people interpret what they see in writing. But even when there is a strong church, belief is almost impossible to control. Leaving aside religious schisms and wars, any church will face an uphill battle in restraining the creativity and devotion of its own flock. A good example is the medieval Catholic Church, which at the time was about as tight an organization as one could hope to find. In many cases, the biggest problem the church faced was not pulling people in to Mass on Sundays. Just the opposite, it was reining in the excessive piety of the country folk, who became enthusiastically devoted to unauthorized local saints and unsubstantiated miracle tales.[5] The difficulty of controlling belief, of course, is that religion poses questions that are too

---

[4] This introduction follows the example of sociologists such as Joachim Wach, who pioneered the idea that religion and religious institutions follow predictable rules, across times and across cultures. Even if this approach might not satisfy historians, it is still an excellent way to understand the big picture. See his frequently reprinted classic, *Sociology of Religion*.

[5] This theme runs through a number of excellent studies of European history. See, for example, William A. Christian, *Visionaries: The Spanish Republic and the Reign of Christ* (Berkeley: University of California Press, 1996); David Blackbourn, *Marpingen: Apparitions of the Virgin Mary in Bismarckian Germany* (New York: Knopf, 1994); and David Warren Sabean, *Power in the Blood: Popular Culture and Village Discourse in Early Modern Germany* (Cambridge: Cambridge University Press, 1984).

important to ignore. Who inhabits the unseen world? Where did the world come from? When and how will it end? What constitutes moral transgression, and how far can I go before I will be punished? A church may answer these questions in its formal doctrine, but the believer will also answer them for himself, in his own heart and in his own way.

But does religion *create* history, or does it somehow follow along behind? Is it an agent of change, or merely a symptom? The answer is that it does and is both. Starting with politics, any sufficiently powerful ruler can, with a stroke of the pen (or brush, since we are in Asia), christen one creed as the state religion and have another outlawed as a vile and contemptible heresy. On the other hand, kings and presidents are people, too, and their decisions are themselves shaped by religious beliefs and ethics. Even if we live in too cynical an age to trust the religious sincerity of our politicians, the fact is that it does not matter whether they are speaking from the heart or simply to their political base. The effect is the same: religious fervor is an extremely potent political force. In the end, it does not make sense to ask whether events such as the Spanish Inquisition, the Islamic Revolution in Iran, or the support of the Christian Right for George W. Bush was more political or more religious in nature. They were fully and equally both.

Beyond politics, religion has always been serious business, financially speaking. Imagine that a national church is (for whatever reason) exempted from paying tax on its landholdings – this was in fact the case at different periods of history in much of Europe and Asia. Such an arrangement is, of course, very good news for the church, in more ways than one. Not only does the church now save money on its own tax payments, but nearby landholders will also discover that they can share the same benefits by placing their own lands under the church's name, as well. As a result, the church becomes a major landholder, perhaps *the* major landholder. This is exactly what happened in medieval China (especially the Tang dynasty, 618–907), a time when powerful Buddhist monasteries owned as much as a third of all arable land. These policies starved the dynasty for revenue, as well as for soldiers, since the tens of thousands of Buddhist monks were exempted from military service. Buddhism alone did not destroy the Tang dynasty, but later Chinese dynasties would remain acutely sensitive to the dangers of allowing religion ever again to become *imperium in imperio*.[6] This includes the modern Chinese state, which remains deeply cognizant of the lessons history has taught it, a fact that we in the West might do well to understand.

---

[6] Arthur F. Wright, *Buddhism in Chinese History* (Stanford, CA: Stanford University Press, 1959), 60, 83–5.

The two-way influence of religion and economics can be seen not only on property, but also on a variety of services. In medieval Europe, it was very common for wealthy gentry to will their lands to the church as a deathbed atonement for what had perhaps been a less than pious life. For similar reasons, they also made very significant donations to the poor. But these donations were not charity – they were an advance payment for prayers that the recipients would endeavor to say for the soul of their patron. This practice (what the historian A. N. Galpern called "a cult of the living in service of the dead") was more than just a quaint local custom – it was a significant engine of exchange between rich and poor. By 1482, as many as one-sixth of the twelve thousand residents of the French city of Reims may have relied on such donations for their livelihood.[7]

Under the right circumstances, an organized church could corner the market for ritual services. The key was usually an alliance with political power. Under the Tokugawa shogunate, the military government that ruled Japan from the seventeenth through the mid-nineteenth century, Buddhist monasteries acted as loyal agents of the state. They kept administrative records and served as a first line of defense against the rise of heresy (or, even worse, Christianity). In return, the monasteries received lavish state patronage, as well as a lucrative monopoly on religious services. For two and a half centuries, every Japanese, from the lowliest commoner to the imperial family, was required to register as a member of a Buddhist sect. When he died, he received a Buddhist funeral. And for every amulet, blessing, and ritual it provided, the monastery received a payment. Over two and a half centuries, this added up to colossal wealth.

Of course, wealth breeds power and corruption, and, over time, disaffection among the rank and file believers. Perhaps the most dramatic example of this is the corrosive effect that a monopoly on lucrative religious services had on the medieval Catholic Church. Abuses of this monopoly, such as the sale of indulgences, were the spark that ignited the Protestant Reformation. But even after the Church had curtailed its worst abuses, the specter of gilded papist corruption continued to haunt later Protestant groups, such as the English Puritans, who came to regard material simplicity as a cardinal virtue. In Japan, as we shall see, the uneven favor of the Tokugawa government ended by souring centuries of good relations between the priests of Buddhism and those of Shintō, the native religion. It also led to a popular tradition of belief

---

[7] A. N. Galpern, *The Religions of the People in Sixteenth Century Champagne* (Cambridge: Harvard University Press, 1976), 20.

in a higher teaching, one that the Buddha had revealed in secret only to the laity, not to the monks.

This final example leads us to what I would argue to be the most important interaction between religion and history – the power religion has to transform *ideas*. These are not just ideas about the divine realm, but about the human world as well. Ideas are the glue that holds a culture together over time. Individual governments, economic systems, and even religions themselves (in the sense of ecclesiastic institutions) may come and go, but this substrate of ideas remains and evolves. This is the real continuity of history. Consider two of the foundational ideas of Judeo-Christian tradition: the existence of free will and the individual soul. Look hard enough, and you can trace a great deal of Western cultural history to one or both of these beliefs. Humanism, democracy, natural rights, capitalism: each relies on a particular understanding (one that is so fundamental that it often does not need to be expressed) of individual human dignity. This includes even the right *not* to believe in God. The principle of religious freedom, itself a relatively new idea in most Western states, derives from a post-Reformation understanding of belief as a personal quest for God. (The medieval Catholic Church viewed matters very differently, hence its persecution of heresy.) The Reformation view was itself not new: its roots can be seen in biblical stories such as the conversion of Paul of Tarsus or the temptation of Jesus, each of whom made a choice to follow God. But to be significant, that choice had to be made freely and willingly.

The most graphic – in a literal sense – and immediate reflection of the interaction between religion and ideas is in art. The next time you find yourself in an art museum, take some time to marvel at the overwhelming transformation of European painting that took place between the eleventh and fourteenth centuries. Certain changes are obvious: techniques become more sophisticated; the figures develop depth and proper perspective; classical themes come to join religious ones. Yet even within staid Christian iconographic themes, such as paintings of the Virgin and Child, the evolution is striking. Earlier paintings such as the altarpiece shown in Figure 1.1A tend to depict both figures as radiant but distant, calmly staring directly at the viewer. These clearly are objects to be worshipped. In later ones, such as Figure 1.1B, the figures are equally holy but take the form of a much more accessible and familiar family. The focus shifts from the divinity of the figures, and instead to the affection of a mother for her child; they are quite naturally looking at each other, rather than staring at the viewer. The reason for the change is obvious. The first painting is meant to inspire devotion; the latter, affection for the Holy Family, and respect (and

Figure 1.1 Two views of the Virgin and Child. **A**. Italian (Latin Kingdom of Jerusalem), *Diptych with Madonna and Child and Crucifixion*, 1275/85, Mr. and Mrs. Martin A. Ryerson Collection, 1933.1035, The Art Institute of Chicago. Photography © The Art Institute of Chicago. **B**. Jacopo (Jacopo da Ponte) Bassano, Italian, c. 1510–92, *Virgin and Child with the Young Saint John the Baptist*, 1560/65, Oil on canvas, The Art Institute of Chicago. Photography © The Art Institute of Chicago.

possibly employment) for the artist. But that change would not have been possible without a new understanding of God, man, and the relationship between them.

Similar sorts of transformation can be seen in Chinese religious art. Buddhism, as many readers will know (and as we will discuss in more detail in the next chapter), is not native to East Asia. It comes from India, or more precisely, an Indian kingdom in what is now Nepal (an unremarkable nine-hour bus ride from Kathmandu). By the time it reached China, Buddhism had already spread up and down the Indian continent and throughout Central Asia, along the way incorporating artistic traditions from as far away as Greece. The Buddha who went to China was thus, in the words of one scholar, a "swart, half-naked Indian."[8] And for many centuries, he stayed that way. Eventually, however, China entered a period of introspection, losing interest in the Silk Road and the steady stream of foreign cultures that it had brought, and it was during this time that the Buddha began to look more and more Chinese.

Even more striking is the transformation of the deity known in China as Guanyin, and in Japan as Kannon. Guanyin is deeply beloved by Buddhist faithful throughout East Asia. Early Christian missionaries writing in English often referred to her as the Goddess of Mercy, sometimes likening her to the Virgin Mary. In China, Guanyin is usually depicted as a middle-aged woman with a kindly smile, wearing long white robes. Sometimes she is shown with numerous arms radiating out from behind her; these are a representation of her limitless mercy and power.

Originally, however, Guanyin appeared quite different. For one thing, she was a man. The first reference to this deity, here by his original name of Avalokiteśvara, presents him as a bit player in a very crowded scene: as one of hundreds of deities assembled in heaven to hear the preaching of the Buddha. Over time, he grew into an independent deity and arrived in China looking much as he had in India, as a richly clad young man, usually portrayed with the slight mustache shown in Figure 1.2A. In China, Avalokiteśvara adopted his Chinese name (*Guanyin* literally means the "hearer of sounds," referring to his desire to answer the prayers of the faithful) and occasionally appeared in feminine form. The real change to Guanyin occurred after the debacle with the Buddhist monasteries, a period when Buddhism was gradually banished from political life. During this time, Buddhism became increasingly associated with the private household, with mercy, and with women. As a result, Guanyin not only remained female, but further

---

[8] Wright, *Buddhism in Chinese History*, 98.

Figure 1.2 The transformation of Guanyin. **A**. This painting from tenth-century Dunhuang shows the deity Guanyin in
Central Asian style, including the telltale mustache. Freer Gallery
of Art, Smithsonian Institution, Washington, D.C.: Purchase
F1930.36.

transformed into the caring, matronly figure seen in Figure 1.2B. This
is the incarnation you are most likely to see today.[9]

This brief introduction has sought to explain to the reader why this
book was written, and what it hopes to accomplish. Before we continue,
a few points are worth repeating.

The first is that religion is a fundamental historical force. This is
probably the least controversial point, particularly to any student of
Western history. Every milestone in Western civilization, from the
decline of the Roman Empire to the American-led invasion of Iraq, was
somehow propelled, diverted, accelerated, or transformed by religion.

[9] Chün-fang Yü, *Kuan-yin: The Chinese Transformation of Avalokiteśvara* (New
York: Columbia University Press, 2000).

Figure 1.2 **B**. Guanyin rescuing sailors at sea. This image comes from a popular Chinese scripture that shows a more typically feminine looking Guanyin saving people from fire, snakes, and jail, not to mention hell. *Guanyin jiuku tu* [Illustrations of Guanyin saving from disaster], Wuxi, 1928.

The second is that religion and its impact are exceedingly diverse. Religion is larger than formal ecclesiastic institutions: it is also the ideas, beliefs, and organizations that exist outside any identifiable church. And while politics and statecraft may provide the most visible and dramatic examples of historical change, religion has in some way shaped every aspect of human society, from how we grow our food to how we spend our money.

The third is that Asian religions have historically interacted with society in a manner that is no less significant than those in the West. Assuming that most readers will be more familiar with Western history, this introduction has used events such as the Protestant Reformation to illustrate the diverse impact religion has had on states and ideas. But the same principles apply to Asian religions and Asian history. The point is not to establish Western history as a standard, but rather to demonstrate that certain phenomena are fundamental to human society and thus not unique to any one culture. Any church that has wealth and power will recognize the need to protect its status. The interaction of state and church always proves a mixed blessing for both. Religious ideals are beyond any church to dominate. Such principles have been demonstrated again and again over the course of Western history, and, as we will see, are equally true for Asia.

And with that, on to our story.

2   Ming China: The fourteenth century's new world order

I. Religious foundations of late imperial China

Religion in China is both singular and plural. For the great majority of Chinese people today, religion consists of a combination of three distinct traditions: Confucianism, Daoism, and Buddhism. Each of these traditions can be seen as its own intellectual and organizational entity, and this chapter will begin by presenting each one separately. In practice, few believers would think to choose one over the others. The idea of exclusive religious membership, that one should be a Buddhist or Daoist, but not both, simply does not apply. Even those believers who are particularly devoted to one teaching will often incorporate elements of the other two, sometimes without even recognizing them as such. The point is not that Chinese people are irreligious. Quite the contrary: the "three teachings," as they are called, are inseparable parts of a single system of beliefs, morals, and rituals that pervades Chinese life.

It was not always so. The three teachings evolved in relation to, and sometimes in conflict with, each other. The current state of equilibrium is relatively recent, at least by Chinese standards, meaning that it is less than a thousand years old. Before that time, the balance among the three teachings was much more fluid, and occasionally more violent, than what we see today.

Confucianism

Properly speaking, Confucianism is less a religion than a political philosophy, one that developed long before the birth of Confucius himself. Rather, the origins of Confucianism lay in a very *un*-Confucian kingdom known as Shang.

The Shang kingdom, which lasted from roughly 1600 to 1050 BC, is commonly regarded as the origin of Chinese civilization. Like many ancient civilizations, it grew up adjacent to a river, in this case, the silty banks of the Yellow River (Huang he). The Shang marked the leap from scattered Neolithic cultures to a large organized society. It was a rough contemporary of other ancient civilizations, such as the pharaonic kingdoms of ancient Egypt, and, like them, the Shang celebrated its new power by building big. The largest Shang cities were surrounded by packed earthen walls that would have required tens of thousands of laborers many years to build. The tombs of Shang kings, although nothing on the scale of the terra cotta armies that would guard the body of Qin Shi Huang, were still immense structures that descended tens of meters into the earth and were attended by the bodies of freshly sacrificed soldiers, musicians, and concubines. Shang armies, armed with horse-drawn chariots for the nobility and state-of-the-art bronze weapons for the infantry, one by one devoured most of their closest neighbors. Their kingdom soon occupied much of what is now northern China. The Shang kingdom was, in short, a superpower of its day: more organized, powerful, and ambitious than anything that part of the world had ever seen before.

What gave the Shang its edge was political sophistication, in particular the sort of political legitimacy held by Shang kings. For seven centuries, one single ruling house held power, and this house included not only living members, but dead ones as well. The power of Shang kings was based to no small degree on their ability to communicate with dead ancestors, of whom they asked questions about important matters of state such as war, harvests, sickness, and royal births. The way they did so was by carving a question into either a tortoise shell or the shoulder blade of a cow, which was then heated until it cracked. The shape of the fissure then provided a rough yes or no answer.

After their use, the bones were discarded and forgotten – that is, until the early 1900s, when a peasant digging a well uncovered a large cache of them. Seeing ancient bones with writing on them, he and his fellow villagers promptly called them "dragon bones" and pulverized them for sale as medicine. Luckily, this trade was soon put to a halt, and a bit more digging (this time by archaeologists) has since revealed thousands more. These bones record not only some of the earliest Chinese characters, a style of script that is called, not incidentally, "oracle bone writing" (*jia gu wen*), but also a remarkable record of politics and even daily life in ancient China. For example, the inscriptions on one single bone could record that a certain king wished to go to war with a neighboring state, asking, "will he be victorious?" Farther down, a note will indicate that the prognosis was positive or negative, and, later, a further indication whether the battle was indeed won or lost. Oracle inscriptions also asked about harvests, hunting, rainfall, the correct time to perform sacrifices. With enough of these bones (as well as other sources, such as inscribed bronze vessels), scholars have pieced together quite a good history of the kingdom, as well as its ideas of medicine, marriage, and the afterlife.[1]

The significance of all this is that the Shang kings ruled by virtue of good luck in a sort of spiritual lottery. For the most part, ordinary people did not have access to the type of divination used by kings. But the Shang ancestors or their living descendants were not seen to have been particularly good or deserving, just powerful. The spiritual realm that produced this whole system, including a shadowy deity known as Shangdi, made no demands of personal morality. (The similarity of this deity to the name of the Shang kingdom is mere coincidence – his name simply means "highest lord.")[2] Many centuries later, Western missionaries would use the name *Shangdi* to denote the Christian God, but at this early stage, Shangdi was little noticed, amorphous, and, importantly, not really concerned with human morality.

Shang political dominance lasted for more than five centuries but eventually did come to an end, when the kingdom was overrun by the Zhou, a neighboring polity to the west. This was not only very bad news for the Shang, it also presented a problem for the new rulers, who now needed to answer certain very important questions. Why had the Shang lasted for so long but only now fallen? What made the new Zhou rulers uniquely qualified to come along and replace them? The answer was morality. In this new understanding, political authority is not doled out by chance, but bestowed by Heaven, the highest power of the universe, who, very unlike Shangdi, does care for the fate of humankind and,

---

[1] For examples, see Robert Eno, "Deities and Ancestors in Early Oracle Inscriptions," in Donald S. Lopes, ed., *Religions of China in Practice (RCP)*, Princeton Readings in Religions (Princeton, NJ: Princeton University Press, 1996), 41–51; David N. Keightley, "Oracle Bone Inscriptions of the Late Shang Dynasty," in William T. de Bary and Irene Bloom, eds., *Sources of Chinese Tradition (SCT)*, 2nd ed. (New York: Columbia University Press, 2000), 1:3–23.

[2] Although the two terms are homophonous in modern pronunciation, they are written with two different characters. By way of context, you should know that Chinese is not phonetic, meaning that the writing does not correspond to the sound of the spoken language. This can be a difficult concept for English speakers to grasp. Not only can one write the same sound with different characters, but the same character will be pronounced differently in different Chinese dialects, and in languages such as Japanese, which also uses a variant of Chinese script. Nor are most Chinese characters really pictures, although they are shapes with meanings. The best comparison may be with written numerals: show a stranger from any country a card with 285 written on it, and you will both understand its meaning, regardless of how each of you will choose to pronounce it.

moreover, grants the right of rulership to the most moral and upright family in the kingdom. This right, known as the Mandate of Heaven (*tian ming*), was granted conditionally – it could also be taken away when the ruling house fell into moral decline. The idea of the Mandate of Heaven appeared early on in the Zhou reign. The first known mention is dated to 998 BC, just decades after the new kingdom had come to power, referring not to the deposed Shang, but to another, even earlier kingdom called Yin, which had lost the Mandate when "the greater and lesser lords and many officials sank into drunkenness."[3] In other words, this new political standard was used retroactively to rewrite history as a cycle of moral rise and decline. In this new telling of events, the Shang ruling house had once been good and upright and took the Mandate from the Yin, which had gained it from an even earlier one known as the Xia. Even if this account of pre-Shang history is largely mythological, it does reveal just how deeply political legitimacy had become rooted in morality.[4]

The ideal of moral governance formed the core of Confucianism. Having developed five centuries before his birth, these ideas were by no means the personal creation of Confucius (551–479 BC) himself. During these years, many theories of ethical governance were maintained and developed by a class of scholars and political functionaries known as *ru* – what we term Confucianism is actually called the "*ru* teaching" (*ru jiao*) in Chinese. What Confucius did was to formulate these existing political ideas into a school of social philosophy, one that later generations would also turn into a religion. Again, the basic elements of moral philosophy had already been developed and accepted centuries earlier – although debate existed on how best to put them into practice. But such questions were becoming increasingly urgent. Technically speaking, the Zhou lasted for nearly eight centuries, from 1045 BC to 256 BC, but in reality, actual power quickly devolved into the hands of a number of kingdoms. Within the Zhou reign, we thus divide the stable Western Zhou (1046–771 BC) from the Eastern Zhou (770–256 BC), by which point central power was already falling apart. Another name that roughly coincides with this latter era is the Warring States period (476–221 BC). The Warring States period was pretty much just what the name implies: a time of intense political and military competition, in which each kingdom desperately sought to gain an edge over

---

[3] John Lagerwey, *China: A Religious State* (Hong Kong: Hong Kong University Press, 2010), 19–45.

[4] Although the Shang was predated by numerous Neolithic cultures, scholars disagree on the historical existence of the Xia kingdom.

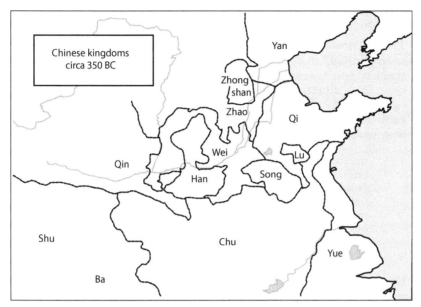

Map 2.1 Chinese kingdoms circa 350 BC.

its neighbors. The political landscape shown in Map 2.1 is really just a snapshot. In reality, boundaries were constantly shifting as kingdoms waxed and waned. The result was a golden age of military and political philosophy. For the battlefield, there was Sunzi's great classic of military stratagems. For the court, there would be Confucius.

The man we call Confucius was born as Kong Qiu in the small state of Lu. (He was later given the more honorific title *Kong fuzi*, from which derived the Latinized *Confucius*.) Confucius emerged from the *ru* tradition and, like others of this class, spent much of his adult life seeking a position as a court adviser. In an ironic twist that has given solace to generations of underappreciated scholars, Confucius – the patron and very image of scholarship – never actually found a job. Disappointed, he returned to his native kingdom of Lu and taught his ideas to a school of eager disciples.

Confucius's particular contribution to *ru* philosophy of governance was to expand it into a larger philosophy of social harmony and personal perfection. The lynchpin was still the king. A virtuous ruler would inspire others in positions of authority to care for those under their charge, and those being cared for would in turn regard their betters with gratitude and loyalty. The result would be a stable and prosperous society. For this reason, the lines of authority must always remain

Box 2.a. Confucian familial relations

The traditional ideal for a Chinese family was to have "five generations under one roof," that is, an extended family that would include great-great-grandchildren. Given the importance of Confucian propriety, it was vital to know where different members of the extended family stood in relation to each other. This created a complex vocabulary of family relations, to distinguish clearly, for example, the son of your brother (*zhizi*) from that of your sister (*waisheng*). For uncles, you have no fewer than six possibilities:

father's older brother	*bo fu* 伯父
father's younger brother	*shu fu* 叔父
father's sister's husband	*gu fu* 姑父
mother's brother	*jiu fu* 舅父
mother's older sister's husband	*yi fu* 姨父
mother's younger sister's husband	*yi zhang* 姨丈

Hierarchy revolved not around age, but around generation (*beifen*). Thus, a young uncle would have higher status than his chronologically older nephew. To keep these lines clear, it was common for all the male children of a particular generation to share an auspicious character in their names. This example comes from a genealogy of the Jian surname published in Taiwan.

First generation	Second generation "Wen 文"	Third generation "Jin 金"
Jian Qilin 簡麒麟	Jian Wensheng 簡文生	Jian Jinneng 簡金能
		Jian Jinchou 簡金丑
		Jian Jinyuan 簡金元
	Jian Wenzhen 簡文陣	
	Jian Wenchang 簡文長	Jian Jinlu 簡金露
		Jian Jinfa 簡金發
	Jian Wentong 簡文統	Jian Jinli 簡金利
		Jian Jinzhi 簡金枝
		Jian Jinchuan 簡金傳

clear. Confucianism is deeply concerned with hierarchy and considers a good society to be one in which people act according to their social roles. Responsibility begins at the top, the dominant person in the relationship. If the king behaves like a king (i.e., with kindness and virtue), his ministers and subjects will follow him. The same logic applies to the relationship between father and son, teacher and student, and older and younger brothers. The only relationship in Confucian thought that is *not* hierarchical is that between friends. (Confucius had little to say about the relationship between husband and wife. Apart from a general sense that they should behave as dutiful wives and caring mothers, women had no real place in this stage of Confucian thought.)

Not being burdened by a court appointment, Confucius had ample spare time to perfect himself, to become what he called a superior man (*junzi*, often translated as "gentleman"). Confucius described this ideal man as one who is respectfully attuned to the world around him. A superior man becomes perfected through ritual, music, and, most importantly, study and introspection. The Confucian gentleman is wise yet humble, commanding yet detached. He performs music to calm his spirit, and ritual to express respect for Heaven and gratitude to his king and his ancestors. Confucius is quick to make clear that rituals are not simply a way to appease spirits. On questions of gods and spirits, Confucius himself was agnostic. His single statement on the topic of the supernatural was superbly ambiguous: "worship the spirits," he said, *"as if they were present."*

Confucius was never recognized during his life, but his disciples recorded his teachings, and over the next generations, the fame of his school began to grow. Local rulers soon discovered that Confucian disciples – all men of letters and loyalty – made top-notch civil servants. Within a hundred years of Confucius's death, his disciples found themselves in much greater demand. One of these disciples, a man named Meng Ke and known to us as Mencius (372–289 BC), profoundly shaped the ideas we know as Confucianism today.

Many schools of thought – religions included – are founded as a two-step process. An iconic figure lays down the basic ideas, but a second, perhaps less celebrated disciple gives them direction as they are adapted to society. Such was the case, for example, with Jesus and Saint Paul in the founding of Christianity. In the same way, many of the ideas we associate with Confucianism were never uttered by the Sage himself, but by his well-traveled and influential disciple Mencius.

The key question that Mencius answered was whether humans are by nature good or evil. For a social and political philosophy that is founded on the moral influence of a virtuous king, this is a rather significant question. If people are naturally good, they will respond to a virtuous king like flowers growing toward sunlight. If they are naturally evil, the king must take more aggressive steps to train them. As with the existence of spirits, Confucius himself took no stand on the question of human nature: "people are neither good or evil," he said, "except that study makes them so." Mencius, on the other hand, was much more hopeful and claimed that people are born with an innate desire to do good. Anyone, he insisted, who saw a baby fall into a well would rush to help. If a ruler would provide his people with the right environment and a bit of inspiration, goodness would follow like water flowing down a hill.

But it is important to remember that Confucius was not the only interpreter of the *ru* tradition, and that Mencius was not the only interpreter of Confucius. These are merely the ones that we best remember today. Many other schools answered the question of morality and human nature very differently, and, for a time, these were the voices that carried the day. The school of Mozi (470–391) criticized the Confucians for being too ritualistic and formulaic, and only concerned with people tied to them by blood or obligation. The greatest criticism of Mencius came from one of his own contemporaries, a man named Xunzi (312–230 BC), who insisted that people are naturally evil, lazy, and degenerate. The only way to govern successfully is thus to force people to act *against* their instincts. It is perhaps no surprise that rulers found the more pessimistic view of Xunzi the more convincing. And one ruler in particular would make this view the law of the land.

This was none other than King Zheng of Qin, better known by his later title of Qin Shi Huang. In his short lifetime, Qin Shi Huang did phenomenal things. He was also the first ruler to unify the warring kingdoms – it is only from this point onward that we refer to China as an empire.[5] The name of Qin was carried by traders to ancient Rome, giving us the word by which we know the country today – *China*. Qin Shi Huang unified his empire's currencies, weights, and measures, and he linked up smaller defensive structures into the first Great Wall. His massive tomb, still not completely excavated, is easily a match in grandeur to anything in the ancient world.

Qin Shi Huang was a brilliant man, but, at least as important, he was a ruthless one. This was no moral monarch: Qin Shi Huang would have made Machiavelli blush. And neither Qin nor his advisers would have seen this as anything to apologize for. The people need rules and order, and more than anything else, they need a strict, ruthless ruler, ready to dole out the harshest of punishments for the slightest infraction of the law. What they most certainly did not need was Confucianism. Qin Shi

---

[5] Just as with religion, it is worth remembering that our political vocabulary is also of Western origin. Terms such as *empire* and *emperor* refer to the very specific model of Roman *imperium*, which is why later European states would continue to use them. I will follow the general convention of referring to the rulers who followed Qin Shi Huang as emperors, but a more precise translation would be "Yellow Thearch."

Huang loathed the Confucians – in a famous essay, one of his political advisers, named Han Feizi (280–233 BC), warned his sovereign about the "five vermin" that any good ruler must root out. These included tax dodgers and people who evaded military service, but none were so insidious as the *ru* scholars, who confused the people with their nonsensical talk about virtue and morality. Qin had the Confucian texts (these were written on slips of bamboo tied together with string) burned. In an act that would live in infamy for millennia, he invited a hundred scholars to the palace and had them buried alive.

Obviously, Qin Shi Huang was something less than successful in ridding China of Confucianism. To his great chagrin, Qin Shi Huang could control everything except death – as we shall see presently, in trying to cheat death, he may actually have poisoned himself. Almost immediately after Qin Shi Huang was placed in his impossibly grand tomb, his empire was torn apart by disgruntled generals, subordinates, and peasants. In fact, pretty much everyone was disgruntled. It seems that ruthless efficiency may have been a fine way to take power, but not to keep it. When the dust had settled and the new rulers, an empire known as Han (from which we have the term *Han Chinese*), had taken power, they took this lesson to heart. The Han certainly had no objection to ruthless efficiency, but they also realized the value of Confucian moral rhetoric, of ruling in the name of goodness and virtue. The result was the proverbial iron fist in a velvet glove. Over the four centuries they ruled China, the Han perfected a system that combined the efficiency of their short-lived predecessors with the moral pretensions of the Confucians. Scholars refer to it as the *Han synthesis*.

After the fall of the Han, China entered a period of prolonged political fragmentation, during which other religions, especially Buddhism, would come to the fore. But although Confucianism was for a time out of favor, the teaching would begin to make a comeback toward the ninth century. In the meantime, it continued to evolve, adding, among much else, a theory of metaphysics. After many centuries of official neglect, Confucianism returned to the political limelight during the Song dynasty (960–1279) and, with a brief interruption during the Mongol reign, would remain the state ideology until the entire imperial system came crashing down in 1911. But it was a teaching that Confucius himself might not have recognized as his own.

Daoism

Of China's three religious traditions, Daoism may be the most difficult to grasp. This is true for a number of reasons. First of all, Daoism is the home of much of Chinese mysticism. Daoist poets wrote tales of mythical beasts and flying mountains. Its philosophers specialized in the abstruse and mysterious. In contrast to straight-laced and straight-forward Confucianism, Daoism is in a way *supposed* to be confusing. To paraphrase the first line of the classic scripture *Daodejing*, if you can clearly explain it, it isn't Daoism.

The second reason is that Daoism is often used as the odd sock drawer of Chinese religions. Having read the previous paragraphs, you should have a relatively clear idea of what Confucianism is and what it is not. The same, as you will see further on, is true of Buddhism. The problem is that a great deal of Chinese religious life is not identifiably Confucian or Buddhist. Nor is it particularly Daoist, but since Daoism is the most conceptually permeable of the three religions, anything that is not clearly one of the first two invariably is dumped into the third. Such varied expressions of Chinese religious life as men parading around the streets dressed as ghosts, spirit mediums going into a trance to channel the words of the gods, or devotees praying for good health in a local temple might all be called Daoism. This is not to say that such a label is incorrect, but rather that we will be better off examining specific aspects of this tradition independently.

Daoism itself is very diverse. Just as Confucianism slowly transformed into the foundation of imperial governance, Daoism developed from a philosophy into traditions of worship, mysticism, and a clerical tradition. It also interacted with a tradition of understanding the cosmos that became the foundation of Chinese science. If you have ever had acupuncture, you have experienced this tradition firsthand.

However, beginning where the study of religion often does, let us start with philosophy. According to the tale, Daoism was the invention of a man named Laozi, who lived at about the same time as Confucius. Unlike Confucius, however, Laozi probably never existed, thus explaining some of the more incredible details of his life, such as the story that he emerged from his mother's womb as an eighty-year-old man. Staying with the tale, Laozi is said to have had a simple existence. Originally living in happy obscurity as a court librarian, Laozi developed such a reputation for wisdom that he was constantly harassed by kings and officials who came seeking advice. Laozi, however, desired only peace and quiet and fled his post and rode on a water buffalo to the western border. Just as he was about to leave the country, he was stopped by a guard who convinced him to write down just a sample of his wisdom. These jottings became the book we now know as the *Daodejing*, or "the Book of the Way and Its Power."

The key element of this book is *Dao*. The word itself simply means "way," but, as in English, can mean either a physical road (*dao lu*) or a path to a more metaphoric or spiritual destination. In the latter sense, we know it as the *do* in the Korean martial art *taekwondo*, or Japanese *judo* or *karatedo*. The formal Japanese tea ceremony is an art known as "the way of tea," or *sado*. In the *Daodejing*, *Dao* is literally everything. It is the totality of all things and forces. It is beyond comprehension or description. "The Dao that can be spoken of," says the very first line of the text, "is not the Dao."

The Dao is not just things: it is things in motion. The Dao is not so much a box packed full of stuff, as a finely tuned clock kept moving by the balance and counterbalance of forces. This is expressed by the symbol known in Chinese as *taiji*, which shows the two alternating forces of yin and yang swirling together. We will hear more about yin and yang presently, but I raise the point about forces because the name of the text mentions not only the Way, but also its *power*.

We often think of Daoism as an exclusively personal philosophy, but in reality it is political. It makes sense to discuss this philosophy after introducing Confucianism, because Daoism in many ways developed as its counterpart. Even certain elements of the Laozi tale hint at a long-standing antagonism with Confucianism. The idea that Laozi had to flee to the west in order to escape the attention of princes and courtiers is an obvious reference to Confucius's own rather conspicuous inability to gain a court appointment. The reason for this antagonism is that political Daoism was a direct competitor with Confucianism – it provided different answers to the same questions. To a king who asked, "how do I rule my country more effectively?" a Confucian would answer, "work harder, study harder, meditate on your own failings, and do more for the welfare of the people." The *Daodejing* says precisely the opposite: "I do nothing, and the people are transformed by themselves ... I take no action, and the people become prosperous by themselves." In other words, a good ruler is one who keeps some distance from his people and allows society to develop without interference. In one famous Confucian exchange, a king described to Mencius how he had worked tirelessly on behalf of his people, routinely relocating them from regions of famine to those of plenty, but still could not increase the population of his kingdom. Mencius answered that the king was obviously insincere in his desire to help the people, because his actions were insufficient to move their hearts. In contrast, I suspect that a Daoist would tell the king that perhaps the people would be happier if he stopped forcing them to move house so often.

The political philosophy of hands-off governance reflects the broader Daoist ideal of *wuwei*, or nonaction. Here again the difference from

Confucianism could not be more clear. Whereas Confucianism seeks personal perfection through effort, Daoism sees power in *non*effort. Resistance is not just futile: it can actually get you hurt. Tall trees might appear to be the strongest and most enduring things in the forest, but they are also the first to be knocked over in a storm. If anything survives, it will be the soft grass that bends in the wind.

Combine these two elements – the motion of forces within the Dao and the philosophy of finding strength through bending with the wind – and you can begin to understand the *power* in the title of the *Daodejing*. It is a desire to harness, rather than fight, the visible and invisible forces of nature. Understanding these forces is also the foundation of much of Chinese science. The two most elemental ones, yin and yang, are seen to flow through everything, creating the image of the swirling *taiji*. Yin and yang are hard to describe in a single word: since all things have these two basic elements, they can appear in different ways. Yin is all that is dark, heavy, slow, downward sloping, and female (among much else), while yang is the opposite: bright, light, quick, upward, and male. It is the interaction of yin and yang within the body that gives life, and the basic task of Chinese medicine is to keep these forces in balance and in proper regulation. Acupuncture, probably the best-known medical treatment, opens or closes the channels within the body. Pharmaceutical treatments are prescribed to correct an overflow of yin or yang. Sometimes the best medicine is simply a change in diet. Foods like meat (particularly beef or mutton), garlic, and chili peppers are very yang, and too much of them can cause insomnia, nervousness, pimples, or other "heat" conditions. Fruits such as pears and watermelon are high in yin. On their own they can balance overactive yang, but eating too many leads to weakness, sweating, and anemia. The root called ginseng fetches such high prices in Asia because certain varieties are known to contain a type of yang that boosts sexual energy.[6]

The same basic principles apply to another of the well-known Chinese sciences known as feng shui. As they do in the body, different forces (these are known broadly as *qi*, but just as with yin and yang, there are many different types of *qi*) circulate through the natural world. The art of feng shui (literally meaning wind and water) aims to organize human life around these flows by positioning buildings and furniture to receive positive and avoid negative energies. In recent years, feng shui has

---

[6] Actually, ginseng grown in different places has different properties. The two main varieties, Korean and American ginseng, have exactly *opposite* effects, boosting yin and yang, respectively.

Figure 2.1 *Taiji* and the eight trigrams. From the main gate of the Jinjiang Chan temple in Singapore. Photo by author.

taken on a certain fashionable quality, and some readers may associate it more with California than China, but do not be fooled: the basic elements of feng shui are as old as China itself. The basic principles are quite straightforward: since yin *qi* flows from north to south, one should not have a front door that faces north. (Think of it as something akin to Daoist weatherproofing.) Within the home, a couple's bedroom should not face onto a bathroom for fear of letting in the appropriately named "smelly *qi*." Sometimes the more advanced principles of feng shui require the services of a professional to decipher and can literally shape the urban landscape. The façade of one twenty-story building near downtown Singapore is covered in tile, making it look more like an art deco fortress than a place of business. The reason for the unique design is that the building faces a current of bad *qi*. Before construction, the owners were cautioned to create a bulwark that would shunt the *qi* aside. Perhaps the most striking example is the Bank of China in central Hong Kong. The architecture of this building, the icon and crowning glory of the world's most expensive skyline, was repeatedly altered in order to assuage concerns about its effects on the flow of *qi* through the business district. The resulting edifice, which from many angles looks like a giant meat cleaver aimed directly at the headquarters of a competing bank, suggests that the accommodations to feng shui were not merely defensive.

Box 2.b. Cosmic correlation

Daoist divination relies on the idea that all things are connected and interact in predictable cycles. The familiar image of the *taiji* shown in Figure 2.1 depicts this cycle in a binary form, with the two forces of yin and yang creating and devouring each other. But these cycles can also be measured in other numbers. The *taiji* is surrounded by the eight trigrams (*ba gua*), which can also be arranged into sixty-four hexagrams. The cycles of these groups of two, eight, or sixty-four represent the natural motions of the universe, like the phases of the moon or tides of the ocean. Daoist divination relies on understanding these cycles and connecting them to external phenomena, such as stars, weather, or health. The chart, taken from a text called the *Precious Scripture of the Five Sages* (*wu sheng baojuan*), illustrates yet another way of arranging these connections, this one based on the number 5:

Element	Water	Fire	Earth	Wood	Metal
Color	Black	Red	Yellow	Blue	White
Body Channel	Kidneys	Heart	Spleen	Liver	Lungs
Sensory Organ	Ear	Tongue	Mouth	Eye	Nose
Body Part	Bones	Blood	Flesh	Blood Vessels	Skin
Direction	North	South	Center	East	West
Constellation	Xuanwu (Dark Warrior)	Zhuque (Vermilion Bird)	Gouchen	Qinglong (Blue Dragon)	Baihu (White Tiger)
Star	Invisible (*tai yi*) Water Star	Fire Star at the Beginning of All Things (*tai chu*)	Absolute (*tai ji*) Earth Star	Wood Star at the Beginning of Form (*tai shi*)	Star Before the Beginning of Substance (*tai su*)
Mountain	Jiuhua	Emei	Puto	Wutai	Baohua
Season	Winter/ Storage	Summer/ Growth	All Year/ Five Grains	Spring/ Birth	Autumn/ Harvest
Buddha	Dizang	Puxian	Guanyin	Wenzhu	Junti

From here it is no great leap to imagine how such ideas also became the foundation of superscience, that is, magic. If you have ever seen a Hong Kong–style kung fu film with heroes flying back and forth over rooftops, shooting balls of energy from the palms of their hands, and punching their way through stone walls, you were watching a popular version of this tradition in action. For centuries, Daoist adepts (among others) have sought ways to harness the deeper powers of the universe, using a variety of medicines and exercises to replace the yin and yang in their own bodies with purified *qi*. Whatever the route they chose, all of this inquiry and experimentation had the same goal: to become what is often called an "immortal" (*xian*) but might more accurately be thought of as a superman, one who not only lived forever, but also gained exactly the type of powers we see popularized in kung fu films, plus infinite wisdom to boot. As far as we know, nobody has ever succeeded. The failures are easier to trace. Qin Shi Huang, and a number of emperors who followed him, poisoned themselves by taking daily doses of concoctions that contained, among other less-than-therapeutic ingredients, mercury, lead, and arsenic. Regardless of the failures, pharmaceutical experimentation was – just like European attempts to turn lead into gold – an important foundation of the science of chemistry. The Chinese name for these experiments was much more evocative. They called it *xuanxue*: the "dark science."[7]

Arts such as feng shui suggest yet another aspect of Daoism, its tie to geography. John Lagerwey, the great scholar of Daoist liturgy, has recently suggested that we can think of imperial China in two ways. The first is in a *lineage* mode, one based on heredity. In politics, this mode is seen in the succession of emperors within a dynasty. In religion, it explains the Confucian concern with family and ancestors. But there is also a *territorial* mode. Returning to the Shang, the very earliest records demonstrate a strong concern not merely with taking and holding territory, but also with rituals such as physically transporting earth from the capital to sanctify new conquests and mark them as part of the realm. This tradition evolved at a national and a local level, through the Heaven and Earth sacrifices practiced by the emperor and the intensely local world of village worship. Both sorts of ritual have the aim of purifying the earth, ridding it of malevolent forces (Daoism also has a strong exorcistic tradition, which we cannot discuss in detail here). From here, it is a small leap to see yet another way for Daoism to enter politics: through its tradition of marking territory and pacifying the gods who live there, Daoism introduced yet another form of political legitimacy. Daoist territorial worship often merged with ideas of moral governance (for example, by saying that the gods themselves were moral and virtuous), but it did not need to. As we will discuss in Chapter 6 on apocalyptic thought, China has had a number of minor or peripheral kingdoms that were ruled entirely on the basis of Daoist theocracy. In the years following the fall of the Han dynasty, during what we might

---

[7] *Dark* here simply means mysterious, rather than evil.

think of as China's Middle Ages (roughly speaking, the years 200–1050 AD), this aspect of organized Daoism emerged as a mainstream political force. During this time, it faced competition not from its old Confucian rivals, but from a new, foreign teaching called Buddhism.[8]

Buddhism

According to a popular saying, Daoism is the only truly Chinese religion – since Confucianism is not really a religion, and Buddhism is not really Chinese. In the case of the latter, this is only partially true. Buddhism did in fact develop in India and evolved there for around five centuries before one particular branch of it reached China. But once it did, Chinese Buddhism developed into something quite unique. This is the Buddhism that spread through much of East Asia and only loosely resembles anything you might see in places like Thailand, Cambodia, or Tibet.

The first thing to know about Buddhism is that it was not invented by someone named Buddha. The founder was Siddhārtha Gautama, the son of a noble family of the Śākya clan, in what is now Nepal.[9] Since the story of Gautama's life has been embellished by two and a half millennia of retelling, it is hard to separate fact from myth, but the basic details are clear enough. For whatever reason, Gautama's father determined early on that his son was to live a life entirely free of pain or suffering. Gautama thus grew up in what was essentially a golden prison, surrounded by lush gardens, flowing fountains, and young, beautiful servants to cater to his every whim. He married and had a child, all the while remaining blissfully unaware that another world existed outside the palace walls – that is, until one day when he managed to sneak out and have a wander around. There he saw for the first time the crowded markets; the dirty, shoving crowds; the toil and destitution of daily life. He also saw people the likes of whom he had never seen before: some of them looked weak and listless, some were frail and ashen, and some were not moving at all. He had had, in other words, his first glimpse of sickness, old age, and death. It was an unpleasant and unsettling revelation, but the worst part was when he found out that such was the fate of all things – even him.

Even after returning home, Gautama found that he could no longer be happy with his golden palace, its gardens and treasures, his servants,

---

[8] Lagerwey, *China: A Religious State*, 20.

[9] The dates of his life remain a matter of scholarly dispute. Most estimates place his death in the fourth century BC.

even his wife and child, knowing that they would all suffer the same fate of decline and decay. Fixated on the impermanence of all things, Gautama abandoned his life of luxury, leaving his family (a point that Confucians would ever after find particularly loathsome) to become a forest ascetic. Never one to do something halfway, Gautama went all out in his rejection of the material world, denying himself all comfort, food, and shelter. Rather like Catholic iconography of the Crucifixion, statues and pictures of Gautama during this period often dwell on his physical suffering, showing him in an exaggerated state of emaciation. According to legend, he became so thin that he could touch his abdomen from the front, and feel through to his spine – quite an accomplishment, but still not enough to rid him of doubt. The two extremes of luxury and deprivation having failed him, Siddhārtha decided that he would sit under a bodhi tree and not move until he had attained wisdom (this is, incidentally, why many monasteries have a bodhi tree somewhere on their grounds). Over the course of one night he sat in meditation. (Like Gautama's birth, the events of this night are interpreted in numerous different ways. Some retellings involve a battle between supernatural forces of good and evil.) By the next morning, Siddhārtha Gautama had attained true wisdom and, being alone, touched the earth to serve as witness of his transformation. For his wisdom, later admirers could refer to Gautama with the honorific name of Śākyamuni, or the Sage of the Śāykas. But it is only from this point that we refer to him with the title of *Buddha*, the Enlightened One.

The teaching of the Buddha revolves around the pain of impermanence. The essence of his teaching, elegantly summed up in the first three of the Four Noble Truths, is that

1. Life is suffering.
2. Suffering is caused by desire.
3. Stop desire and you stop suffering.

Put simply, we suffer because we want things that we can never have. We want to hold on to our possessions, our loved ones, our health, and our lives, even though these, like all things, are fleeting. Being poor is certainly no fun, but the people who make themselves most miserable over money are often the ones who have more than enough to spare. Death only occurs once, yet instead of learning to love life, we live in constant fear of its end. We exist, in other words, as prisoners in a cage of our own making.

Life may be suffering, but ironically even death provides no respite. The teachings of the Buddha developed out of a society that already had rich theological beliefs, one of the most fundamental of which was that all life is interconnected. Because all life is essentially one force, we do not disappear at death but will instead return through the endless cycle of birth and rebirth known as reincarnation. As many readers will know, this tradition also says that the circumstances of rebirth are dictated by our actions, known as karma. Most people will think of karma as something akin to a point system – do something good, you earn a point; do something bad and points are taken away – and when you die, the grand total determines whether you win or lose. Win and you may be reborn as someone richer or smarter or better looking; lose and you will be reborn into a lower station, or possibly even as an animal or demon. One medieval Chinese text called the *Ultimate Book of Cause and Effect* (*Taishang ganying pian*, here meaning "reward and punishment") was quite literally a guide to the number of points you would lose for beating a dog versus a human (you lose even more for beating a Buddhist monk), or the number you would gain for giving food to a beggar, reprinting Buddhist scriptures, or restoring a temple. For centuries, people used guides such as this to calculate very carefully exactly how many pious acts they would need to keep on the good side of karma.

The way to escape this cycle is to tame desire. The last of the Four Noble Truths is that the way to do so is to travel the Eight-fold Path, which is essentially an eight-step road to wisdom. We need not worry about the details, but the essence is to change perception, to learn to see things as they truly are, to recognize and meditate on impermanence. As we lose our attachment to things, status, and people, we are liberated of desire and are made truly free. Eventually, we even lose our attachment to ourselves, our cleverness, our happiness, and our existence. This is the final hurdle that we must cross on the way to enlightenment. Once we have done so, we are freed from the cycle of birth and rebirth. When an enlightened being dies, he is not reborn but instead enters nirvāna, which, in contrast to popular use of the term, is *not* paradise. Because all life is suffering, nirvāna, the highest attainment of Buddhists, literally means snuffing out a candle. What is being extinguished is not life, but rather the individuated consciousness that results from desire. Nirvāna itself is neither existence nor nonexistence.

Buddhism spread throughout South Asia for centuries before reaching China. As religions do, it broke into branches and sects, each one evolving into a slightly different variation on basic teaching. One of the basic divisions was between two branches known as the Way of the Elders and the Greater Vehicle. The Way of the Elders (Theravāda) teaches that the pursuit of nirvāna is restricted to monks. For this reason, its detractors refer to it unaffectionately as the Smaller Vehicle

(Hīnayāna). This type of Buddhism is common in Southeast Asia, explaining why countries such as Thailand and Cambodia have large numbers of monks. The Greater Vehicle (Mahāyāna) is, as the name suggests, intended to be more expansive. In Greater Vehicle Buddhism, anyone can seek nirvāna, not just monks. The reason is that while monks may be slightly better than ordinary people, Greater Vehicle Buddhism sees the pursuit of good karma as something far beyond the power of any human to attain on his own. Humans are too weak, our sins are too great, and all of us, monks and laypersons alike, must rely on the mercy of the Buddha to take us to nirvāna. Luckily for us, this teaching adds a twist on the story of the Buddha. Whereas the Way of the Elders views him as a historical personage (this is why they focus more on his actual life and death), Greater Vehicle treats the Buddha as transcendent, in other words, divine. In Mahāyāna Buddhism, the Buddha existed before his arrival on earth and continues to exist today.

The Mahāyāna ideal of a transcendent Buddha opened the door for Buddhism to develop a number of ideas and practices that we might naturally associate with religion. Most obviously, it meant that devotion could center on the Buddha himself. If human effort is insufficient to overcome bad karma, we must rely on the mercy and compassion of the Buddha, as well as on a group of divine figures known as bodhisattvas, for compassion and mercy. Over time, this caused religious practice to shift from meditation to prayer. It also meant that the teaching of the Buddha, like the Buddha itself, was alive. For Theravadins, the Buddha arrived, taught, and left. The canon of his teachings is fixed and unchanging. However, if you believe that the Buddha still exists, it opens the door for further revelation. The most famous Mahāyāna scripture, the *Lotus Sutra*, centers on a parable of a man who rescues his children from a fire by lying to them, promising them toys in order to coax them away from the dangerous scene. The analogy is that the Buddha, realizing the limits of human wisdom and understanding, will also tell us pretty lies in order to guide us toward something greater. Since the oblivion of nirvāna will seem to our unenlightened minds to be a rather bleak ending, the Buddha instead promises the virtuous rebirth in a paradise called the Pure Land. One lifetime in this land of earthly delights can last hundreds of thousands of years, an ideal easier for humans to understand and strive for.

It was Mahāyāna Buddhism that reached China, sometime around the first century AD. It entered from Central Asia, along a route that passed the gargantuan Buddhist statues that once stood in the Bamyan Grottoes of Afghanistan, and the famous cave frescoes in Dunhuang. Buddhism quickly took root in China but retained this link with Central

Asia. In the centuries following the fall of the Han, China interacted far more closely with Central Asia than ever before. Some of the ruling houses, including that of the glorious Tang dynasty, were even of mixed ancestry. These were the glory days of the Silk Road, a time when a flood of Central Asian artistic, architectural, and religious influences swept through Chinese culture. Up until the twentieth century, the Tang stood out as the most cosmopolitan period of China's long history. Politically it was also a time of experimentation. Successive emperors alternately favored Buddhism or Daoism. As mentioned earlier, this is when the teachings of Confucius were pushed somewhat into the background. Some Tang emperors spent huge sums of money on Buddhism. They commissioned expeditions to India to retrieve original sutras (one such trip provides the plot of the famous novel *Journey to the West*), supported Buddhist scholarship and rituals, and exempted the monasteries from taxes. Wu Zetian (625–705), the only woman to ever reign as empress (as opposed to the unofficial exercise of power by figures such as the late Qing empress dowager, Cixi), was a fantatstic supporter of Buddhism. To the profound disgust of later generations of Confucians, Wu even declared herself to be the earthly incarnation of the Maitreya Buddha (a figure we will see again when we talk about the apocalypse).

Eventually, the winds would shift back. Sapped in no small part by the money it had spent on religion, the Tang dynasty fell into decline, paving the way for Confucianism to return with a vengeance. Buddhism and Daoism did not disappear entirely, but neither one would again rise to the same level of political significance. Nearly two thousand years after it reached China, Confucian literati of the last dynasty still harbored a grudge against Buddhism and continued to grumble about the pernicious influence of that "foreign religion."

Three become one

With this quick overview of Confucianism, Daoism, and Buddhism, we return to the question raised earlier: does China have three religions or one? The answer for the great majority of people is one. Over the next few chapters, we will encounter certain people who were particularly devoted to one or another of the three religions, but even they would have found it difficult to reject or ignore the other two completely.

And there really was no need for them to try. None of the three religions of China is exclusive. In contrast to Western religions, none of the three Chinese religions has anything comparable to the biblical third commandment, directing followers to follow one god exclusively. At their core, each of the three Chinese teachings is less a religion in the

Western sense than a philosophy that includes ideas that we associate with religion: morality, the nature of the universe, the fate of the soul, and the like. Because there is no single creator god, Chinese religion does not have a strong impetus against idolatry or false worship. (There is most certainly an idea of *heresy*, but we shall leave that question for later.)

A second reason that the three religions could coexist is that they did not directly overlap. In practical terms, each one found its own specialized place in the life of the believer. This arrangement took time to develop. For eight centuries between the fall of the Han and the fall of the Tang, both Buddhism and Daoism were active in court life and competed for political patronage. Over the centuries, more than a little blood was shed, as one ruler favored Buddhism, whereas his successor purged it. But by the beginning of the Song dynasty in 960, Confucianism had begun to eclipse both of these as the official political religion. (Again, the brief period of Mongol rule of 1271–1368 is an exception.)

In practice, the three religions constitute a single whole. Most rituals freely combine elements of two or all three traditions. The *pudu* ritual, celebrated in some form or another throughout the Buddhist world, derives from a Buddhist festival of the dead. In China, it often features the story of the Buddhist monk Mulian, who travels to hell to rescue the soul of his mother. But even this very Buddhist festival also incorporates Daoist elements. The date is calculated according to a Daoist calendar, to coincide with the beginning of the seventh lunar month, a time when the ghosts are believed to be released from hell. Even the story of Mulian, who risks life and limb to save the soul of an undeserving parent, suggests a strong element of Confucian filial piety.

Conceptions of death and the afterlife show how the three traditions are distinct yet inseparable. In death as in life, Confucianism remains focused on the family but also promotes the metaphor of the "celestial bureaucracy," a system of ranks and promotions for the dead that mirrors the imperial civil service. Daoist territorial deities play their part in this bureaucracy by keeping watch over a locality, enforcing order over the realm of spirits, and preventing harmful ghosts from wreaking havoc among the living. Buddhism adds the idea of reincarnation, as well as the most elaborate mortuary ritual and a devotional tradition of chanting prayers and sutras to transfer good karma to the deceased. But regardless of whether we call them Confucian, Daoist, or Buddhist, these conceptions all merge into each other.

The point is that in terms of both beliefs and practice, China's three traditions effectively combine to form one religion. Many traditions of thought, including one that we will revisit when we talk about the apocalypse, have evolved to explain how the three teachings relate to each other, but all return to the same point, summed up in the phrase "the three religions are one" (*sanjiao he yi*).

II. The emperor monk: Zhu Yuanzhang and the new Confucian state

Historians trade in the marking of time: dividing and naming eras and finding those distinct milestones that mark the truly momentous transformations. In the case of political history, this does not present much of a challenge – it does not require much imagination to decide that the reign of a queen named Elizabeth should be called the Elizabethan era. In other cases, these divisions might be less clear and, as a result, more controversial. What we call the Age of Discovery is usually taken to begin with the nautical wanderings of the likes of Christopher Columbus or Vasco de Gama. It could be argued, however, that this period actually began centuries earlier, with the voyages of their equally intrepid Arab or Viking predecessors. More than a few have said that the term should be dropped altogether, since the civilizations of the New World were doing quite well long before the Europeans ever got around to "discovering" them.

As far as giving names goes, one of the more contentious questions is where to mark the beginning of the "modern" era. You will no doubt notice the quotation marks that mark the word *modern* as something I want to put in someone else's mouth. Most historians would do something similar. The reason is that when we call something "modern" it conjures up the idea that all civilizations are naturally striving toward a single destination – a sort of "World of Tomorrow" complete with Moon colonies and robot dogs. There is a moral dimension to this, as well. Societies that placed too much confidence in being "modern" at any cost often ended up in some very bad places – this was the case with some of the more conspicuous ideological failures of the past century. It is worth remembering that for a time, fascism was considered by more than a few observers to be the next great revolution in human history, and figures such as Mussolini were regarded by many of their contemporaries as unique visionaries. Apart from these moral questions, placing too much emphasis on the modern era is simply a bad way to view history, as it tends to ignore everything that did not succeed. In effect, such a perspective dismisses all of the false starts, failed kingdoms, and dead languages as insignificant, simply because they did not lead directly to us. That said, there is merit in looking for those moments when the world did change, truly and irreversibly. In Europe, this would no doubt include events such as the Enlightenment or the French Revolution. In China, a good candidate would be the founding of the Ming dynasty.

The Ming dynasty was aptly named. The word *Ming* itself means "bright," and when the dynasty was founded in 1368, it marked the end of nearly two rather dark centuries of Mongol rule. The dynasty would last for three hundred years, and even after it fell, many of its innovations in law, governance, culture, and diplomacy would remain in place for centuries, until the moment that the whole imperial system came crashing down in 1911. What is more, many of these sweeping changes came about during the lifetime, and at the initiative of, one man: the dynasty's founder, Zhu Yuanzhang.

Zhu Yuanzhang (1328–98) was a truly unique individual. Born into abject poverty, he fought his way to power, captured the city of Nanjing before his thirtieth birthday, and crowned himself emperor of China at the age of forty. For the remainder of his long life, Zhu turned his boundless energies to the duties of office, waking before dawn to pore over communications from an army of lower officials whom he relied upon but never trusted. By the time of his death in 1398, Zhu had left his mark on China in a way few have done before or since. Zhu was literally larger than life. Later stories about his rise to power attribute his success to supernatural assistance, alternately to the protection of the Buddha or to a pact with demons. As we will see, Zhu had very personal experiences with, and equally strong opinions about, religion.

Before we delve any deeper into Zhu himself, first a word about names. Each dynasty in China was given a name, one that has nothing to do with the surname of the ruling family. The Ming dynasty was thus ruled by a family named *Zhu*, not a family named *Ming*. Indeed, the only place one will find a person named Ming is in Flash Gordon comics – it does not exist as a surname in China. (The surname *Zhu*, coincidentally, has the same sound as the word for pig, which means that for three centuries, sensible people in China assiduously avoided making pig jokes.) The emperor himself had many names. Beyond his personal name, an emperor also had one or more reign names, which also provided a way of marking the years on the calendar. Thus 1370 is recorded in Chinese sources as the second year of the Hongwu (meaning "vast military") reign. To avoid confusion, remember that this was a descriptive title, not a personal name. (Thus we refer to "Zhu Yuanzhang, the Hongwu emperor.") To complicate matters further, most literate people had a number of pen names, and each emperor also had a special "temple name" given to him at death, for use in various types of funerary ritual. Fortunately we need not concern ourselves with those here.

As just mentioned, Zhu Yuanzhang was a truly unique individual, and this begins, unfortunately, with a uniquely traumatic upbringing. Zhu was born in northern Anhui province. This is a poor region cursed with salty soil, and its inhabitants are still characterized by many of their wealthier neighbors as ill-mannered bumpkins. If Zhu himself ever felt the sting of such comments, it was certainly the least of his problems. While he was still a teenager, a particularly devastating famine swept the region, and Zhu could only watch helplessly as most of his family succumbed to disease and starvation. He and his older brother could not even afford coffins for their parents' burial, a situation made even more intolerable by Chinese culture's profound concern with honoring ancestors in death.[10] Zhu was entrusted by his brother to a local Buddhist monastery, which housed him for a time but eventually sent him into the world to live the life of a mendicant monk, which is to say that they threw him out and told him to go begging. Zhu did eventually return to the monastery and remained there for four years, learning to read Buddhist scriptures and studying Buddhist doctrine.

However, when Zhu did finally leave the monastery for good, it was not to embark on a life of peaceful contemplation. These were the waning years of the Mongol occupation, and while they had been peerless conquerors (no empire before or since has been as vast), the Mongols did not prove to be especially effective or competent as administrators. As a result of their misrule, much of the country was in chaos. And as Mongol power fell into decline, numerous rebel bands had risen to fill the vacuum. Zhu began his career as a foot soldier in one of these many armies. Within five years, he was commanding his own force, the one that would eventually capture the city of Nanjing and give him claim to the emperor's throne.

During these early years, Zhu needed all the friends he could find, and among his early allies was a group of rebels known as the Red Turbans. The name of this group derives from their practice of sending soldiers into battle with a red sash wrapped around their heads or waists. This was actually a well-established tradition among rebels – there had been a number of so-named Red and Yellow Turban rebellions in Chinese history, perhaps the most famous being the second-century Yellow

---

[10] In addition to expressing gratitude and respect toward the parents themselves, a proper burial is vital for assuring the postmortem salvation of the spirit. Without such a burial, a spirit may continue to exist as a tortured ghost and wreak vengeance upon the living.

Turban revolt that opened the epic novel *Romance of the Three Kingdoms*. The practice of wearing colored sashes into battle was thus more than just a convenient way of identifying who was fighting on which side. It recalled a long history of popular rebellion and implied a unity of purpose with these other short-lived expressions of peasant utopianism. In the case of the second-century Yellow Turbans, this utopianism had been fed by religious ideas, specifically a kind of millenarian Daoism that venerated and awaited the return of Huanglao, a divine manifestation of Laozi. For a brief period, this rebellion was able to sustain an independent state in the remote Southwest. (It was inspired by a teaching called the the Way of Great Peace [*taiping dao*], a term that we will be hearing again in a later chapter.)

The Red Turbans whom Zhu encountered were very much products of this same tradition. Indeed, the tradition was so strong and central power so weak that these were not the only Red Turbans around, but only one of a number of roughly allied movements. Like the second-century Yellow Turbans, these groups took their religious beliefs seriously, preparing for battle with elaborate sacrifices and rituals. For this reason, the group with whom Zhu found himself allied was also styled the "Incense Army" (*xiang jun*) by contemporaries. They followed a youth named Han Lin'er (d. 1366), who was said to be the heir of the deposed Song dynasty (the last Chinese dynasty before the Mongol invasion), and given the title of *Lesser Radiant King* (*xiao ming wang*). This name was more than mere flattery: it hinted at a core belief of the Incense Army.

Few of the men (and occasionally women) who joined the ranks of groups like the Red Turbans were career soldiers. Most were peasants. Some were driven by desperation, others perhaps by the promise of plunder, but all were at least to some degree motivated by faith in their cause. For such a movement to succeed, its cause had to be truly momentous. People will not willingly leave home and risk their lives in defense of a pretty good idea, but they will do so for a great one, and this is why mass movements such as peasant rebellions so often contain religious elements. We will revisit the question of apocalyptic belief in a later chapter, but for now, suffice it to say that for mass movements to succeed, they must believe themselves to be part of events of cosmic significance.

China had a long tradition of such movements. The Yellow Turbans had been messianic; their goal was to realize the divine reign of Huanglao on earth. The Red Turbans were similar. Han Lin'er's grandiose title of Lesser Radiant King identified him as the pivot of such a transformation, the precursor of a portended *Greater* Radiant King (*da ming wang*), who would usher in a new era of history. The message worked. The Red Turbans raised a large and devoted army and for a brief period even managed to control a small region of Central China that they styled the Song kingdom. Like the Kingdom of Heavenly Peace, this new Song kingdom was a religious polity: its leaders were equally military men and priests of a handful of messianic deities. Worship of any other deities was strictly prohibited.[11]

However, neither the Red Turbans nor the Song kingdom was destined to last for long, a fact that Zhu seems to have welcomed. Zhu rose to prominence alongside the Red Turbans and was by all accounts a loyal ally, but as the Song declined in the 1360s, he happily left them behind. Although the name he would chose for his own "bright" (*ming*) dynasty did echo the luminous imagery of the messianic Radiant King, the fact is that Zhu never shared in their ideology. He did, however, learn from it. Through his alliance with the Red Turbans, Zhu had become keenly aware of the power of religious belief, especially of the type that made radical, utopian promises to the poor and disaffected. When he gained power, Zhu assiduously erased from the historical record all references to his earlier dalliance with the Song and went to great lengths to ensure that such a force would never have the chance to threaten his own rule.

The full extent of Zhu's ideological about-face was plainly evident by the time he rose to power. Just before he founded his Ming dynasty, as he was completing his conquest of northern China, Zhu prepared an open proclamation to justify his overthrow of the erstwhile Mongol order. This letter contained no talk of messianic deities, presaged divine kingdoms, cycles of cosmic transformation, leveling of wealth, or any of the other millenarian ideas that had characterized the political rhetoric of groups such as the Red Turbans. Instead, Zhu returned to the core political value of Confucian governance – the personal morality of the ruler. In a somewhat formulaic fashion, Zhu praised the virtue of early Mongol rulers but condemned later ones precisely for their lack of Confucian propriety. China was in chaos not because the rulers were foreign but because they had "ceased to follow ancestral instruction and ruined moral norms." According to an open declaration made by Zhu on the eve of his proclamation as emperor, the Mongols' worst

---

[11] The radiant imagery derives from a religion called Mancheism, which arrived from Persia centuries earlier and became deeply integrated with Maitreyan belief. Ma Xisha, "Lishi shang de Milejiao yu Monijiao de ronghe" [The historical integration of the Maitreya teaching and Manicheism], in Ma Xisha, ed., *Dangdai Zhongguo zongjiao jingxuan congshu: Minjian zongjiao juan* (Beijing: Minzu chubanshe, 2008).

crime was their perversion of the natural laws of social hierarchy. Under Mongol misrule, "superior and inferior were interchanged without regarding it as unnatural. They deeply profaned and disrupted the proper relations between father and son, ruler and minister, husband and wife, older and younger."[12]

In a sense, Zhu was just doing what any wise political figure would have – changing his political rhetoric to appeal to a new and wider power base. Millenarian ideals that demand the overthrow of society are extremely effective in mobilizing the poor and dispossessed but hold little attraction for those who have a stake in restoring or maintaining a degree of social stability. His new appeal to classical moral rhetoric made Zhu acceptable to a much wider swath of Chinese society, including the Confucian scholarly class. This pool of scholars had indeed suffered under the Mongols, not the result of any persecution, but because members of the imperial family had instead lavished their favor on competing schools of Daoist and Buddhist advisers. Most importantly, the Confucians had been evicted from their traditional role as government officials. Lucrative positions in the civil bureaucracy were instead given to foreigners, particularly the Central Asians known as the colored eyes (se mu), whom the Mongols considered more trustworthy. Some Confucian literati had indeed served under the Mongols, but most members of this once-prominent class chose instead simply to withdraw from public service. There, in a comfortable obscurity, they could write long poems bewailing the state of the world, while waiting patiently for a return to a Chinese style of governance that would allow them to reclaim their proper political role. However this class might have felt about an upstart like Zhu personally, the language of his proclamation was music to their ears.

It was not, however, mere rhetoric. Once in power, Zhu did reinstate Confucianism as the official political orthodoxy of the imperial order. He put into place policies that took seriously the paternalistic role of the state as an agent of moral transformation. Under Zhu, the state would not only care for matters of politics: it would in essence become teacher and father to the people, as well. It would not, however, be a carte blanche for the Confucian class.

One need only recall the circumstances of Zhu's rise to power to appreciate the sort of ruler he would become. In twenty years, Zhu had risen from half-starved wandering monk to rebel captain to emperor of

---

[12] Edward L. Farmer, *Zhu Yuanzhang and Early Ming Legislation: The Reordering of Chinese Society Following the Era of Mongol Rule* (Leiden: E. J. Brill, 1995), 54.

Figure 2.2 Zhu Yuanzhang at middle age. This portrait shows
the aging emperor in a dignified pose. Other less flattering images
emphasize a protruding lower jaw, suggesting that the august
Ming ancestor might not have been a particularly handsome man.
National Palace Museum, Taiwan, Republic of China. Image supplied by National Palace Museum, Taipei.

China. It hardly needs mentioning that he was a man of phenomenal
ambition, will, and talent. As emperor, he was dynamic to a superlative
degree. Zhu transformed the entire government by centralizing power
in the hands of the emperor, an innovation that worked well when the
emperor was strong and competent but would prove disastrous when
less capable men sat on the throne. He vastly expanded the bureaucracy, at the same time instituting numerous layers of redundant
systems and internal checks to keep it honest and, as much as possible,
directly accountable to him.

Even as emperor (Figure 2.2), Zhu would always remain deeply
suspicious of the officials who staffed his government. Like many of
the headstrong emperors who would follow him, Zhu considered his
officials untrustworthy, uninterested in the problems of the people,
and far too adept at the use of moral double-talk to cover over their

own incompetence, laziness, and greed. This tendency presented two problems. Not only did Zhu require competent and honest officials; he moreover appears to have been sincerely devoted to the ideals of moral transformation. The very men whom Zhu so distrusted not only staffed the state apparatus, but were also the keepers of the Confucian tradition. Scholar-officials were trained from an early age in the Confucian classics and commentaries and recruited through an examination system that tested precisely these ideals.[13] In Zhu's eyes, however, they were also the least likely to uphold them.

The answer was to go directly to the people, to use the power of the throne to introduce proper teachings, rituals, and norms to all of his subjects. It may not sound it, but this was a very radical solution. For one thing, Chinese imperial governments had extraordinarily little real influence over the lives of common people – as the saying goes, "the mountain is high, and the emperor is far away." Even in the fourteenth century, China had a population of about sixty-five million, and, administratively speaking, the Ming state was very light on the ground. The lowest official bureaucrat, the county magistrate, might preside over an area with a population of tens of thousands. And he, you will remember, was not fully trusted by his own boss. Precisely to prevent them from becoming too friendly with the locals, officials were rotated in and out of positions every few years. This policy ensured that officials would not have an opportunity to become corrupt, but it also kept the state bureaucracy chronically ill informed and ineffective at the local level. Thus, while Zhu presided over a larger and more streamlined government than any China had ever seen before, it was still nowhere up to the task of any sort of direct interaction with the population at large.

But beyond the question of manpower, Zhu was attempting something no ruler before him had ever done, to influence the behavior of his subjects directly. As you will remember, virtue in the Confucian ethos is contagious and flows downward. When the superior member of any social relationship behaves well, the inferior will naturally be inspired to do the same. (Again, this is why Confucian thought treats nearly all relationships as hierarchical.) Goodness does not need to be actively propagated: a concentration of virtue at the top will naturally spread through the whole system.

The system Zhu set in place was quite different. For one thing, he used law. The Ming legal code was far and away the most elaborate

---

[13] The idea of recruiting by examination had already been around for centuries. What was relatively new was basing these exams on the interpretation of Confucian texts.

yet seen in China, and it specifically mandated all manner of propriety and moral behavior. In its original conception, Confucianism was
adamantly opposed to the use of law to coerce correct behavior – the
resort to force was itself a sign that the ruler no longer had the moral
ability to lead by example. But as the Confucian tradition was incorporated into real government, state power and the rhetoric of morality
became increasingly intertwined. (This was the iron fist–velvet glove
arrangement established by the Han dynasty.) The innovation of the
early Ming was to expand and universalize existing laws and statutes
vastly and to wield the power of the state much more aggressively.

It is an irony of history that attempts at social control are often
directed at the privileged classes. George Orwell expressed this (among
much else) especially well in his *Nineteen Eighty-Four*, in which it was
the party elite, not the common citizens, who suffered the real scrutiny of the Big Brother society. In a similar fashion, many (indeed
most) of the rules instituted by earlier dynasties had been directed at
the official classes. The Ming maintained this tradition but also added
new rules intended for more general consumption. Typical of the latter are the requirements set forth in the two legal milestones of the
early Ming: the *Great Ming Commandment* (*Da Ming ling*) of 1368, and
the *Great Code of Ming Law* (*Da Ming lü*) of 1374. In increasing detail,
these two codes legally established precisely how and for how long one
was to mourn a relative. At the death of a parent, for example, surviving sons were to remain in mourning for a period of three years.
For a brother, such mourning lasted only one year. At least on paper,
this type of obligation extended far beyond the immediate family to a
degree of complexity that explains the need to maintain detailed family genealogies. The death of a father's agnatic female first cousin (that
is, a female cousin of your father on your grandfather's side) would
require you to mourn for three months (although it might take that
long to figure out that such a person was related to you at all). With
the exception of very close family members, only patrilineal relationships mattered. Even within the immediate family, the male relative
took precedence. Both parents were mourned for the same period, but
for the father the regime was harsher and more demanding. Those
in high mourning, as for a father, refrained from certain foods, from
sexual intercourse, and from taking the civil service examinations
(because these examinations were the all-important starting point for
an official career, an untimely death could inflict significant financial hardship on a family). Anyone in mourning was required to wear
hemp sackcloth, with the degree of coarseness related to the closeness
of the relationship.

Box 2.c. Ming mourning regulations

The *Great Ming Commandment* was announced by Zhu Yuanzhang in 1368, as a companion to the existing code of laws. (The complete Ming code was promulgated a few years later.) In addition to outlining all manner of crimes and punishments, the commandment established an extremely precise set of ritual protocols, including the grades of mourning to be observed at the death of various relations. The accompanying box is a sample that gives an idea of the level of detail:

Grade	Duration	Clothing	Relationship of Deceased
1	Three years	Unhemmed coarse sackcloth	Son for father Unmarried daughter for father Wife for husband
2	Three years	Hemmed fine sackcloth	Son for mother Stepmother for eldest son Wife for husband's mother
3	One year	Hemmed sackcloth and staff	Son for a mother who has remarried Paternal grandson for grandmother, if grandfather is still alive Husband for wife
4	One year	Hemmed sackcloth	A married woman for her parents For paternal uncles and their wives Husband's parents for daughter-in-law
5	Five months	Hemmed sackcloth	Paternal great-grandparents
6	Three months	Hemmed sackcloth	Paternal great-great-grandparents Stepfather if now living apart
7	Nine months	"Greater coarseness"	Married daughters Brothers who die early or in late teens Divorced mother for her daughters

Box 2.c. (*continued*)

Grade	Duration	Clothing	Relationship of Deceased
8	Five months	"Lesser coarseness"	Paternal great uncles and their wives Husband's brothers' wives for each other Unmarried daughters and granddaughters of paternal grandfather's brothers
9	Three months	Coarse hemp	Father's married paternal cousins Husband's female paternal cousins Daughter's son's wife

Source: Farmer, *Zhu Yuanzhang*, 164–71.

It should be noted that mourning was only compulsory for members of one's own family. One was not required to mourn the death of a friend. Indeed, mourning a relationship based purely on emotion was considered unseemly and actively discouraged. The reason was that the goal of mourning laws had less to do with providing any emotional release for the bereaved than with visibly maintaining hierarchical social propriety. This sensitivity to one's place within a relationship (as well as the sense of responsibility or deference it would imply) was trained and grounded in the family but extended to the structure of society as a whole. For example, Confucian ethics treated commerce with a disdain bordering on disgust. Merchants were officially considered to be parasites, a slippery class that fed off society but contributed nothing to it. Despite their often considerable wealth, merchants were legally forbidden to dress, act, or live in a manner above their station.

Conversely, although he mistrusted the Confucian elite, Zhu firmly believed in the need to maintain their exemplary status visibly. Commoners were strictly forbidden to ride in sedan chairs, build elaborate roofs or fly flags outside their homes, or wear imperial insignia; all of these privileges were reserved solely for the degree-holding elite. This was not to discriminate against the common people, but rather to educate them, to ensure that they would recognize their betters and develop the proper attention to social hierarchy. Zhu was especially keen to see such values contribute to social stability within rural society, particularly within village communities. In 1381, he mandated a ritual called the Wine Drinking Ceremony, which was meant to boost the moral authority of village elders. In this annual ritual, all males in the village were to assemble, line up according to age and accomplishment, and decorously drink a cup of wine together. Of course, it was impossibly impractical to enforce this decree, but the intent is clear: even in the most remote village, everyone was to know his place.

Another of Zhu's innovations was to reach the people directly through moral texts and monuments. Moral exhortation in the style of the Confucian classics was, essentially, an elite tradition – many among these classes considered commoners to be simply incapable of receiving instruction. Zhu sought to disseminate moral messages to all of his subjects and even penned some of the tracts himself. Following a 1385 incident of treachery among his own officials, the emperor spent four years composing a series of moral exhortations called the *Grand Pronouncements* (*Yuzhi da gao*). These were printed and distributed throughout the country at state expense and designed not only as a warning to serving officials, but also as edification for the common people, especially for village leaders. Their content is simple: proper social relationships are a matter of national security. "Loyalty to the ruler and filial piety to relatives," Zhu wrote, "this is the essence of it. If these can be carried out, it will bring good fortune. If it cannot, it will bring disaster." Anyone who needed a reminder need only recall how the once-mighty Mongols had been done in by their own depravity. Zhu reserved special bile for Mongol family relationships. "First cousins of the same surname married each other, younger brothers inherited their elder brothers' wives, and sons got their fathers' concubines. These were the customs of the former Mongol Yuan." The Mongols were not merely incestuous: by twisting the natural hierarchy of the family, their customs perverted society. And in the end, no amount of military might could have saved them.

In a variety of ways, Zhu conveyed Confucian morality to the people. Like the *Grand Pronouncements*, other texts with didactic value were printed, distributed, and, for the sake of the illiterate or semi-literate majority, read aloud. One of the most famous of these was a folk classic, still read by many schoolchildren in places such as Taiwan and Korea, called the *Twenty Four Filial Examples* (*Er shi si xiao*). This short book was originally written by a Chinese Confucian literatus during the Mongol period (he was at the time mourning the death of his father and presumably did not have much else to occupy himself) and consists of twenty-four short poems, each followed by a longer text, explaining a tale of family responsibility taken to an often ridiculous but otherwise admirable extreme. In one, an impoverished family realizes that they are too poor to care for both their child and the husband's aged mother.

The man's wife, explaining that they can always have another child but never replace the kindness of a mother, suggests that they dispose of the child by burying it in the wilderness. In a twist somewhat reminiscent of the biblical story of Abraham and Isaac, their resolve to make the ultimate sacrifice is not unrewarded: in the hole they had dug to be their child's grave, they discover a fortune in gold. In another story, a poor scholar is unable to purchase meat to serve his ailing mother and slices off a piece of his own thigh to boil into soup. (Although this leaves one a bit puzzled as to how he managed to get dinner to the table, it does show how religious ideas travel between traditions. According to the scholar Chün-fang Yü, this custom of "iatric cannibalism," serving a piece of one's own flesh to ailing parents in hopes of a miraculous cure, did in fact become a feature of medical practice during this period. I have seen newspaper accounts from the 1940s confirming that the custom survived well into the twentieth century.)

In addition to spreading these heartwarming stories, Zhu ensured that the law itself was made accessible to the common people. In 1398, the final year of his rule, Zhu promulgated the *Placard of People's Instructions* (*Jiaomin bangwen*). This was just what the name implied: an extensive

---

Box 2.d. *Twenty Four Filial Examples*

The *Twenty Four Filial Examples* are known throughout China. Many of the stories (such as the one depicted in Figure 2.3) contain an element of the supernatural, of divine rewards for filial behavior:

Tears make the bamboo sprout

During the three kingdoms, there was a man named Meng Zong, also called Gongwu. His father died when Meng was a child and his mother was very ill. One winter she wanted to eat soup of boiled bamboo shoots. [But, because bamboo shoots were out of season] Meng had no way of obtaining them. He went out to a bamboo grove, seized a bamboo stalk, and began to cry. His filial piety moved heaven and earth. Instantly, the earth broke open and many stalks of bamboo shoots appeared. Meng gathered them and returned home to make soup for his mother. As soon as she had eaten it, she recovered.

A poem praises him, saying:

> Tears fall, the north wind is cold
> And blows through a stand of bamboo;
> But winter bamboo shoots emerge!
> Harmony is Heaven's desire.

Figure 2.3 Tears make the bamboo sprout. This scene is painted on wall tiles at the Pushan (Spreading Kindness) temple in Singapore. Like the Christian Stations of the Cross, images from the *Twenty Four Filial Examples* are so well known that there is no need to add an accompanying explanation. Photo by author.

list of the rules that the people are to live by. Like earlier promulgations, it recognized the authority of natural community leaders to make binding decisions. While serious crimes of murder and theft were to be reported to civil officials, lesser disputes were to be mediated by the village elders, who should by right be the moral backbone of the community. This faith in the ability of Confucian values of hierarchy, respect, and deference to transform every village into an ideal community is why the visible expression of authority in rituals such as the Wine Drinking Ceremony was so vital to Zhu's vision. But local leaders did more than punish. Village elders were also to report cases of exemplary moral virtue to higher authorities, so that filial sons or chaste widows could be included in local records or even recognized by the construction of a plaque or memorial arch at the entrance to the village. A few of these monuments survive today, in places like the historic village of Xidi, recently named a UNESCO World Heritage Site.

While many of these rules may seem alternately draconian and wildly impracticable, it must be remembered that Zhu's attempt to extend moral transformation beyond the small circle of scholarly elites, unique in the history of China, did not derive from mistrust of the common people. Just the opposite, it reflected his confidence in their basic unspoiled goodness and sense. Zhu sincerely cared about the welfare of the ordinary peasant – after all, he was one. He distributed fallow land to whoever would till it, partially to help production recover from years of destructive warfare, but also out of a sense that land should by right belong to the farmer. This level of concern is also why he became so consistently exasperated with his own bureaucracy. Imagine how it must have felt for someone with Zhu's personal history to discover that a corrupt local official had sold emergency grain supplies for profit, or that some bureaucrat's cavalier incompetence had allowed a remediable famine to get out of hand. And what better compliment for the people than to speak to them directly – to give them the benefit of his own moral leadership without the mediation of a class of pampered scholars? In another era, this same instinct would lead Mao Zedong, in many ways a very similar figure to Zhu, to chastise his own Communist Party and to speak directly to the revolutionary masses. Edward Farmer, the great scholar of Ming society, aptly calls it "imperial populism."

Such confidence aside, Zhu also used law in a more coercive sense, to delineate the boundaries of acceptable religion clearly, and in particular to outlaw anything resembling the millenarian beliefs of his erstwhile allies, the Red Turbans. Ming law proscribed much of what we might think of as magic: fortune-telling, books of prophecy, and any sort of shamanistic possession. It also divided deities and religious teachings into three groups: orthodox, illicit, and heretical. The final group was strictly banned. The Ming statute, which was adopted to the letter by the subsequent Qing dynasty and would remain in force until 1911, demanded strangulation for "all teachers and shamans who call down heterodox gods, write charms, chant incantations over water, perform spirit writing and pray to sages ... or call themselves the White Lotus Society of Maitreya ... or learn heretical techniques, or hide pictures of heterodox gods or gather in groups at night to burn incense." Followers got off relatively lightly with banishment to a borderland at least 3,000 *li* (about 1,000 miles) distant. Like much else from the early Ming, the instinct to divide legitimate and illegitimate religion would resurface again and again, in slightly different forms, over the following centuries.[14]

---

[14] This was not the first legal ban on such groups, but certainly the most comprehensive.

Besides Red Turban–style beliefs, the other great target of Zhu's cleanup campaign was Lamaist Buddhism. Overall, Zhu was friendly toward Buddhism. In 1378, he sent the monk Zongle (1318–91) to Tibet to recover lost sutras and published lavishly printed and gilt editions of Zongle's scriptural commentaries. He funded a spate of temple construction in Nanjing and other major cities. When his beloved Empress Ma died, Zhu assigned Buddhist advisers to each of his princes to ensure that they said devotions for the repose of her soul. Of course, part of the bargain implicit in bestowing patronage on Buddhism was that Zhu also extended his control over the institution. Zhu made it more difficult to become a monk by raising the age and scholarly requirements for ordination. He created special departments of Buddhism and Daoism within his own Ministry of Ritual (*li bu*), effectively making the two religions part of the state bureaucracy.

These courtesies did not, however, extend to Lamaist Buddhism, the school favored by Tibetans and Mongols, which was tainted by its association with the previous dynasty. The Mongol rulers of the Yuan were indeed deeply religious and devoted to their lamas. One Chinese minister in the Mongol court estimated with obvious alarm that two-thirds of state expenses were being spent on construction and support of elaborate lamaseries. As we will discuss further on, Lamaist Buddhism was also central to Mongol identity and political authority. The association between the two was such that Chinese hatred of the Mongols was equally directed against the lamas. Rumors spread of all manner of depravity taking place within the lamaseries, of orgies within the monks' quarters, and of lamas routinely deflowering Chinese boys and girls on the eve of their wedding.[15] Zhu sought in vain to rid China of the lamas as part of his systematic erasure of the Mongol legacy. He supported other schools of Buddhism in order to weaken the Lamaist influence but was never able to purge them from the court completely.

[15] This latter custom may remind some readers of *jus primae noctis*, the "law of the first night," which gave European lords the right of sexual congress with village maidens on the night before marriage. The two are indeed similar, particularly in the sense that neither one actually existed, at least not in the form that later retellings would lead us to believe. European lords did indeed have a right of *primae noctis*, but this was more economic than sexual in nature. Tibetan lamas were generally not expected to be celibate, and in some medieval schools of Central and Southeast Asian Buddhism, sexual congress was employed in religious rituals, such as those involving exorcism. In any case, no society, particularly one as concerned with family and ancestors as China's, would tolerate two centuries of the routine rape of their wives and daughters. Of course, as the producers of films such as *Braveheart* would certainly agree, the apocryphal version does still make an outstanding device for advancing the plot in historical dramas.

Moreover, Zhu was unable to lessen the influence of the sect in its homelands of Tibet and Mongolia, areas over which he had no control. In retrospect, this was a good thing for the subsequent Qing dynasty, in which Manchus, Mongols, and Tibetans ruled over the China we know today, their alliance lubricated by their common devotion to Lamaist Buddhism.[16]

We began this chapter with the suggestion that the first years of the Ming dynasty were a watershed in Chinese history, an important step toward the creation of the China that we know today. In many ways, this burst of energy did set the stage for much of what would occur later. Even keeping in mind the caution against viewing history solely from the modern perspective, we can still see evidence of Zhu Yuanzhang's innovations in China. Previous dynasties had sought to control religion, but Zhu was unique in wanting to control it *directly*. From this point onward, Chinese regulation of religious institutions would remain strict, if unevenly enforced, and later states would emulate his paternalistic attitude toward popular morals. Few of his descendants would be able to duplicate his connection to the common people, but Zhu was for a while able to envision an order in which the virtue of an energetic emperor would do more than inspire the loyalty of the bureaucracy: it would invigorate and transform the entire nation. The influence of Zhu's ideas is plainly evident in religious policies that began later, including those of the People's Republic. One can only wonder what Zhu might have thought of China's state-controlled churches or its campaigns against religious groups that are said to harm public morals, but he would no doubt have found the logic behind these initiatives far more familiar and sensible than the criticism that such policies often provoke in the West.

[16] Zhao Yifeng systematically compares Ming policies toward Han and Tibetan Buddhism. *Mingdai guojia zongjiao guanli zhidu yu zhengce yanjiu* [Research on the national religious regulatory apparatus and regulations of the Ming dynasty] (Beijing: Zhongguo shehui kexue chubanshe, 2007), 145–94.

3 The Buddha and the shōgun in sixteenth-century Japan

I. Religious foundations of medieval Japan

As we leave China and move to Japan, it is worth considering some of the reasons why these two close neighbors are so very different.

The best place to begin is by looking at a map. China is a massive piece of territory: the geographic anchor of East Asia. With Taiwan included, China is slightly larger than the United States. The Ming Empire was significantly smaller – just over half the size of the People's Republic of China today – but that is still roughly as large as the entire European Union. It was also exceedingly diverse. Even after the expulsion of the Mongols, Ming dynasty China was still home to a large variety of non-Han peoples. It was also surrounded by all the cultures of Asia: the Indic-influenced kingdoms of mainland Southeast Asia, Buddhist kingdoms in Tibet and modern Mongolia, Central Asian Muslims who traded along the Silk Road, and Chinese-style polities in Korea and Manchuria. Chinese call their country the Middle Kingdom, and for centuries, it very much was the great cultural behemoth that sat squarely at the crossroads of the world.[1]

Japan, in contrast, is an island (or more precisely, an archipelago). In size, Japan is about as large as the state of California, but before the large northern island of Hokkaido was fully incorporated in the late nineteenth century, it was roughly the size of Italy or the Philippines. And while Japan was originally settled by a variety of peoples and still has a wide diversity of regional cultures, it is far more internally homogeneous than China. Historically, its external relations were also rather

---

[1] The name *Middle Kingdom* (*Zhong guo*) is often mistaken as an expression of Chinese cultural chauvinism. In fact, the term comes from the preimperial period, a time when the territory of modern China was divided into competing kingdoms. Historically, people would refer to the country not as the Middle Kingdom, but rather by the name of the dynasty.

straightforward. As it was an island nation, Japanese sailors fished, traded, and settled along the continent and into Southeast Asia. But the most overwhelming cultural influence had one source: the world of Sinic culture that reached Japan through the Korean Peninsula, only ninety kilometers away. Thus, while China drew upon all the cultures along its borders, Japan was more like a pendulum, at times welcoming continental culture and at times rejecting it.

Thus, while Chinese religion is an ever-evolving combination of three beliefs, the religion of Japan is a more dualistic exchange of native and foreign influences. Like Japan itself, the history of Japanese religion is largely that of the changing relationship between the two.

The story begins with the native tradition, which is naturally the older of the two. We know this tradition today as Shintō, although that name has not always been used. The term *Shintō* literally means "Way of the Spirits," with the *way* being written with the same character as *Dao* in Chinese. Here the word does not refer to Daoism, but rather, to a philosophy or school of thought – rather like the English suffix *-ism* in English. (As mentioned earlier, this same character also appears in the names of martial and other arts, such as the formal ceremony of preparing and serving tea.) The name *Shintō* was adopted to give Japanese beliefs and traditions a certain completeness and gravitas, but as we will see, that all came later. In its early stages, there was not much to this tradition that we associate with a formally structured "religion." Indeed, it might be better for historians if there had been. An ecclesiastic religion would probably have written scriptures, rules, and records – Japanese indigenous worship of the time had none of these. Much of what scholars do know about early Japanese religion dates from a time *after* the indigenous tradition had already met and mingled with the great continental import: Buddhism.

But we can with some confidence piece together the basics. Early Japanese religion was based on the worship of spirits called *kami*. Some of these *kami* were anthropomorphic, meaning that they were thought of as individuals with names, personalities, and family relations. Many were not. Many *kami* derived directly from nature itself, as the essential spirit of a tree, a mountain, or a river. Both types of *kami* were connected to nature; that is one reason why much of Shintō ritual revolves around agriculture. People worshipped *kami* at key points in the planting season, and rural communities took *kami* as their patrons and protectors. Political families did, as well. Important clans, including the royal clan, each worshipped their own *kami*, who protected the family. The political significance of this sort of worship can be seen in the grand shrines that dot the medieval capitals of Nara and Kyoto (such as

Figure 3.1 Shintō shrine in Kyoto. The great gate of the Kamigamo Shrine. Photo by author.

the Kamigamo Shrine shown in Figure 3.1), but had already taken root during the fifth and sixth centuries, as the early kingdom of Yamato solidified its power over central Japan. It was also during this time that the royal clan began to venerate Amaterasu, the *kami* of the Sun, not only as a patron deity, but as the blood ancestress of the royal house. At every level, pleasing the *kami* was understood as vital to the collective fate of the group: the village, clan, or nation.[2]

Japan probably began regular, sustained contact with the Asian continent some time in the first or second centuries. Not much of this early interaction is well documented. On the basis of clues from literature, scholars once theorized that the islands had been invaded by horse-mounted warriors from Korea, but they have since become more doubtful.[3] A more peaceful sort of interaction probably resulted from

[2] It is a bit misleading to speak about "early Japanese religion" as if it were one single entity. While the details are not important here, you should be aware that Japanese religion and its relation to politics had already been evolving for centuries before Buddhism arrived on the scene. Matsumae Takeshi, "Early *Kami* Worship," in Delmer Myers Brown, ed., *The Cambridge History of Japan* (*CHOJ*), *Ancient Japan* (Cambridge: Cambridge University Press, 1993), 1:317–58.

[3] For an overview of the long-debated problem of horses in Japanese archaeology, see William Wayne Farris, *Sacred Texts and Buried Treasures: Issues on the Historical Archaeology of Ancient Japan* (Honolulu: University of Hawaii Press, 1998).

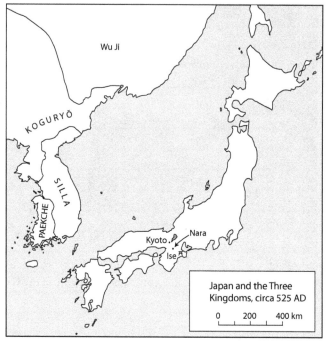

Map 3.1 Korea and Japan circa 525 AD.

traders, fishermen, and diplomats making the crossing from the tip of Korea to the southern island of Kyūshū. It is very likely that some Buddhist monks would have been among these early visitors.

But the real arrival of Buddhism in Japan can be clearly dated to the year 538, when an envoy arrived from the Korean kingdom of Paekche carrying sutras, a statue of the Buddha, and a proposition. For some time, the Korean Peninsula had comprised the three competing kingdoms shown in Map 3.1: Paekche in the West, Silla in the Southeast, and Koguryŏ in the North. Militarily, these three kingdoms were evenly matched, and in delivering Buddhism to the Japanese court, the Paekche king was hoping to seal an alliance to tip the balance. The Korean envoys understood that Buddhism was a very potent political force. Two centuries earlier, in the year 372, an ambassador from the court of the short-lived Chinese kingdom of Former Qin (Qian qin) presented the Koguryŏ king Sosurim (d. 384) with a gift of Buddhist sutras and statues. Three years later, Koguryŏ completed its first Buddhist monastery, and within twenty years had named Buddhism as its state religion.[4] By adopting Buddhism, the rulers of Koguryŏ at once cemented their own spiritual authority, entered into a world of religious diplomacy, and drew upon the power of the Buddha himself, who, judging from the success of their powerful neighbor to the south, was a potent deity indeed. The story is not precisely the same for the other two Korean kingdoms, since each one adopted a slightly different form of Buddhism, transmitted from different parts of China, but nevertheless we can say that when King Sŏngmyŏng (r. 523–54) of Paekche formally presented the gift of Buddhism to his Japanese counterpart Emperor Kinmei (509–71), the last thing either party was worried about was seeking inner peace.[5]

The Japanese, for their part, understood the idea of divine patronage very well and received the Buddha as another *kami*, albeit one whom the native *kami* might not especially welcome. For this reason, Kinmei was unwilling to offend native deities by accepting the Buddha himself. He initially allowed another clan named Soga to do so, but when a pestilence struck the capital, he ordered the practice stopped and had the statue unceremoniously dumped into a canal. Most of the other aristocratic clans were equally happy to put the incident behind them, until something strange began to happen. The Soga remained faithful to the Buddha and began to prosper, both in the court and on the battlefield. Within a few decades, worship of the Buddha had spread to other clans and among the populace; most importantly, it had been accepted by the royal family. Some historians might dispute the image of Prince Shōtoku (574–622) as a great Buddhist thinker, but he and Kinmei's reigning daughter, Suiko (554–628), laid the legal foundation for Buddhism to prosper. Especially after internal political machinations removed the Soga from power in 645, Buddhism became increasingly connected with the royal clan. Buddhism itself was not all that was at stake. The historian Joan Piggott suggests that diplomacy with the Chinese court may have prompted Suiko to reinvent elements of Japanese kingship, by establishing Buddhism as a sort of "royal cult."[6] In the decades that followed, the Buddha became enshrined as the patron and protector of

---

[4] Oikawa Giemon, *Manshū tsūshi* [Complete history of Manchuria] (Tokyo: Hakubunkan, 1935), 57–8; Daigan Matsunaga and Alicia Matsunaga, *Foundation of Japanese Buddhism* (Los Angeles: Buddhist Books International, 1974), 9–17.

[5] I follow convention in translating the title of the Japanese sovereign as "emperor." Joan Piggott makes a strong case for avoiding this term, and instead using "king," even in the case of female sovereigns such as Suiko. Joan R. Piggott, *The Emergence of Japanese Kingship* (Stanford, CA: Stanford University Press, 1997), 8–9.

[6] Although Shōtoku was technically appointed as her regent, Suiko did exercise real political power. See Piggott, *Emergence of Japanese Kingship*, 79–83.

the Japanese state, and worship of the Buddha was mandated at every level of society: an imperial order of 685 demanded "every house set up a Buddhist altar, with an image of the Buddha and Buddhist scriptures, for worship and offerings of food." In 741, to put a stop to a series of poor harvests and rampant disease, the emperor Shōmu (701–56) required each province to build at least one major Buddhist temple. A few years later, he capped his great building project by ordering the casting of a massive statue of the Buddha to sit in the Great Eastern Temple (Tōdaiji), which dominated the new capital of Nara.

With state support came state regulation. After the coup of 645, the entire government was restructured to resemble the Chinese administrative bureaucracy. This new system relied on a vastly expanded legal code, which also regulated Buddhism. New laws restricted who could be ordained Buddhist monks and how they would be trained. Special care was taken to deal with unregulated holymen who tried to pass themselves off as genuine Buddhist priests, and especially those who used the power of religious belief to interfere in politics. Two successive codes specifically outlined punishment for monks who "discuss matters relating to state, delude the common people, or read military books."[7]

But it is important to remember that even if they sought to keep the monks under control, the Nara kingdom did not simply view Buddhism from the outside. Buddhism was integral to the state itself. Like Confucian morality in China, Buddhism became an important foundation of the evolving imperial institution. Other ideas, such as divine ancestry and ritual purity, were not forgotten, but integrated into a cosmology of kingship that placed Buddhism on an equal level. The law of the sovereign (obō) and the law of the Buddha (Buppō, i.e., the dharma) were likened to two wheels of a cart. (Over the centuries, this same analogy would be put to a variety of purposes, but in this case it is important to remember that what is called the law of the Buddha simply refers to sacred authority more generally.) Likewise, state-mandated construction projects, such as the edict requiring every province to build a temple, were not merely expressions of imperial piety; they were also the anchors of a sacred geography, one that simultaneously pacified and protected the nation, and integrated Buddhism into the state structure. In a similar way, Tōdaiji itself was more than a great cathedral. It undergirded state authority, centered the sacred geography on Nara, and served as a single point from which the state would try to keep the expanding Buddhist institution under surveillance and control.[8]

---

[7] Stanley Weinstein, "Aristocratic Buddhism," in *CHOJ*, 2:450.

[8] To appreciate the complex interaction of political and religious power fully, see Piggott, *Emergence of Japanese Kingship*, 236–79. For a shorter overview, see Neil McMullin,

By accepting Buddhism, Japan opened the door to a flood of continental high culture. Along with Buddhism, state-of-the-art architecture, sculpture, medicine, statecraft, and philosophy were introduced. Chinese characters, often used in a uniquely Korean way, had already reached Japan before the age of Nara Buddhism. But the influx of Chinese high culture and the votive act of copying Buddhist sutras by hand or later by print put Chinese characters into even more widespread use. The reason why scholars can never know for certain precisely what Japanese religion might have looked like before Buddhism is that precious few written records exist from before this time. Even the great classics of ancient Japanese literature, the *Record of Ancient Matters* (*Kojiki*) and *Chronicles of Japan* (*Nihongi*), were not actually written down until Buddhism had already become very well established. The new texts entering from China were linguistically complex. Moreover, some of the sutras were meant to be chanted out loud according to their original pronunciation in Sanskrit or Pali. What was needed was a way of glossing the text to represent grammar and sounds, and over time, the hybrid system further adapted to become the foundation of what would later become the characteristic Japanese phonetic system known as *hiragana*.[9]

Early Japanese Buddhism was a distinctly high culture. Rather than a single school, the Buddhism of the Nara period (710–94, so named after the location of the capital) consisted of six separate schools, all of which were headquartered in Tōdaiji. The Tōdaiji monks' hearts may have been with the Buddha, but their minds were busy absorbing the most cutting edge philosophy from China. Each of the six schools represented this profoundly intellectual tradition, one that was concerned with the metaphysical nature of matter, existence, consciousness, and time. Had they the chance to meet, the scholarly monks in Nara would have very much appreciated their counterparts in Christian Europe, who posed such questions as how many angels would fit on the head of a pin.

The native tradition was never purged. Even if some of its shrines and deities were to some degree pushed into the background, at least initially its overall relation to Buddhism was more symbiosis than competition. Some of the more ardent Buddhist apologists did express their dislike of the native tradition, such as the emperor Kōtoku (596–654), who in 645 proclaimed that he "honored the Way of the Buddha and

Buddhism and the State in Sixteenth Century Japan (Princeton, NJ: Princeton University Press, 1984), 17–21.
[9] Christopher Seeley, *A History of Writing in Japan* (Leiden: E. J. Brill, 1991).

Figure 3.2 Great Buddha of Tōdaiji. The cost of materials used in casting the giant statue nearly bankrupted the Nara court. As with many of Japan's cultural treasures, both the building and statue have been reconstructed after damage by fire and earthquakes. Photo by Misako Suzuki.

despised the Way of the *kami*." But even those sovereigns who supported Buddhism did not feel compelled to *disbelieve* the existence of the native *kami*. In 741, before the emperor Shōmu commissioned the colossal Buddha statue for Tōdaiji shown in Figure 3.2, he first visited the shrine at Ise to report his plans to the *kami*. When a Buddhist monk tried to place himself in line for the throne in 769, the dying empress Shōtoku (718–70, not to be confused with the prince of the same name) sent an envoy to a Shintō oracle to make sure that such an arrangement was in fact the will of the *kami* Hachiman. (As events turned out, it was not.) Even this devoutly Buddhist sovereign was still conscious of her blood tie to Amaterasu.

But even if Buddhist deities had for the moment stolen the limelight, they and the native *kami* continued to share the same stage. Two decades before he foiled the monk's plans to become emperor, Hachiman asked that his shrine be moved to Tōdaiji, so that he too might worship the

Buddha. Over time, the relationship would become a bit more equitable. By the end of the eighth century, the beginning of what is known as the Heian period (794–1185), the great wave of continental culture had permeated Japanese soil. Chinese culture had begun to feel less exotic, less foreign, and indeed had transformed into a hybrid culture that was as advanced as anything in China, but also was truly Japanese. Even as China itself fell into a rapid political decline with the waning of the Tang dynasty, all of its refined arts – literature, poetry, and art – remained in full flower in Japan.

Buddhism was now fully Japanese and had merged seamlessly with native beliefs. Not only were Buddhist and Shintō shrines built together on the same premises, but the idea began to arise that Buddhas and *kami* were in fact two names for the same deities. As in China, this arrangement was inspired by the Mahāyāna idea that the Buddha's teaching is always contingent and evolving – that he tells us only what we are able to understand at that moment but will reveal more when we are ready to learn it. The idea, then, was that the deities had introduced themselves as *kami* simply as a way of preparing the ground for revealing their true nature as Buddhas and bodhisttavas. Thus, it was claimed that the *kami* Hachiman was actually the bodhisattva Amida, and that Amaterasu, progenitress of the imperial household, was in fact the kindly deity Guanyin (known in Japan as Kannon). The name given to this theology of dual identity was "substance and manifestation" (*honji suijaku*, more precisely translated as "true nature and apparent traces"), and is depicted in the Kasuga mandala in Figure 3.3. The more common interpretation, at least for the time being, was that the Buddhist identity represented the first half of this equation – the genuine substance. Shintō was the latter: it was not exactly incorrect, but it did represent an inferior reality. Later generations would retain this formulation but would interpret its content very differently.

This is also the period when Tiantai and Zhenyan, two schools of Chinese Buddhism, crossed the sea and began to develop into something distinctly Japanese. Although very different from each other, these two schools, better known by their Japanese pronunciation of Tendai and Shingon, shared certain common features. In contrast to the sterile intellectualism of Nara Buddhism, both were highly devotional. The founders of these two schools, Saichō (767–822) and Kūkai (774–835), had begun as friends, but doctrinal differences sent Tendai and Shingon in very different directions. Tendai devotion was based primarily on meditation and on the recitation of scripture, especially of the *Lotus Sutra*. Shingon turned its attention to secret knowledge and

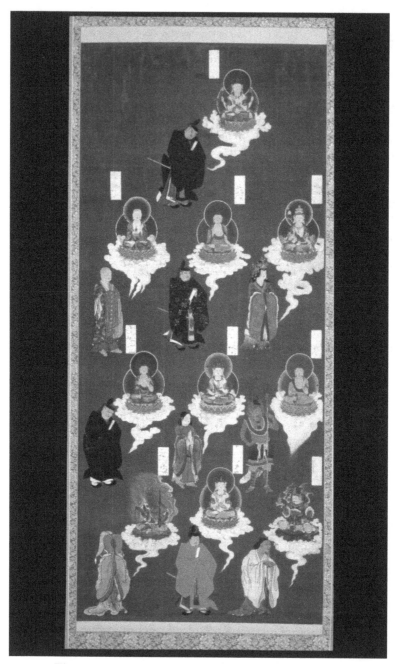

Figure 3.3 Depiction of *honji suijaku*. This detail of the Kasuga mandala shows historical and Shintō figures and their inner Buddhist identities. Image kindly provided by Hōzanji Temple, Nara.

mystic arts known collectively as tantra.[10] Over time, the differences
between these schools would sharpen, particularly once they began
competing for resources, and especially for imperial patronage (since
its rituals could be used both for healing and for the protection of the
state, Shingon generally fared better in this contest).

But Tendai and Shingon were not so different. Both believed that
scripture recitation and ritual were important; the vital question was
which was *more* important, or to put it in the language often used, which
was the *true essence* of Buddhism. And people did have to choose one
path or the other. Unlike the Nara schools, which mixed freely in places
like Tōdaiji, these new schools were exclusive. Saichō pioneered the
sectarian monastery, that is, a temple filled with monks from only one
school, which would later become standard for Japanese Buddhism.[11]
Becoming a Tendai monk took no less than twelve years of intense training and devotion. Shingon was no less rigorous. Not surprisingly, these
two schools sought to separate themselves from society – each one set
up headquarters on a mountain. Tendai built a massive temple complex
on Mount Hiei near Kyoto. A bit later, Shingon established its center on
Mount Kōya farther south. Together, both of these highly demanding
schools are sometimes referred to as Mountain Buddhism.

The name *Heian* literally means "peaceful and secure," and for the
most part, it was. The periods that followed, the military rule of the
Kamakura (1185–1333) and Ashikaga (1336–1573) shogunates, were
somewhat less so. They were also, however, periods of renewed interaction with China. Together, these two trends produced yet another wave
of innovation within Buddhism, one that carried the teaching down
from its mountain temples and into the life of the lay believer. Two of the
three schools associated with this wave, Zen and Pure Land, had orig-
inated in China but further evolved in Japan, while a third, Nichiren,
was original to Japan and patriotic to the point of chauvinism. What
each of these schools shared in common with the others was simplicity.
Both Tendai and Shingon demanded a lifetime of devotion, learning
secret tantric arts or chanting sutras, but in either case pursuing a
course that was professional, lifelong, and essentially selfish. But these
newer teachings were for the nonexpert, the sincere layman.

Hōnen (1133–1212), the founder of Japanese Pure Land Buddhism,
began his career as a Tendai monk. Instead of chanting the complete

---

[10] Because much of their ritual was intended for insiders only, schools such as Shingon
are often called Esoteric Buddhism. However, despite its image in popular culture,
tantra has relatively little to do with creative sexual techniques.
[11] Weinstein, "Aristocratic Buddhism," 471.

text of the *Lotus Sutra* as he had learned in his thirty years on Mount Hiei, Hōnen directed his followers instead to repeat the name of Amida. This practice, of "calling the Buddha" (*nembutsu* in Japanese, or *nian fo* in Chinese) over and over, thousands of times, marks a fundamental shift in Buddhist thought. While earlier schools ran monks through years of rigorous training, this new practice was based on the idea that the world had become so degenerate that no amount of prayer or ritual could do the job alone. The only way to be saved (that is, to be reborn in the Pure Land) is to rely on the infinite mercy of divine beings. The most merciful of these is Amida, who in the *Lotus Sutra* vows to save anyone who calls out to him with a pure heart (this is called the "original vow," or *hon gan*, a term you will be hearing again shortly). Earlier Tendai teachers had encouraged monks to visualize Amida's vow mentally while chanting the entire sutra, and Hōnen just took the next logical step of focusing directly on Amida himself. Other schools varied this theme of simple, sincere recitation. Nichiren told his devotees to recite "praise to the Holy *Lotus Sutra*" (which some readers will recognize as the phrase "*namu myōhō renge kyō*"). In the mid-thirteenth century, the monk Shinran (1173–1263), one of Hōnen's own disciples, founded a new sect called the True Pure Land (*jōdo shinshū*), which simplified this practice even further: devotees only had to call the name of Amida *once*, but with complete faith and sincerity.[12] Not surprisingly, this very simple, sincere, and devotional Buddhism became very popular with the common people. (The simplicity of Zen, which is rather less simple to explain, is the subject of a later chapter.)

Most of these various Buddhist schools lived side by side, but the relationship was not always peaceful. Centuries earlier, schools such as Tendai had needed to fight for their own survival and now had little patience for their newer rivals. The practice of *nembutsu* was especially divisive: by claiming that sincere recitation was the *only* path out of hell, schools such as the Pure Land broke a long-standing tradition of mutual tolerance among schools. In 1207, Hōnen and Shinran both discovered the danger of offending the Buddhist establishment when they were accused of heresy and banished from the capital.[13] And when different schools or different factions within the same school attacked each other, the result was often violent. Nichiren, who was particularly aggressive in spreading his teaching, was repeatedly jailed to prevent him from causing disturbances.

---

[12] In English, this school is sometimes referred to as Shin Buddhism.

[13] Ōsumi Kazuo, "Buddhism in the Kamakura Period," in Yamamura Kōzō, ed., *CHOJ, Medieval Japan* (Cambridge: Cambridge University Press, 1990), 3:565.

As always, one very important source of conflict was money. As temples grew increasingly wealthy, competition for resources grew ever more intense. Just as they did in China, the Buddhist faithful in Japan made large donations of land to monasteries, which in turn invested their wealth in town enterprises and merchant guilds. Since pilgrims and traders plied the same roads, many of these walled temples grew into commercial centers known as *ji nai chō*, literally a "town inside a temple." And none of them was taxed: military officials were barred from even entering the temple precincts. The reason behind this preferential treatment was the importance of Buddhism as a protector of the nation. People continued to place political and religious power on the same level, as two wheels of the same cart. The Buddha was, after all, still a protector of Japan. Twice during the thirteenth century, the Mongols, who had already overrun China, Korea, and pretty much everywhere else you could imagine, turned their eyes on Japan, and the Buddhists of the country responded by organizing marathon prayer sessions. When the ships carrying the Mongol warriors were caught not once, but twice, in sudden typhoons, there was no doubt that Japan had been spared by the Buddha. The typhoons became known as a "divine wind," the original source of the term *kamikaze*.[14] As central authority fell into decline during the second half of the Heian period, many monasteries sought to maintain a more conventional form of defense. Many began keeping bands of armed monks (*sōhei*) to guard their interests, to threaten rivals, and, in some cases, to put pressure on political authorities. The wealthiest temples were built on mountains and surrounded by elaborate military fortifications.[15]

But the newest types of Buddhism had another type of power altogether. Established schools like Tendai and Shingon seemed to hold all the cards: close ties to political power, learned institutions, artistic and cultural treasures, and vast landed wealth. It probably is not too great a stretch to compare these schools to the Catholic Church in medieval Europe – or to liken the rise of new teachings based on simple piety and sincerity to the Protestant Reformation. Both cases reveal one very important similarity: a church that amasses wealth and power also makes itself vulnerable. When England's Henry VIII found himself simultaneously feuding with the Catholic Church and in need of cash, he had little difficulty in simply seizing church property (as did the short-lived Wuzong emperor, 814–46, of the Tang dynasty). Similarly, even if some Japanese monasteries, such as the massive Tendai complex

---

[14] Although probably not with that particular pronunciation.
[15] McMullin, *Buddhism and the State*, 20–1.

on Mount Hiei, were themselves armed and fortified, they still relied on vital landed and commercial interests for their upkeep.

In contrast, the newer schools were less centralized and, relatively speaking, less reliant on clergy. Some schools, such as True Pure Land, had a clear hierarchy of authority but rejected the monastic life entirely. Their temples, such as the Honganji (the Temple of the Original Vow; the suffix -*ji* simply means "temple") did have significant business interests but also relied heavily on lay donations directly to the main temple. Other schools kept order by maintaining a hierarchy of monasteries, but lay piety was much more difficult to control: even the Honganji could not claim complete control over its faithful. As do those of any religion, the disciples of True Pure Land broke into sects and factions and had to balance their own interests against any directives that flowed down from the top. But when they needed to, schools like True Pure Land could organize more than money. During the late 1400s, armed networks of lay believers participated in a series of uprisings. Unshakable in their convictions, the Buddhist faithful fought with such courage and discipline that they became known as *ikkō*, or "single-minded." Even regional branches could quickly raise tens of thousands of well-equipped volunteers, all without having to pay to support an army in the field. When the time came, these lay networks would prove an extremely formidable force.[16]

II. Burning monks: The assault on Buddhism

By the middle of the sixteenth century, Japan resembled nothing as much as a giant board game brought to life. A rich and mighty realm, once united under the military rule of the Ashikaga shōgun, was now divided into the fifty-four independent domains shown in Map 3.2. Each of these domains, known as *han*, was in many ways a kingdom in itself – each one had its own army, natural and man-made defenses, and, perhaps most importantly, each had its own military ruler, a daimyō, or "great name," who often had great ambition to match. As the power of the shōgun waned, that of the once-docile domains grew. For half a century, Japan would be thrown into chaos, as each of these daimyō became a player in a fifty-four-part civil war, from which even the victors would emerge bloodied.

---

[16] Carol Richmond Tsang, *War and Faith: Ikkō ikki in Late Muromachi Japan* (Cambridge: Harvard University Asia Center, 2007), 288; McMullin, *Buddhism and the State*, 51–2.

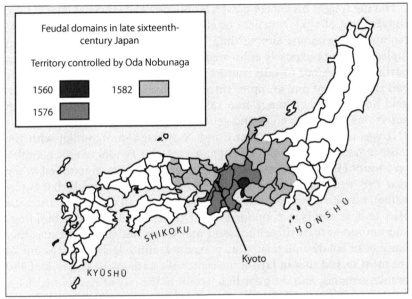

Map 3.2 Feudal domains in late sixteenth-century Japan.

The most important figure to emerge from these chaotic times was Oda Nobunaga (1534–82). Nobunaga,[17] the first of three generals, who, in succession, would eventually best their rivals and found a new shogunate, had a reputation as a brute of the first order. The son of a military family in the central domain of Owari, Nobunaga would, through a combination of daring, skill, and ruthless diplomacy, command his own army and rise to the rank of daimyō. He was a brilliant and audacious tactician, on one occasion defeating twenty-five thousand men with a force of only eighteen hundred. By means of such talent, he one by one bettered and absorbed his local opponents and so came to establish himself as the strongest power in central Japan, the wealthy and important region that contains the imperial city of Kyoto. By the end of the 1560s, Nobunaga was rapidly emerging as the man to beat, and all other forces faced the choice of either joining him or trying to hold together an alliance to oppose him.

[17] In all Chinese and Japanese names, the surname is given first. However, because they are such familiar figures, and in order to distinguish them from other members of their families, it is also common to refer to the three founders of the Tokugawa by their given names, as Nobunaga, Hideyoshi, and Ieyasu, respectively.

Having fought his way to power, Nobunaga had little patience for the conventions of silky courtiers or effete monks. This is not to say that Nobunaga was some simple thug; he was a master of Machiavellian diplomacy and purposely cultivated his image as a ruthless foe. He was particularly vicious toward traitors within his own ranks – he famously had the heads of one group of turncoats cleaned of flesh, lacquered in gold and silver, and made into sake cups, which he then used when entertaining his own allies and generals.

It was just such a case that drove Nobunaga into conflict with the most famous of the mountain monasteries, the Tendai temple complex on Mount Hiei. The central Enryakuji temple had been founded in the year 788 (near the beginning of the Enryaku reign, from which it got its name), but the complex itself was more like a small city. Altogether, the Hiei temple complex contained about thirty-eight hundred buildings and housed at least three thousand monks, as well as many times that number of lay disciples, support personnel, and pilgrims. It was one of the most sacred sites in Japan, the center of a nationwide network of 380 branch temples, and the guardian temple of the city of Kyoto, which lay nestled in the valley below. For practical purposes, the Enryakuji was inviolable, or so thought two of Nobunaga's rival daimyō, who in 1570 were defeated on the battlefield and fled to the mountain seeking refuge. (As with Christian churches in Europe, the independence of major monasteries effectively made them places of political sanctuary.) Never one to give quarter to a weakened foe, particularly not one so close to his own capital, Nobunaga marched his army to the entrance and presented a simple ultimatum: surrender the two men and the temple would retain its rights and landholdings; refuse and the temple would be destroyed.

The monks, unwisely, chose the latter, and one year later, Nobunaga returned with thirty thousand men to make good on his promise. Now quite alarmed, the monks attempted to buy Nobunaga off, but without success. Nobunaga quickly overwhelmed their defenses and embarked on a week of slaughter. All of the priests, as well as the lay population, were hunted down and beheaded, countless cultural treasures destroyed or looted, and every structure burned to the ground. (For reasons explained in a subsequent chapter, the temple was rebuilt by Nobunaga's successors. Buildings at the site today, such as the main hall seen in Figure 3.4, are all of this more recent vintage.)

As a result of his actions, Oda Nobunaga quickly became the target of a massive uprising of the Buddhist faithful. As religious sects often do, the various schools of Buddhism frequently fought among themselves, but the unthinkable violence that accompanied the destruction of the

Figure 3.4 Enryakuji, Mount Hiei. As with all of the buildings currently at the Enryakuji, this main hall was reconstructed. Photo by Jack Meng-Tat Chia.

Enryakuji gave everyone pause, particularly when Kennyo (1543–92), the abbot of Honganji in Kyoto, sent out a nationwide letter to all high-ranking priests, branding Nobunaga an "enemy of the law" (that is, an enemy of Buddhism) and urging them to resist his forces in any way possible. The problem was, while Nobunaga may have shocked the world by burning the Enryakuji, he also patronized other temples. Kennyo's missive aside, most people realized that Nobunaga was less an enemy of Buddhism than he was a ruthless foe of anyone who got in his way. Moreover, while many schools of Buddhism were indeed wealthy and powerful, most were landholders like the Enryakuji. They knew that it would present little difficulty for Nobunaga literally to march right in and strip them, one by one, of their wealth and weapons – particularly if any were to take the foolish step of declaring war on him first.

The exception to this was the network of the new Kamakura schools of Buddhism, particularly those of Kennyo's own True Pure Land. This school had only a thin stratum of monks at the very top, but otherwise very little in the way of leadership. What it did have was faith, very strong faith, in its mission and the righteousness of its cause. The faithful of this school responded to the call to oppose Oda Nobunaga by reorganizing *ikkō* networks on an even larger scale than they had in the past. For ten years, they fought Nobunaga's forces with an unparalleled ferocity, knowing that their cause was just, and that death in battle would earn them reincarnation in the Pure Land. They proved almost impossible to defeat. For ten years, Nobunaga's generals would fight the *ikkō* in one location, only to have them reappear in another. Because they were lay-based, they did not rely on clergy and could immediately resurrect their networks wherever the faithful were present, which clearly was just about everywhere. Eventually, in 1576, Nobunaga did manage to corner the most important leaders and the bulk of the remaining followers in the citadel of the Ishiyama Honganji,[18] a heavily fortified branch of the temple near Osaka. After a lengthy siege, requiring four years, sixty thousand men, and a naval blockade (to prevent the arrival of aid from rival families, who were only too happy to see Nobunaga thus occupied), Oda Nobunaga destroyed the temple and the rebellion once and for all. But for ten years, it had been an uprising of devoted Buddhists, not the armies of his daimyō rivals, that presented the greatest challenge to Oda Nobunaga's dreams of conquest.

Armed Buddhism would never again become a significant force in Japan, but Oda Nobunaga would not be around long to enjoy his victory. Not surprisingly, he died a violent death in 1582, after being betrayed by one of his own generals, and was succeeded by Toyotomi Hideyoshi (1537–98). Hideyoshi was easily as ruthless as Nobunaga, but arguably more clever. Hideyoshi was a colorful character, who had risen from complete obscurity as a foot soldier to become one of Nobunaga's inner circle of generals – his life remains a popular topic for television dramas in Japan. (He is rather less celebrated in the rest of Asia, because of his two ill-fated attempts to invade China through Korea.) The common schoolyard rhyme about the three founders of the Tokugawa shogunate is that Nobunaga, Hideyoshi, and their successor Tokugawa Ieyasu each wanted a bird to sing: Nobunaga threatened to kill the bird if he did not sing, while Hideyoshi offered the bird a treat if he would consent to do so. (Tokugawa, who would eventually found the shogunate that bears his name, was more clever still and simply waited until the bird wanted to sing – this, no doubt, in reference to his enviable talent for being in the right place at the right time.)

Hideyoshi had been instrumental in many of Nobunaga's military offensives and in 1585 initiated his own campaign against the heavily armed Negoroji, an equally august and revered temple complex

---

[18] As many temples share the same names, they are often written together with the name of the place.

associated with Shingon, burning all but the main pagoda to the ground. After this, the remaining Buddhist schools were largely willing to fall into line. It was from this point that Hideyoshi would demonstrate the tactical skill for which he would become so well remembered. After destroying or emasculating the wealthy and powerful monasteries of medieval Buddhism, Hideyoshi now sought to portray himself not only as a sincere Buddhist, but as a great patron of Buddhism.

In doing so, Hideyoshi began the process by which Buddhism would become the foundation of a complex system of social control that would remain in place for another two and a half centuries. Once the military reunification of Japan, begun by Nobunaga, was nearly complete, Hideyoshi in 1588 embarked on the great "sword hunt," a massive disarming of the populace. From this point onward, only the samurai, a hereditary warrior class, would be allowed to carry swords (or wear the topknot hairstyle still worn by sumo wrestlers today). Everyone else was forced to surrender his sword, for the ostensible reason that in iron-poor Japan, these items were needed to provide nails for the reconstruction of Buddhist temples and to cast images of the Buddha, such as the massive statue Hideyoshi commissioned for his new temple (Hōkōji) in Kyoto. In 1593, near the site of the former Negoroji, Hideyoshi built the elaborate Diamond Peak temple (Kongobuji, the name being a reference to the Diamond mandala used in the characteristic meditative practices of the school). Monks were allowed to return to this and other rebuilt temples but in doing so were required to submit to the new civil authorities. They were required to swear oaths of allegiance to the shogunal authorities and encouraged to report misconduct within the temples. And as we shall see in a later chapter, the monks themselves were just the beginning. The Tokugawa shōguns not only exerted control over Buddhism itself, but also put the monks to use as administrators.

4   Opportunities lost: The failure of Christianity, 1550–1750

I. The Society of Jesus comes to Asia

Although separated by two and a half centuries, the early years of the Ming dynasty (1368–1644) and Tokugawa shogunate (1600–1868) present certain obvious similarities. Both regimes emerged from periods of chaos and warfare, and each one went to great lengths to transform society and thus establish a more durable political order. Bitter experience had taught the ambitious founders of each of these new governments that religion could be both a threat and an ally. Each enshrined new policies toward religion, supporting some, banning or ignoring others. Of course, the two were working within fairly different religious landscapes: the Ming emperor built up Confucianism but also faced the destabilizing influence of apocalyptic belief, while the early Tokugawa rulers had first to tame and then to harness Buddhist piety. To appreciate fully the comparison between these two, we need to see how each one reacted to the arrival of a new religion: Christianity.

The first Christian missionaries, Iberian Catholics of the Jesuit order, reached Japan in the mid-1500s, and China a few decades later. In each place, they found allies among the political elite and faced opposition from a variety of conservative figures, particularly Buddhist monks. Similarly, Christian missionaries in both Japan and China experienced an initial period of success, which was abruptly terminated by a sudden reversal of political fortune. By the early seventeen hundreds, Western missionaries had been expelled from both countries, and their religion banned by law.

What led to such an outcome? The fact that the Christian religion rose and fell in the same spectacular fashion in these two very different countries might suggest that it was simply doomed to fail in East Asia. But upon closer inspection, the story behind Christianity's initial success and ultimate demise was very different in Japan and China.

Iberian Christianity came to Asia by sea – on the decks of ships that first plied the world's oceans in what Western history usually calls the Age of Exploration. This was the time of Christopher Columbus, Vasco de Gama, and Ferdinand Magellan, one in which religious fervor, trade, and colonization were inseparable from each other. This is a point to which we will return later, but for now you may merely keep in mind that from the European perspective, religious mission was never solely a question of piety; it was also a matter of financial and national interest.

During the sixteenth century, the European powers one by one made their way to Asia. The first to arrive were the Portuguese. Under the sponsorship of a series of royal patrons (including the rather absurdly misnamed Henry the Navigator [1394–1460], who did most of his "navigating" from the safety of his palace) Portugal had pioneered the circumnavigation of Africa, captured the strategic Indian city of Goa, and established a stronghold at Malacca, the city at the center of the impossibly lucrative spice trade. From there, it was an easy trip up the coast to China. The Portuguese trader Rafael Perestrello first reached China in 1516 and was followed one year later by Tomé Pires, who was sent by the king of Portugal to act as an envoy to the Ming court. In 1535, Portuguese traders were given permission to establish a small settlement on the isthmus of Macao and from there would monopolize the foreign trade into and out of Canton. A few years later, in 1542 or 1543, three Portuguese traders who had been thrown off course in a typhoon became the first Europeans to reach Japan.[1]

The Portuguese were followed by the Spanish, who sailed not by way of Africa, but directly across the Pacific from the New World. Magellan had first made the crossing in 1521, landing on a group of islands that he claimed for Spain, just before being killed by natives who were none too pleased with the idea. By the 1560s, Spanish colonists had formed a permanent settlement on the islands (which they named the Philippines after their king, Philip II) that soon became the terminus of a thriving galleon route that traded Asian luxury goods for Mexican silver. Spanish envoys reached the Chinese coast in 1575 and were given permission to trade along some of the southern provinces, but not to set up residence. Spanish friars established a base in Taiwan in order to begin missionary work on the island.

By the time the Dutch arrived in the early 1600s, the field was already getting crowded. The Dutch government had granted the Netherlands East India Company permission to raise troops and declare war, and the company immediately did both: it seized Sumatra, Java, and the

---

[1] J. F. Moran, *The Japanese and the Jesuits: Alessandro Valignano in Sixteenth Century Japan* (London: Routledge, 1993), 1.

Moluccas from Portugal, and Taiwan from the Spanish. For a time, Portuguese influence was sufficient to keep the Dutch out of both Japan and China, but before long, Dutch (and later, British) envoys were making fast friends with any and all who had misgivings about Portuguese inroads into the halls of power.

As European traders extended their reach into Asia, Christian missionaries followed in their wake. Here again, Portugal was at the lead. The 1494 Treaty of Tordesillas granted to Portugal *padroado* in all newly discovered lands east of the Atlantic, meaning that Portugal would have exclusive right to convert and thus govern any non-Christians they found. The string of Portuguese trade settlements along the coasts of Africa and the Indian Ocean also became the backbone of a Catholic missionary network. Initially this emerging empire was placed under the Portuguese diocese of Funchal, but in 1533, Goa was named a diocese in its own right and two decades later was elevated to archdiocese.[2] Even as the number of new dioceses continued to grow (see Map 4.1), Goa would remain one of the most important centers of Catholic mission in Asia.

The pioneers of this missionary enterprise were the priests of the Society of Jesus, better known as Jesuits. This society had been founded by Ignatius of Loyola (1491–1556) in 1540, a time when the Catholic Church was reeling from the Reformation. Before long, the Jesuit order had become known not merely as priests, but also as an elite corps of devoted and disciplined scholars. They opened schools and universities in Europe and excelled not only in theology and classical languages, but also in the more technical fields of astronomy, naval design, and siegecraft. The Jesuit order was at the forefront of Catholic mission into Asia, establishing itself first in Goa and from there to other Portuguese settlements along the coast of India, and eventually throughout Asia.

Japan

In 1549, the extraordinarily energetic Jesuit missionary Francis Xavier (1506–52), along with three other priests, landed on the southern island of Kyūshū. In every sense, Xavier's journey to Japan had been a long one. A friend of Ignatius Loyola, and one of the core members of

---

[2] Of course, only the Catholic powers recognized this right of governance. The Treaty of Tordesillas was signed by Portugal and Spain and mediated by the Vatican but was meaningless to the Protestant powers of Europe, much less to the various "undiscovered" peoples the treaty sought to govern.

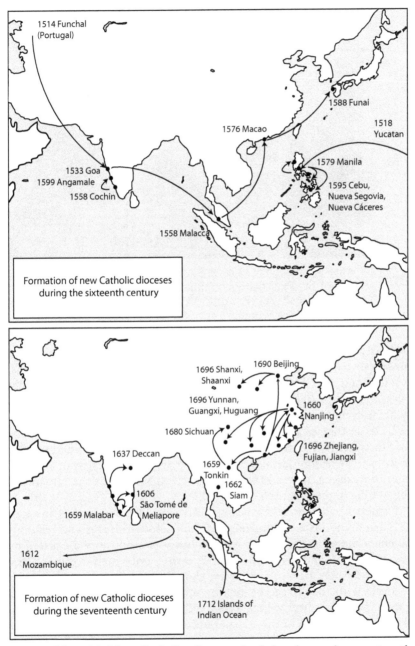

Map 4.1 New Catholic dioceses in Asia, sixteenth–seventeenth centuries.

Figure 4.1 Statue of Francis Xavier. This statue stands before the ruins of St. Paul Catholic Church in Malacca. Francis Xavier's remains were kept here until 1553, when they were moved to Goa. Photo by Ryoko Nakano.

the early Jesuit order, Xavier had decided as early as 1540 to devote his life to Christian mission in the lands of the Portuguese *padroado*. Xavier knew very little about the lands he would travel to, except that he would not be likely to return from them. To Loyola, he gave a very final farewell: "For what is left of this life, I am well assured, it will only be by letter that we are together – it is in the other that we shall embrace face to face." Xavier traveled up the African coast, remaining for a few months in Mozambique and finally taking up residence first in Goa and later in Malacca, where his statue still greets visitors at the remains of the old Portuguese church (Figure 4.1).

Francis Xavier's first few years in Asia were frustrating but instructive. He found little to admire in the indigenous cultures and religions he encountered in India and Malaya but was even more disgusted by the corruption and brutishness of his own countrymen overseas. To a friend in Lisbon, he wrote: "Do not allow any of your friends to be sent to India with the charge of looking after the finances of the King.... There is here a power, which I may call irresistible, to thrust men into the abyss." Because of these experiences, Xavier was relatively unique among missionaries of the time, in that he did not equate Christianity with becoming culturally Portuguese, or even European. And despite conspicuously lacking linguistic ability himself, Xavier would place great emphasis on preaching sermons and hearing confessions not only in local languages, but using native religious concepts as well.[3]

It was while living in Malacca that Xavier first heard of Japan. Even before leaving port, he was already convinced of the great potential of this new land, and once he arrived in the southern domain of Satsuma in 1549, he became positively effusive. "The people we have met so far is [sic] the best that has until now been discovered," he wrote, "and it seems to me that among the heathen peoples no other will be found to surpass the Japanese."[4] In Satsuma, the mission was received courteously by the daimyō himself, who granted permission for Xavier and his colleagues to set to work immediately.

The first task was to learn the language. Even with the help of Japanese whom they had taken back with them from Malacca, this would be no easy task. For a while, the inability to communicate actually worked in the missionaries' favor. Having heard that the strange, bearded holymen had arrived from the West, people assumed that they were in fact Buddhist monks from India. The mistake was compounded by Xavier's own preference, already realized in Goa, for using native religious terminology to explain Christian ideas. In their first Japanese translation of the Bible, the Jesuits thus rendered the term for God as *Dainichi*, which Xavier had been given to understand signified an omnipotent deity but actually referred to Vairocana, a Buddha particularly venerated by the Shingon school. Xavier's first attempt to read a sermon in Japanese was reportedly so garbled that the crowd burst out laughing. Over time, as they grew more proficient in the language, the missionaries finally were able to explain both their religion and their purpose in traveling to Japan. Although this new clarity brought their once cordial relationship with the local Buddhist clergy to a quick end, the Jesuit missionaries continued to invest their time and energy in learning language, producing translations of Christian texts, and accommodating themselves to the customs and dress of their hosts. Pioneered in Japan, this strategy of cultural adaptation would become a hallmark of Jesuit mission in East Asia.[5]

The Jesuits had arrived in Japan at a portentous time. As discussed in the previous chapter, by the middle of the sixteenth century, the two-hundred-year reign of the Ashikaga shogunate (1336–1573)

---

[3] Andrew Ross, *A Vision Betrayed: The Jesuits in Japan and China, 1542–1742* (Maryknoll, NY: Orbis Books, 1994), 14, 18.

[4] George Elison, *Deus Destroyed; The Image of Christianity in Early Modern Japan* (Cambridge: Harvard University Press, 1973), 14; Ross, *Vision Betrayed*, 24.

[5] Ross, *Vision Betrayed*, 28–9.

was drawing to a close, and real power was devolving to its once-loyal domains. Xavier may have known this when in 1551 he left the small daimyō courts of Kyūshū to travel to the capital of Kyoto. Being unaware of court protocol, the strange visitor was unable to gain an audience with anyone of significance. But over the next few years, his successor, Gaspar Vilela (1525–72), learned the art of how to appear in court – the importance of correct speech and ritual and of arriving in possession of proper credentials and presents (not to mention having bathed). In 1559 Vilela finally received an audience with the Ashikaga shōgun, Yoshiteru (1536–65), who granted him permission to spread Christianity throughout Japan. Within a few years the Catholic faith had made a promising foundation in Kyoto, particularly among members of the samurai class, who, it seems, were genuinely moved by its message.

But the real action was taking place back in Kyūshū. Regardless of the efforts that Gaspar Vilela had expended trying to secure the support of the shōgun for their mission, it was obvious that the Jesuits would also need to seek patronage among individual daimyō. But although they had been treated with courtesy in the courts of Kyūshū, the Jesuits still had no reliable patron. Some daimyō families, such as the Matsuura of Hirado, had been violently hostile to the missionaries, despite the possibility that they might help them to tap into the lucrative Portuguese trade networks, especially the annual visit of the *nao* ships laden with Chinese silks from Macao.

In the end, it was a clan named Ōmura that would come to the rescue of the Jesuits in Kyūshū, and vice versa. The Ōmura were a clan of middling power and outsized ambition. They were based in Sonogi, a small and mountainous strip of land wrapped around an ocean bay. During the recent wars the Ōmura had managed to establish themselves as daimyō of their small domain, but they were surrounded by stronger neighbors. The Jesuits desperately needed a patron, and Ōmura did have one asset that the Portuguese needed: location. The Sonogi domain was located on the tip of Kyūshū, and its sheltered bay was ideal for the deep-keeled Portuguese *nao*.

The merger of interests became official in 1563 when Sumitada (1533–87), head of the house of Ōmura, was baptized a Christian, adopting the name *Bartolomeu*. Ōmura granted safe haven to the missionaries, who returned the favor a few years later by sending Portuguese ships to aid him in defense against the predations of the neighboring Saigō clan. He also opened Nagasaki, at the time a small cluster of villages, to foreign trade. Nagasaki would quickly grow into a thriving trade port, and the epicenter of European and Christian influence in Japan.

In 1574, Ōmura converted his subjects as well, ordering the destruction of all Buddhist and Shintō shrines within his domain. Finally, in 1580, with a coalition of neighboring daimyō threatening him from all sides, Ōmura played his final card: he gave his domain to the Jesuits. In the words of the agreement,

> I make the free donation for always to the said Society and to its P^e Visitator[6] of the settlement of Nangasaqui, and with all the terrains and arable lands which are within its confines, without any exception; and thus I and over from now on the possession thereof. And thus the said padres of the Society may put as captain over the said place whomsoever they please, and remove him from his charge: and to whomsoever they should select I give the faculty, that he may kill and exercise all the justice necessary for the good government of the land and for the chastisement of those who should break the laws thereof.[7]

As George Elison points out, this act, known as the Donation of Bartolemeu, may indeed have been sincere, but it also served obvious self-interest. Not only did it protect Ōmura from attack, it also ensured that the Portuguese would not divert their trade to some other harbor under some other daimyō. It may have also discharged Ōmura of debts previously incurred in the defense of his domain. For the Jesuits, the stakes were equally high. The order now possessed more than an ally: it had an actual colony, one in which it had to exercise real governance. As an expedient, it allowed Ōmura to retain suzerainty but also took the prudent step of erecting fortifications around the city of Nagasaki.

Wealth poured into the new colony, and with its fame, so grew the fortunes of Japanese Christianity. Church law generally forbade priests to engage in commerce, but a special dispensation was made for the Jesuits to use profit from the *nao* trade with Macao to support their activities in Nagasaki.[8] During the 1570s, two more daimyō became Christian, and like Ōmura, they marked their conversion by ordering the Buddhist temples and statues within their borders destroyed. Buddhist monks in these domains were required to become Christian or leave. Jesuit success was such that in the years following the Donation of Bartolomeu, it became possible to imagine converting the entire island of Kyūshū, and from there, the whole of Japan.

---

[6] The office of "visitor" is unique to the Jesuit order. It signifies a special envoy of the province (in this case, the province of Asia headquartered in Goa), who has authority over all other Jesuits.

[7] Elison, *Deus Destroyed*, 94–5.

[8] Moran, *Japanese and the Jesuits*, 117.

In retrospect, we can now see that there was never any real chance that the daimyō on the southern island would form a Christian military alliance. Even if they shared the same religion, these daimyō were still locked in cutthroat competition. They could not band together long enough even to defeat their largest regional rival: the powerful Shimazu clan on the southern edge of the island. To do this, the Christians required outside help. In 1586, Ōtomo Sōrin (1530–87), the strongest of the Christian daimyō, and the Jesuit Gaspar Coelho went to meet the most powerful man in Japan: Toyotomi Hideyoshi.

China

In contrast to Japan, Christianity was not new to China. Long before the seaborne connection was made, Christianity had already been spread to China along the trade routes of the Silk Road. Centuries before the birth of Christ, trade and communication had linked the Qin Empire with Syria and Egypt, but the connection between China and Europe remained a thin and mediated one. Goods traveled from one end of the Silk Road to the other, passing through many pairs of hands along the way. Before they would ever reach Europe, the silk brocades from China would first be traded at any number of wealthy commercial cities of Central Asia: Turfan, Kashgar, Bukhara, Samarkhand, and eventually Damascus or Constantinople. Ideas traveled the same way. Christianity had trickled into China during the Tang dynasty, the heyday of the Silk Road, but the Christianity that reached China was Nestorianism, a branch that had been rejected by Rome and separated from the Western church in the fifth century. And it apparently did not stick. What few records remain suggest that the small Christian community fell victim to persecution by Buddhism toward the end of the dynasty.

After his success in Japan, Francis Xavier had dreamed of spreading the Catholic faith to China. He finally reached Macao in 1552 but died of a fever almost immediately after his arrival. It would be another twenty years before the Jesuits would return to China, but when they did, they returned in force: forty-two priests arrived from Lisbon in 1577 and immediately set to work learning Chinese.

By the time they reached China, the Jesuit order in Asia was firmly committed to a policy of acculturation. Alessandro Valignano (1539–1606), the newly arrived visitor of the Jesuit mission in Asia, was well acquainted with successes in Japan and was keen to apply these lessons to China.[9] The priests would adapt themselves to China, learning

---

[9] Moran, *Japanese and the Jesuits*, 3; Ross, *Vision Betrayed*, 18–19.

the language and spreading their message in a manner that respected cultural contours. As in Japan, this meant converting from the top down: winning over the political, intellectual, and religious elite and presenting the Catholic faith using terms and concepts from native religions. It also meant emulating local religious leaders in behavior and deportment. Jesuits in Japan dressed in kimono and explained their own organization using the system of ranks and titles used by Zen monasteries. In China they initially emulated Buddhist monks, shaving their heads and beards, but they soon realized that the monks did not carry quite the same status in China as they did in Japan and instead chose to associate with Confucian scholars.

Jesuits in China not only dressed and comported themselves as Confucian scholars, they eventually mastered the Confucian classics themselves with a surprising degree of sophistication. The decision to emulate the Confucian elite produced some controversy in Goa and Rome. (As with the wearing of kimono in Japan, the problem was not the foreignness of the attire, but the appearance of luxury for priests, who had, after all, taken a vow of poverty.) But the Jesuits stuck hard to their decision because, as it turned out, they profoundly respected Confucian thought. Not only did the Jesuits produce Chinese versions of Christian works in Chinese, they also worked in the other direction, translating Confucian classics into Latin and French. These translations were widely read in Europe, where they earned the admiration of humanists such as Voltaire and would remain unsurpassed for centuries.

The feeling was largely mutual. The Jesuit priests made quick friends with local officials and literati for their discipline, their spartan lifestyle, and, most importantly, their knowledge. Over the years, more priests arrived, gradually drawing the attention of higher and higher officials and eventually taking up residence in the imperial capital itself. Carrying with them the most advanced European arts and sciences, the handful of priests exerted enormous influence. The German Jesuit Johann Adam Schall von Bell (1591–1666) introduced Western techniques of gunnery and became a close friend of the Qing Shunzhi emperor (1638–61).[10] He and the Flemish priest Ferdinand Verbiest (1623–88) introduced Western advances in astronomy and corrected certain mathematical errors in the Chinese calendar. Verbiest refitted the Beijing observatory, casting new state-of-the-art instruments for tracking the night sky. The Italian Giuseppe Castiglione (1688–1766) combined Western and Chinese architectural elements in his design for the summer palace outside Beijing (Yuanming yuan). He literally

[10] Ross, *Vision Betrayed*, 170.

Father, Matthew Ricci, Chinese, Missionary.   Father, Adam Schaal, Chinese, Missionary.

Figure 4.2 Jesuit scholar-missionaries. These drawings show Matteo Ricci (left) dressed as a scholarly official and the astronomer Adam Schall von Bell (right) surrounded by the instruments of his trade. From *Frontispieces of Richard Brookes and Jean Baptiste Du Halde. The General History of China: Containing a Geographical, Historical, Chronological, Political and Physical Description of the Empire of China, Chinese-Tartary, Corea, and Thibet. Including an Exact and Particular Account of Their Customs, Manners, Ceremonies, Religion, Arts and Sciences.* London: J. Watts, 1741.

introduced a Western perspective to Chinese painting. Whereas Chinese painting traditionally represents objects in the distance above those in the foreground, Castiglone introduced the Renaissance technique of portraying lines of sight disappearing into a point in the distance. Jesuit prominence in the imperial court spanned even the change in dynasties. Early Qing rulers, such as the Kangxi emperor (1654–1722), were eager students of all the knowledge the priests could impart.

By far, the most famous and influential Jesuit was Matteo Ricci (1552–1610), depicted with fellow Jesuit Adam Schall von Bell in Figure 4.2. Trained in Rome, Ricci reached Macao at the age of thirty and would remain in China for the next twenty-one years. More than anyone else, it was Ricci and his compatriot Michele Ruggieri (1543–1607) who pressed the Jesuits to comport themselves first as scholars rather than missionaries. Ricci and Ruggieri were superb linguists, and together they compiled the first bilingual dictionary of Chinese and any European language. Ricci was skilled in other arts, as well: in 1584 he drafted a map of the world that was widely reprinted in China and was recreated in precious stones for the Ming Wanli emperor (1563–1620). Although Ricci never met the emperor in person, it was his present of a working clock in 1601 that won permission for Jesuits to reside in Beijing.

But Ricci's greatest gift was theology. In order to win over the Chinese elite, Ricci composed the *True Meaning of the Lord of Heaven* (*Tianzhu shiyi*), a lengthy treatise that presented Christianity in the idioms, culture, and language of Confucianism. Even though Ricci's volume replaced an earlier version composed by Ruggieri, it still required more than ten years to research, write, and gain the approval of authorities in both Rome and Beijing. But it was worth the wait. The text reveals not only Ricci's brilliance, but also the depths of his knowledge and admiration for Confucianism. More than simply using the language of the classics as a vehicle for explaining Christianity, Ricci saw his task as something more akin to the work of Thomas Aquinas, who had produced a theological synthesis when he married Christian doctrine to Aristotelianism.[11] Ricci's work did something similar, presenting each of the pillars of Confucianism – filial piety, benevolence, and especially the cultivation of virtue – in Christian terms, showing how the Christian teaching was the very embodiment of the Chinese moral ideal. He began with the very foundation of Confucianism, political loyalty:

> Among the Five Relationships, the most important is that regarding the king, and the first of the Three Bonds in Human Relations is that between the king and minister. A just man must understand this and act accordingly.... A country can only be united under one lord: could the universe possibly have two? Therefore a superior man could not but know the source of the universe and the creator of all creatures, and raise his mind to Him.[12]

But Ricci was equally careful to explain what Christianity is *not*. Using logic and judicious quotations from Chinese classics, he echoed Confucian disdain for Daoism and Buddhism, as well as for much of

---

[11] Ross, *Vision Betrayed*, 145.

[12] Matteo Ricci, *The True Meaning of the Lord of Heaven = T'ien-Chu Shih-I*, trans. Douglas Lancashire and Guozhen Hu, Jesuit Primary Sources in English Translations, no. 6 (St. Louis: Institute of Jesuit Sources, 1985), 57.

the mixing of philosophy and metaphysics that had taken place in the centuries since Confucius. He was careful to refute the Buddhist concept of reincarnation (even suggesting that Śākyamuni's teaching is nothing more than a bastardization of Christianity) and explained that the Lord of Heaven is neither the Daoist deity known as the Jade Emperor nor the interaction of yin and yang known as the Supreme Ultimate (*taiji*).

Ricci's treatise shows just how deeply the Jesuits had immersed themselves in Chinese classical culture. Although they still had not realized their dream of converting the emperor (although the Qing Kangxi emperor was sufficiently intrigued to quiz the Jesuits on questions such as whether Confucius would be denied entry to heaven), their impact was considerable and growing. In 1651, there were 150,000 Chinese Catholics. By 1700 that number had doubled. Just as it had in Japan, the future of Christianity in China appeared bright.

II. The roots of conflict and the long road home

Japan

The year 1586 was a good one for Hideyoshi. At the time of his meeting with the Jesuit priest Gaspar Coelho and the Christian daimyō Ōtomo Sōrin, Hideyoshi had just secured his succession to the vassal domains and forces of Oda Nobunaga. He had reason to feel magnanimous and certainly appeared receptive to the visitors from Kyūshū. To Coelho, he granted permission to spread the Catholic faith. To Ōtomo, he assured protection for the Kyūshū Christians and gave a promise to aid them in their war with the Shimazu. But what neither Coelho nor Ōtomo could have known was that Hideyoshi was already preparing for a showdown with the Shimazu, who had been weakened in their wars with the various Christian daimyō. He had already presented the Shimazu with an ultimatum and was already preparing an invasion force of 200,000 men. Map 4.2 shows why this new alliance with the Christians was so attractive to Hideyoshi: the best route to reach his one remaining enemy took him through the domains of Ōtomo and other Christian daimyō. The following May, Hideyoshi's forces did just that, marching unopposed through Christian territory and quickly defeating the Shimazu. He could now count among his many domains the island of Kyūshū.

After all of this, Coelho and the Jesuits had expected Hideyoshi to be at least neutral in their struggles, if not an actual ally. In fact, he was neither. On July 24, 1587, Hideyoshi issued an edict banning the spread of Christianity and demanding the expulsion of the priests:

Map 4.2 Southern Japan at the height of Christian influence.

Japan is the Land of the Gods. Diffusion here from the Kirishitan (i.e., Christian) Country of a pernicious doctrine is most undesirable. To approach the people of our provinces and districts and, making them into [Kirishitan] sectarians, cause them to destroy the shrines of the gods and the temples of the Buddhas is a thing unheard of in previous ages....

It is the judgment [of the lord of the realm] that since the Bateren (priests) by means of their clever doctrine amass parishioners as they please, the aforementioned violation of the Buddhist Law in this Precinct of the Sun has resulted. That being outrageous, the Bateren can hardly be allowed to remain on Japanese soil. Within twenty days, they must make their preparations and return to their country.[13]

The Christians were taken completely by surprise, but they should not have been. Hideyoshi and Oda Nobunaga before him had both spent years fighting militant Buddhists. In retrospect, it should have been obvious to all that Hideyoshi would view the Jesuits, with their access to wealth and weapons from overseas and attempt to form an alliance of Christian daimyō, as an immediate threat. The parallel between

[13] Elison, *Deus Destroyed*, 115–16.

the Christians and the armed True Pure Land Buddhists was equally unmistakable. To Hideyoshi, these were different acts of the same play. It was in 1580, the very year that Nobunaga finally completed his decade-long suppression of the Buddhists, that Ōmura signed over the city of Nagasaki to the Jesuits. The day before announcing the public edict against Christians, Hideyoshi prepared an announcement for his own subordinates, in which he made the comparison with *ikkō* more explicit.

> The Bateren sectarian, as it has come to the attention [of the lord of the realm], are even more given to conjurations with external elements than the Ikkō sect. The Ikkō sect established temple precincts in the provinces and districts and did not pay yearly dues to their enfeoffed recipients.... That the daimyō in possession of provinces and districts or of estates should force their retainers into the ranks of the Bateren is even more undesirable by far than the Honganji sectarians' establishment of temple precincts, and is bound to be of great harm to the realm.[14]

Although Hideyoshi was not above feigning indignation at the mistreatment of the gods and Buddhas in his public announcement, the private notice reveals a very different concern. The problem with the Christians was not so much their religious beliefs as their political pretensions. Hideyoshi was said to have been disgusted, for example, by the fact that Coelho – a foreigner and a priest – would try to meddle in affairs of state. But just as the Buddhists were allowed to exist, and even prosper, within strictly defined limits, so too would the Jesuits be discreetly allowed to remain in Japan, so long as they abandoned their political ambitions and kept their missionary work to a minimum. At least, that was the plan.

The year 1580 was momentous not only in Japan, but in Europe, as well. This was the year the royal families of Portugal and Spain merged, producing a brief union of the two Iberian rivals. In reality, this "union of the crowns" was never intended to be a permanent merger of the two countries (the two empires would be administered separately), and the union lasted only for a few decades. But despite its brevity, this union had large consequences. It opened the door for other Catholic orders, such as Spanish Dominicans, Augustinians, and Franciscans, to work in what had formerly been the exclusive territory of the Jesuits under the *padroado* of Portugal. The Jesuits had long lobbied both Lisbon and Rome to prevent these other orders from entering Japan. Beyond

---

[14] Elison, *Deus Destroyed*, 118.

politics, the Jesuits feared that the newcomers' disdain for and ignorance of Japan could easily undermine the position that they themselves had fought so hard to gain. Part of Jesuit success had been their
ability to police their own ranks. Since his arrival in 1579, Valignano
had spent years easing out an earlier generation of missionaries such
as Francisco Cabral (1529–1609), who had refused to learn Japanese
language and culture and referred to even Japanese Jesuits condescendingly as *negros*.[15] Beyond his commitment to language, Valignano was
himself a scion of a prominent Neapolitan family and understood the
fundamental importance of rank and status in Japanese society. The
last thing he wanted was for a group of mendicant friars to inflame an
already precarious political situation by preaching among the poor.

But even after Hideyoshi instituted his ban on Christian mission,
friars of the competing orders began to arrive from Manila. In 1596,
a group of Spanish Franciscans was shipwrecked off Japan and began
preaching as soon as they were rescued. Hideyoshi was uninterested in
differences between orders and began to suspect all of the Christians
of being involved in a plot to prepare Kyūshū as a staging ground for
an invasion of Japan. (He was not entirely mistaken. In the days when
Nagasaki was still surrounded by hostile neighbors, Coelho had repeatedly entreated Manila to send a military force of Spaniards and Filipinos.
The Jesuits, he promised, would serve as guides to the terrain.)[16] The
following year, Hideyoshi raised the stakes by executing twenty-seven
Christians. Valignano did what he could to stem the tide. In 1602, he
wrote to Diego García, Jesuit vice-provincial [sic] of the Philippines,
reminding him that even after a half-century of exemplary behavior,
the Jesuit mission was still balanced on a knife's edge:

> If His Majesty and His Holiness do not put a stop to the coming of so
> many religious by that route [Manila], the result without a doubt will
> be the ruin of Christianity here, and there will be no avoiding it. Either
> there will be another persecution, because now there is one lord of all
> Japan ... or the division which will undoubtedly result in this new
> Church will be such as to do even more harm than a persecution.
>
> I say that there is bound to be some persecution, for if, when we
> were the only ones in Japan, and we came from Macao, where there
> were no armies, and we had no power, and behaved with such con
> sistency, and were so careful to provide no grounds for suspicion,
> accommodating ourselves to such an extent to the customs and the
> way of life in Japan, making ourselves like natives, and all of us having

---

[15] Moran, *Japanese and the Jesuits*, 53.
[16] Moran, *Japanese and the Jesuits*, 73.

Box 4.a. *Deus Destroyed*

While the prohibition of Christianity in Tokugawa Japan was a government initiative, many of the religion's most strident critics were private citizens. One of these, a Japanese former Jesuit with the Christian name of Fabian Fucan, composed his thoughts into the 1620 text *Deus Destroyed*. Fucan sought to disprove Christianity by pointing out the absurdities in its own theology:

The adherents of Deus claim:

After D had created heaven and earth and the myriad phenomena which crowd the universe, he created man to be the master over all the myriad things.... But here also D set down a law, for Adam and Eve to follow: of every herb and tree of the garden he let them freely eat, but not of the fruit called *maçan*....

To counter, I reply ...

The term "sacred law" itself implies something holy, but still, such a precept must contain the stuff of which laws are made. But this business of "Don't you dare eat the *maçan!*" (a fruit something like the persimmon) truly is the height of absurdity! It's just like tricking an old woman or cajoling a crying child. A persimmon does not suffice to serve as direct or indirect cause for such all-important matters as the possession of Supreme Heaven, or the fall to hell. Among the Five Commandments, or the Ten Laws, or all the codes of the School of Discipline [all Buddhist precepts], I have not heard of one precept which cautions against persimmons....

Did D not know that Adam would break his law? If he did not know, then he is not Wisdom encompassing the Three Worlds. And if he did know, then from his position of mercy and compassion he certainly should have taught Adam and Eve the determination not to fall into sin. Either way, the explications of the adherents of Deus are gross invention and completely outrageous.

Elison, Deus Destroyed, 273–5

---

come with the resolve to stay here till death, and therefore setting ourselves with such diligence to master the language ... notwithstanding all this, since this is a land of pagan lords, and we are foreigners here, and we preach a law so contrary to their sects and to many abuses which they have, in the course of the fifty years we have been in Japan we have been persecuted many times.[17]

Hideyoshi died in 1598, on the verge of completing his conquest of Japan. In the end it was Tokugawa Ieyasu who would bring the great

[17] Moran, *Japanese and the Jesuits*, 87.

enterprise to fruition, and his descendants who would subsequently rule Japan for two and a half centuries. Although a devout Buddhist, Tokugawa Ieyasu himself initially had no strong predilection against Christianity, but an incident of corruption and insubordination involving two Christian daimyō in Kyūshū turned him against the faith with a vengeance. In 1614, he outlawed Christianity as subversive and heretical and again ordered the missionaries to leave Japan. Nevertheless, most of the 115 Jesuits stayed on, even managing to add seventeen thousand new baptisms to their existing flock of what may have been as many as 300,000 Christians. But any who were hoping simply to ride out the storm were to be very disappointed. The campaign against the Christians grew increasingly violent. Christian peasants in Shimabara who rebelled against their local lords during the late 1630s were suppressed with particular ferocity. At the same time, the foreigners, both missionary and merchant, were one by one evicted from the Land of the Gods. In 1624, the Spanish were expelled, as were the Portuguese in 1639. When a Portuguese delegation arrived from Macao the following year to request remission of the ruling, all sixty-one members were beheaded. In 1641, it was decided that the only foreigners allowed in Japan would be the Protestant Dutch, who were confined to Dejima, a small island off the coast of Nagasaki. Not only were foreigners kept out: Japanese were kept in. Between 1633 and 1639, a series of regulations forbade Japanese to leave their islands or make unauthorized contact with foreigners. If a sailor or fisherman was accidentally blown off course and landed on foreign soil, that land would be his new home: he was thenceforth forbidden to return. But the real focus was the strange visitors from the West. For them, Japan would remain a *sakoku*, or "sealed country," for the next two centuries.[18]

China

The Jesuits in China were in some ways more fortunate. They too had to face political upheaval, but compared to the complex web of daimyō politics that Valignano and Coelho had attempted to navigate in Japan, the fall of the Ming and rise of the new Qing dynasty were relatively straightforward affairs. The priests had quickly ingratiated themselves with the energetic new rulers, easing the way for large numbers of conversions. But this very success also made them more than a few enemies. The Muslim Chinese astronomer Yang Guangxian (1597–1669) accused Schall von Bell of having caused the death of the empress by miscalculating the proper date for her son's burial. Even after he was

---

[18] The term itself was not used at the time these policies were formed.

dismissed from his post as court astronomer, Yang would spend his newfound free time composing anti-Christian tracts. Buddhist advisers in the court, such as Mu Chennai, were tireless in their efforts to see the Christians expelled.

But the greater threat arose not from China, but from within the church itself. The 1580 union of Portugal and Spain marked a dramatic turning point in the conduct of Catholic mission, not just in Japan, but all across Asia. For years, priests of the Dominican and Franciscan orders had been fighting for just this sort of opportunity to work in what had formerly been exclusive Jesuit territory. More than simply wanting a share of the pie, these orders were vocally critical of Jesuits themselves, particularly their attempts to accommodate the Catholic teaching to a non-European culture. In China, they disagreed, for example, with the use of native terms such as "Heaven," or *Shangdi*, to refer to the Christian God, even as an expedient, preferring instead either "Lord of Heaven" or "Yehuwa," a transliteration of *Jehovah*. In retrospect, some of their complaints seem trivial in the extreme – for example, they objected to Jesuit artists portraying Jesus and the apostles wearing shoes at the Last Supper. Other objections were more fundamental, none more so than their attitude toward Confucius. The Jesuits approved wholeheartedly of Confucius and felt firmly that Confucian thought implied belief in a Supreme Deity, despite the fact that Confucius himself had not known the Christian God. Ricci's masterful synthesis demonstrates the degree to which the more scholarly priests considered Confucius's teaching to be compatible with Catholic doctrine. But the other orders were not impressed. They saw Confucius himself as an atheist and were particularly appalled by the Chinese Christians who performed rituals of veneration for Confucius, and for their own ancestors.[19] The Jesuits had considered these rites to be simple expressions of respect. The Franciscans and Dominicans saw them as nothing less than idol worship.

The Catholic Church is not one to let questions of doctrine go unanswered, and each side took its case to Rome seeking papal approval. The response was bad for the Jesuits in China, and more broadly for Catholic mission throughout the world. The papal bull *Ex illa die*, promulgated by Pope Clement XI in 1715, one by one reversed each of the concessions the Jesuits had made to Chinese culture.[20] Chinese Catholics were banned from participating in or even *watching* the Spring and Autumn rites for Confucius. They were not allowed to visit

---

[19] Ross, *Vision Betrayed*, 147–52.
[20] Papal encyclicals are named simply by using the first three words in the text.

Confucian temples or to perform any rituals for their own ancestors. For good measure, the subsequent pope, Benedict XIV, expanded these prohibitions in 1742 in the bull *Ex quo singulari*. The trend in both of these bulls was to equate the Catholic Church firmly with European ideas, interpretations, and culture. As we will see further on, some of these restrictions were reversed during the Second World War, as the Vatican tried to make its peace with the Japanese empire. But it was not until the Second Vatican Council of 1962 that the church would truly allow non-European Catholics to worship in a manner derived from their own cultures.

Box 4.b. *Ex quo singulari*

It would be hard to think of a greater diplomatic blunder than the papal ban on Confucian worship in China.

Ironically, the two popes who made this decision had also broken with centuries of tradition by *accepting* certain differences in the Eastern churches in Greece, Egypt, and Armenia, such as allowing priests to marry. But they took a different stance toward influences from outside the Christian world. In addition to their position on the Chinese rites, the popes condemned the Malabar Rites in India and the Jesuit "error" of recognizing caste differences among converts. Moreover, both Asian cases were shaped by a growing suspicion of the Jesuit order and shared the bad advice of the papal legate Charles-Thomas Maillard De Tournon (1668–1710).

The 1742 bull *Ex quo singulari* appears in the following. The high-handed tone of its final paragraph shows just how badly the pontiff was informed about China:

Pope Clement XI wishes to make the following facts permanently known to all the people in the world....

I. The West calls Deus [God] the creator of Heaven, Earth, and everything in the universe.... From now on such terms as "Heaven" and "Shangdi" should not be used: Deus should be addressed as the Lord of Heaven, Earth, and everything in the universe. The tablet that bears the Chinese words "Reverence for Heaven" should not be allowed to hang inside a Catholic church and should be immediately taken down if already there.

II. The spring and autumn worship of Confucius, together with the worship of ancestors, is not allowed among Catholic converts. It is not allowed even though the converts appear in the ritual as bystanders, because to be a bystander in this ritual is as pagan as to participate in it actively.

Box 4.b. (*continued*)

III. Chinese Catholic officials are not allowed to worship in Confucian temples on the first and fifteenth days of each month. [These sacrifices are part of their official duties.]

IV. No Chinese Catholics are allowed to worship ancestors in their familial temples.

V. Chinese Catholics are not allowed to perform the ritual of ancestor worship. Such a ritual is heathen in nature regardless of the circumstances.

Despite the above decisions, I have made it clear that other Chinese customs and traditions that can in no way be interpreted as heathen in nature should be allowed to continue among Chinese converts. The way the Chinese manage their households or govern their country should by no means be interfered with. As to exactly what customs should or should not be allowed to continue, the papal legate in China will make the necessary decisions. In the absence of the papal legate, the responsibility of making such decisions should rest with the head of the China mission and the Bishop of China. In short, customs and traditions that are not contradictory to Roman Catholicism will be allowed, while those that are clearly contradictory to it will not be tolerated under any circumstances.

China in Transition, 1517–1911, trans. Dan J. Li (New York:
Van Nostrand Reinhold Company, 1969), 22–4

It is certain that both Clement and Benedict overestimated the influence the church held in China, because their decision left Chinese Catholics in an absolutely unsustainable position. Veneration of Confucius and one's own ancestors had long been regarded as basic human decency. Particularly for the political and cultural elites, with whom the Jesuits had found such affinity, the idea of forgoing the rites was an absolute impossibility. Even if people could somehow be persuaded to abandon the rites, the choice was not really theirs, since the first Ming emperor had made participation in Confucian rites the law of the land. Were they to adhere to church doctrine, Chinese Catholics would not simply be acting in bad taste; they would be in active sedition. For this reason, the papal decisions had immediate political consequences. In 1721, the Kangxi emperor, who had once entertained a friendship with Jesuit tutors, reacted strongly to the news:

Reading this proclamation, I have concluded that the Westerners are petty indeed. It is impossible to reason with them because they do not understand larger issues as we understand them in China. There is not a single Westerner versed in Chinese works, and their remarks are often incredible and ridiculous. To judge from this proclamation, their religion is no different from other small, bigoted sects of Buddhism or Taoism. I have never seen a document which contains so much non-sense. From now on, Westerners should not be allowed to preach in China, to avoid further trouble.[21]

Despite the harsh tone of the pronouncement, the Kangxi emperor did not ban Christianity outright, although later emperors came close. In 1724, the Yongzheng emperor (1678–1735) expelled all but a handful of foreign missionaries to Canton, and in 1736 the Qianlong emperor (1711–99) prohibited the propagation of Christianity under pain of death. Over the century that followed there were a number of small persecutions of Chinese and foreign Christians, but nothing like the purge of the religion seen in Japan. When foreign missionaries again entered China in the late nineteenth century, they found a church that had survived quite nicely in their absence. But for Matteo Ricci and the others who had dreamed of building in China a Catholic kingdom that was larger and perhaps more enlightened than all of European Christendom, these remnants would have seemed very poor consolation indeed.

---

[21] *China in Transition, 1517–1911*, trans. Dan J. Li (New York: Van Nostrand Reinhold Company, 1969), 22; also Ross, *Vision Betrayed*, 197.

5   Buddhism: Incarnations and reincarnations

I. Bodhisattvas and barbarians: Buddhism in Ming and Qing China

There were many factors behind the decline of Iberian Catholicism in China and Japan, but one condition that missionaries in both places shared in common was the determined opposition of Buddhist monks and their allies. The reason behind this opposition, other than simple chauvinism, was that Buddhism was itself fighting for political prominence, and the strange new religion was making that endeavor more difficult. But just as Christianity faced different challenges in entering China and Japan, so too did Buddhism adapt to the rapidly changing political circumstances.

Although Zhu Yuanzhang never persecuted Chinese Buddhism as such, the new preeminence of Confucianism cast a long shadow. Ming laws propagated Confucian values and upheld a Confucian intellectual orthodoxy. The dynasty's elites earned their status not by heredity or imperial favor, but by their mastery of Confucian scholarship. Entire extended families devoted resources to training their most promising children to take these examinations one day. Even if examination success did not necessarily lead to a coveted position in the imperial bureaucracy, degree holders earned privileges that set them apart from other commoners: they had the right to travel by sedan chair, to post a flag in front of their house, and to seek an audience with the county magistrate. Because of their elite status, this class is sometimes termed China's gentry. They were the keepers of the flame, by definition devoted to Confucianism. But as it turns out, many of them also became devout Buddhists, as well.

Not all, of course: some Confucians remained extremely hostile to Buddhism. Some simply clung on to clichéd images: they saw the religion as corrupt, effeminate, vulgar, and, worst of all, foreign. Others raised more substantive objections. They felt, for example, that Buddhist insistence that all existence is illusion denied any moral reality. Buddhism encouraged people to become passive and to turn their backs on moral obligations. Buddhist monks, it was often stated, were parasites who did not pay taxes or perform military service. Perhaps worst of all, they abandoned their families. Dyed-in-the-wool Confucians particularly despised the free mixing of Buddhism into their own moral beliefs, such as when scholarly hopefuls would pray to the Buddha to help them pass the examinations. And those who saw Buddhism as a worm burrowing at the heart of upright Confucian rule did not have to look far for confirmation: much of the corruption that took root in the Ming court was indeed connected with Buddhist supporters, such as palace ladies and eunuchs.

But others found ways to accommodate devotion to both Confucianism and Buddhism. The best way was simply to divide them into two separate spheres. One could, for example, be a Confucian official during one's working life and later retire to a monastery to atone for sins and pray for salvation. Confucius, it was felt, was concerned with the world of the living, Buddhism with the world beyond. Just as they did with Buddhism and Shintō in Japan, some compared the two teachings to the two wheels of a cart.[1] With some creative interpretation, Buddhist sins could even become Confucian virtues. To those who balked at monks who left home, Buddhists could answer that an ordinary filial son at best fed and clothed his parents' bodies, but one who joined the *sangha* cared for their *souls*.

In fact, Buddhism flourished during the Ming, largely owing to the generous patronage of the Confucian gentry. There were many ways that these elites could support Buddhism – and much that they could receive in return. The most obvious sort of support was financial. Wealthy elites gave gifts of cash to build new halls or repair monasteries. This sort of support funded a new wave of Buddhist construction throughout the Ming. People supported temple construction for many reasons, but the association of Buddhism with postmortem salvation ensured that many of the donations were final bequests. Just as in Europe, a deathbed donation was often made in exchange for some particular service, such as keeping the donor's ashes in a stupa at the monastery or reciting sutras for the repose of the soul. Such generosity was also recorded for the sake of the living – names of donors were carved into stele, large stone tablets that were placed prominently in the temple courtyard.

In addition to money or land, elites supported Buddhism by lending the monasteries some of their own prestige. The scholarly elite presented

---

[1] This cart metaphor was also rolled out to explain the relationship between political and religious authority.

Figure 5.1 Buddhist cultural heritage. **A**. Like those in Japan, Buddhist monasteries in China were living museums of art and architecture. Shown here, the main pagoda of the Lingyan Temple in Shandong dates from 1057, but other parts of the complex are centuries older. Photo by author.

them with gifts of literary compositions, calligraphy, poetry, and paintings. Occasionally, they helped the monasteries in more tangible ways, such as in legal matters. In return, the Confucian elites were welcomed into the Buddhist cultural world. Many monks were themselves known as fine poets and calligraphers. When a Confucian scholar presented a gift of his own work to a local monastery, it was not only a display of support, but also an expression of taste, a way to hobnob with cultural peers. Wealthy patrons visited distant monasteries as both pilgrims and tourists. Famous monasteries were storehouses of holy relics and cultural and architectural treasures (see Figure 5.1). Many were located on sacred mountains, and people of all stations would go to worship, but also to enjoy the cool air and spectacular scenery. A poem composed on one of these trips reflects the mixture of culture, art, and spirituality:

Figure 5.1 **B**. Statues of arhats in a temple near Beijing around 1905. Artists usually depicted these early Buddhist disciples in individual poses, often engaging in conversation with each other or lost in thought. Property of the Wason Collection on East Asia, Cornell University Library.

Spring gloom spreads like an ocean, evening lengthens to a year,
I draw water from the spring with the teapot and bring it to a boil.
With me a white bearded monk listens to the rain;
We go off to our beds to sleep under the lamp of the Buddha.[2]

Buddhism also drew China into the world of foreign diplomacy. Even after it had pushed the former rulers of the Yuan back beyond the northern frontier, the Ming court retained diplomatic, commercial, and cultural contact with Central Asia. In part this was a defensive measure – a weakened foe is after all still a dangerous one – but it also reflected the deep and enduring ties between China and the tribes and kingdoms to the north and west. The steppe frontier was often a threat, but it also presented opportunities for trade, for alliances, and for cultural exchange. In the long term, the Silk Road is probably as accurate an image of this relationship as is the Great Wall. China and Inner Asia shared a great deal in common, most notably Buddhism. Regardless of whether relations were friendly, hostile, or indifferent, China and its inland neighbors

---

[2] Timothy Brook, *Praying for Power: Buddhism and the Formation of Gentry Society in Late-Ming China* (Cambridge: Council on East Asian Studies, Harvard University and Harvard-Yenching Institute, 1993).

used Buddhism as their common cultural language. Steppe tribes used it to form political alliances with each other. More often than not, Ming rulers often used it to prevent such alliances from taking root.

Although the world now recognizes a country called Mongolia, the idea of a Mongol people, or more specifically of a Mongol *ethnicity*, is actually quite recent. The people whom we would now call Mongols were historically a diverse collection of tribes spanning the vast space that separated the Indic, Sinic, and Muslim worlds. At times, such as during the heyday of the Yuan, the people of Central Asia were drawn into federations of independent tribes, unified by political marriages and occasionally by the rise of a great ruler. And none was greater than Chinggis Khaghan (c. 1162–1227, more commonly known as Genghis Khan), who unified the tribes into an unstoppable fighting force that would eventually go on to conquer not only China, but also much of India, Persia, and the Middle East.[3]

This empire ruled China as the Yuan dynasty (1276–1368), and as conquerers of a vastly larger Han population, the Mongols naturally adopted certain aspects of Chinese culture, including ideas of political legitimacy. While early Mongol rulers, such as Chinggis himself, had little in the way of court ritual, later ones seem to have adopted the trappings of Confucianism, such as ancestor worship. But much of the similarity is cosmetic. True, the Mongol rulers of China did worship imperial ancestors in an annual ceremony, but the rituals themselves bore little resemblance to anything Confucius would have recognized:

> Every year in the second half of the twelfth month, on an auspicious day, ropes were prepared from the wool of white and black sheep, and the emperor, his consort and the princes were fettered from neck to hands and feet with these woolen ropes. Male and female shamans recited incantations, and fumigated the body of the emperor with smoke arising from a silver bowl in which butter oil and rice hulls were sprinkled on a fire. Then the ropes were cut and the contents of the bowl were offered to the emperor. He then tore red ribbons several inches long, spat three times and threw everything into the fire.[4]

A more important form of political legitimacy came from Buddhism. Rulers throughout the Buddhist world enhanced their reputations

---

[3] While the title of *khan* appears in various forms throughout Central Asia, the term *khaghan*, meaning "great khan," was invented specifically to refer to the ruler of the federated Mongols. It was applied retroactively to Chinggis. See Pamela Kyle Crossley, "Making Mongols" in Pamela Kyle Crossley, Helen F. Siu, and Donald S. Sutton, eds., *Empire at the Margins: Culture, Ethnicity, and Frontier in Early Modern China* (Berkeley: University of California Press, 2006), 80, note 4.

[4] Herbert Franke, *China under Mongol Rule* (Brookfield, VT: Variorum, 1994), 29–35.

by posing as patrons of Buddhism. Political support for Buddhism harkened back to a long tradition of Buddhist kingship, modeled on the Indian emperor Ašoka, who was to Buddhism what the emperor Constantine had been to Roman Christianity. More broadly, Buddhist kingship was based on the ideal of the *cakravartin*, the "wheel turning" emperor. A *cakravartin* is more than a just, pious king: he is a universal ruler of the entire Buddhist world. The birth of a *cakravartin* is a rare event of cosmic significance, marked by divine portents and omens. His enlightened reign is destined to unite and transform the Buddhist world – hence the progressive image of turning the Buddhist wheel. Buddhist historians generally regarded the Indian king Ašoka as a *cakravartin*. So, too, it seems, was Chinggis Khaghan.

Unlike many emperors who sought Buddhist legitimacy, Chinggis Khaghan never claimed this mantle for himself. It was his descendants who did so, specifically *after* they had converted to Buddhism. As did many Chinese emperors, the first Mongol ruler of China, Chinggis's grandson Khubilai (1215–94), opened his court to religious debate. Khubilai invited monks of many schools to present their teachings but found Chinese Buddhism too abstract and intellectual and was instead drawn to the Tibetan branch of Buddhism known popularly as Lamaism. Khubilai was especially attracted to the Lamaist ideal of the vigorous *cakravartin*, who would unite the Buddhist world in the same way that his grandfather had united the fractious Mongol tribes. More than native Chinese religions such as Daoism, the conception of Buddhist kingship was perfect for a multiethnic, multicultural empire like that of the Mongols. As the Tibetan monk P'ags-pa argued, "one has heard of Laojun only here (in China), but the name of the Buddha is known throughout the world."[5]

The image of Chinggis as a *cakravartin* developed retrospectively during the century of Yuan rule. One Chinese text from 1333 describes his birth and rule in the idiom of Buddhist divine kingship:

> At that time a king was born in the Northern Mongol state whose virtuous fortune from previous existences had reached completeness. His name was Chinggis. He first ruled from the North over nations with many languages, like a king turning the wheel of iron.... He adopted the Law of the Buddha and civilized (*hua*) his people according to the Law. Therefore the teachings of the Buddha flourished twice as much as before.[6]

[5] Franke, *China under Mongol Rule*, 52–76, at 59.
[6] Different types of *cakravartins* were symbolized by wheels made of gold, silver, bronze, and iron. The first three types ruled over divine realms; the iron wheel *cakravartin* united the human world. Franke, *China under Mongol Rule*, 55.

Even after the fall of the Yuan, when the Mongol tribes retreated to the northern frontier and again grew politically fragmented, the images of Buddhist kingship and of Chinggis as a divine incarnation remained a potent political force. Two centuries later, Altan Khaghan (1507–82) again introduced Tibetan Buddhism as a way of consolidating an alliance of Mongol federations. It was he who recognized the primacy of the Ge-lugs sect and who endowed its leader, Songnam Gyamtso (1543–88), with the title *Dalai Lama* (*dalai* meaning "oceanic" or "universal"). During the early 1600s, Lighdan Khaghan of the eastern Mongols (there remained a significant political divide between opposing federations of Chakhar Mongols in the East and Khalkha Mongols in the West) threw his full support behind the Ge-lugs sect, building temples, translating texts, and banning the practice of shamanistic folk religion. Lighdan also sponsored the worship of Mahākāla, a cult that bolstered Lighdan's own legitimacy by portraying him as an avatar of Chinggis's own consciousness, and a continuation of his reign as *cakravartin*.

But despite Lighdan's efforts to reunite them, the Mongols would never again rise to their former greatness. Their support of Lamaism and claims to the *cakravartin* throne would instead be taken up by their neighbors to the east. At roughly the same time that Lighdan was consolidating his power, a federation of Jurchen tribes was taking shape under the leadership of Nurgaci (1559–1626). The Jurchen and Mongols were part of the same band of cultures that stretched from Korea into Central Asia. Like the Mongols, the Jurchen tribes were neither a state nor anything resembling a self-conscious "nation." The greatest task any leader faced in ruling the diverse Jurchen tribes was thus to unite them. Nurgaci began by differentiating his Jurchens from their neighbors, commissioning the creation of a distinct script (based on written Mongolian). The Jurchen alliance soon began to emerge as a potential rival to the eastern Mongols. Nurgaci himself was styled Revered Khan (*Kündülün khan*) in 1606, and his son and successor Hong Taiji (1592–1643, sometimes written as Huang Taiji) began to imitate Lighdan's trappings of universal power: the support of the Lamas and claim to embody the consciousness of Chinggis. After Lighdan was overthrown by his own generals in 1634, Hong Taiji was able to lay uncontested claim to the Mongol tradition of universal kingship. Taking the mantle of the long-deposed Yuan (some still referred to Mongols as the "Northern Yuan"), Hong Taiji now assumed the title of emperor and in 1636 proclaimed the foundation of the Qing dynasty.[7] It was not an idle boast. The Ming dynasty to the south was looming on the verge of collapse. In 1644, Qing armies

[7] Crossley, "Making Mongols," 58–82.

captured Beijing, and the final Ming emperor hanged himself from a tree in the Forbidden City. The Jurchen, now styled Manchus, were the new rulers of the Middle Kingdom.

The Qing were very much like the Yuan, in that they ruled China as a part of a larger multiethnic empire. To do so, they gave a great deal of latitude to local custom, allowing the different peoples of their empire to maintain their own traditions and practices, so long as these did not directly contradict Qing law. Within China, they copied Ming institutions to the letter. They adopted Ming law, its system of administration, and its court rituals. They arguably exceeded the Ming in their support for Confucianism. In places like Jiangnan, the wealthy region near Shanghai, Chinese Buddhism continued to flourish much as it had during the Ming.

But along the periphery of what had once been the Ming Empire (see Map 5.1), including the Manchu homeland to the northeast of Beijing, and the sometimes allied, sometimes occupied lands of the Mongols and Tibetans, the Qing continued to emphasize the symbols and institutions of Buddhist universal kingship. Both the Kangxi and Yongzheng emperors promoted the worship of Mahākāla, the same cult that Lighdan had once used to press his claim to be the continued consciousness of Chinggis. But the most active proponent was the Qianlong emperor, whose long reign spanned much of the eighteenth century. By throwing his support behind the worship of Mahākāla, the emperor was able to lay claim to the legacy of Chinggis, to the title of *cakravartin*, and to the legitimate rule of Mongolia.[8] All of the early Qing emperors employed the visual symbols of Buddhist kingship. Imperial tombs were plastered with Buddhist images, not merely of blessings or hope for a peaceful afterlife, but specifically of kingship. And while all of the Qing emperors were frequently painted in the staid poses of the Confucian scholar, brush in hand, surrounded by books, some such as the devoutly Buddhist Yongzheng emperor also chose to have themselves depicted in the pose and garb of a monk.[9] The most striking images are a series of portraits of the Qianlong emperor. These paintings portray the emperor in various guises: in some, he wears the clothes, hat, and symbols of a Buddhist master, but in images like the one shown in Figure 5.2, he is unmistakably meant to be a reincarnated Lama, or the bodhisattva

[8] Pamela Kyle Crossley, *A Translucent Mirror: History and Identity in Qing Imperial Ideology* (Berkeley: University of California Press, 1999), 238–46.

[9] Barend J. ter Haar, "Yongzheng and His Buddhist Abbots," in Philip Clart and Paul Crowe, eds., *The People and the Dao: New Studies in Chinese Religions in Honour of Daniel L. Overmyer* (Sankt Augustin: Institut Monumenta Serica, 2009), 435–80.

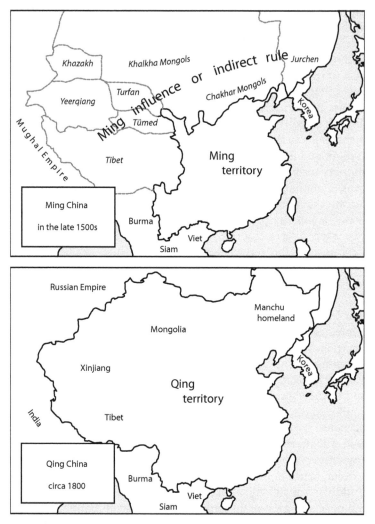

Map 5.1 China and Central Asia during the Ming and Qing dynasties.

Mañjuśrī. These paintings were more than just a testament to imperial vanity. Distributed to Lama temples in Beijing, the summer palace of Chengde, and Mongolia, they are literal depictions of the dual nature of the emperor as both Chinese sovereign and *cakravartin*.[10]

---

[10] In Buddhist art, Mañjuśrī was often meant to represent China, while Avalokiteśvara represented Tibet. See Michael Henss, "The Bodhisattva-Emperor: Tibeto-Chinese

Figure 5.2 Qianlong as bodhisattva Mañjuśri. This painting was commissioned by the emperor and copies were distributed to lamaseries in Beijing, Mongolia, and Tibet. To prevent any possible misinterpretation, it also includes an inscription identifying Mañjuśri as the ruler of the Buddhist world. Freer Gallery of Art, Smithsonian Institution, Washington, DC: Purchase – Anonymous donor and Museum funds F2000.4.

When the Qing emperors claimed the throne of *cakravartin*, they explicitly placed themselves at the center of the Buddhist world. The effect on Buddhism throughout Central Asia was similar to that of the

Portraits of Sacred and Secular Rule in the Qing Dynasty, Part 1," *Oriental Art* 48, no. 3 (2001), 1–16, and David M. Farquhar, "Emperor as Bodhisattva in the Governance of the Ch'ing Empire," *Harvard Journal of Asiatic Studies* 38, no. 1 (1978), 5–34.

Box 5.a. Temples at Chengde

Located to the north of Beijing, the Mountain Palace for Escaping the Heat (*bi shu shan zhuang*) was a summer residence for the Qing emperors, as well as a place of business. This was where the aging Qianlong emperor first met the British envoys in 1793. It was also where the Qing conducted much of its diplomacy with friends and foes in Central Asia. Nestled in the mountains behind the palace complex were the Eight Great Temples (*ba da miao*), Buddhist monasteries that also served as working residences for emissaries from Tibet and the Mongols. The Lamaist influence is obvious in the temples themselves. The Puto Zongcheng temple shown in Figure 5.3 is a miniature copy of the Potala Palace in Lhasa.

Figure 5.3 Puto Zongcheng temple, Chengde. Photo by author.

centralization of early Christianity on the city of Rome. In both cases, the rise of a new center also rewrote the entire religious geography. In the case of Catholic Europe, Church Latin eclipsed the use of vernacular languages, and the existing constellation of local saints, cults, and festivals was reinterpreted within the framework of the Church Universal. Something similar happened to the many Buddhisms of Central Asia. Even more than earlier rulers such as Altan or Lighdan, the Qing emperors promoted one school of Lamaism – the Ge-lugs school of the Dalai Lama – to the detriment of all others. The alliance of Qing emperors and Tibetan lamas created a new Buddhist orthodoxy that transformed Mongol Buddhism, along with its rituals and sacred sites. Scriptures and liturgies were replaced with new, standard versions, written in Tibetan. Even Chinggis himself was now worshipped through reverence to the Qing emperors, as the vessels of his living consciousness.[11]

Looking back, scholars often group the Ming and Qing dynasties together as a single historical era. This is because, despite their foreign origins, the Manchu Qing took great pains to preserve many of the cherished legal, financial, and political institutions of the previous dynasty. And just as they had been for the erstwhile Ming dynasty, Confucian ethics, scholarship, and ritual lay at the heart of Qing governance and society. But Buddhism never lost its significance. Throughout the Ming, Buddhism always retained a place in the heart of elite society. For the Qing, Buddhism was even more fundamental. Buddhism was, in a sense, an alternate diplomatic universe – a unique set of ideas and images for the Manchu rulers to establish their authority over allies and neighbors to the west.

II. The gilded cage: Funerary Buddhism during the Tokugawa

Buddhism was many things in late imperial China: a source of solace for the faithful, a cultural diversion for the gentry elite, and a political idiom for the Qing and its allies. But it never became a religion of the state in the way it would in Tokugawa Japan. Under the reign of the new shōgun, Buddhism was promoted far more forcefully than at any other point in Japanese history. There were many reasons behind the Tokugawa interest in Buddhism. Personal piety, for example, cannot be discounted entirely. But whatever else motivated them, Tokugawa rulers were driven by a desire to reshape and control society. To this end, Buddhism would become a close ally.

The first concern of the new regime was political. Having emerged from decades of civil war, the Tokugawa naturally sought to ensure that no new rivals would ever arise to challenge their power. The daimyō were kept in place, but they were also kept in check. Each daimyō was required to maintain a lavish abode in the capital of Edo (modern Tokyo). Every few years (the frequency was determined in part by whether a particular domain had supported or opposed Tokugawa's rise to power), the daimyō would be required to visit the capital, taking his entire retinue in tow. These trips were phenomenally expensive: in

---

[11] Johan Elverskog, *Our Great Qing: The Mongols, Buddhism and the State in Late Imperial China* (Honolulu: University of Hawaii Press, 2006), 104, 118–20, 124.

some cases, they might eat up half of the daimyō's entire income. This was, of course, precisely the idea.

But the new regime's plans went beyond politics. Like Zhu Yuanzhang at the beginning of the Ming, the early rulers of the Tokugawa regime sought to establish order by regulating society. They copied the four-tier Confucian social structure, with peasants placed above artisans and merchants below them. (In Japan, the very bottom was occupied by a subclass of people such as leatherworkers or animal slaughterers, who by virtue of their occupations were considered impure.) At the top of this hierarchy, the position occupied by Confucian scholars in China, they placed the hereditary warrior class of samurai. As in China, this structure was maintained by marks of status. Just as the Confucian elite in China were given exclusive right to display their status, so too did the samurai literally wear their rank, in their clothing, their hairstyle, and their sword. They were legally allowed to defend their honor by killing a commoner who offended them. Conversely, merchants were forbidden to display their wealth, for example by wearing silk. (Of course, the more fashion- and status-conscious found ways around this rule by wearing common cloth on the outside but allowing layers of more expensive silk to peek through at the collar and sleeves.)

The early years of Tokugawa governance were, in short, overwhelmingly devoted to two goals: weakening potential rivals and establishing a strict social order. The suppression of Christianity (to which we will be returning) was but one part of this larger transformation, as was state support for Buddhism. Bearing in mind that Buddhism consists of a number of competing schools and interests, rather than a single institution, we can still say that Buddhism as a whole had fared quite badly during the later decades of the sixteenth century. The Tendai temples on Mount Hiei, along with their scholarly and cultural treasures, had been put to the torch by Oda Nobunaga, who then spent the next ten years hunting down and killing the True Pure Land armies that rose up to oppose him. True, his successor, Toyotomi Hideyoshi, had built new temples and commissioned the casting of the gigantic Buddha in Kyoto, but his support had a high price: Buddhist schools and temple networks lost their economic independence, not to mention their military strength, the private forces of armed monks.

Buddhism continued to flourish under the rule of the Tokugawa, but it did so in a strictly controlled fashion. Like the Ming, the Tokugawa relied heavily on law. The Tokugawa vastly expanded the scope of existing codes and enacted a series of new laws to regulate Buddhism, as well. The architect of these new policies was the monk Ishin Sūden (1569–1633, also known as Konchiin Sūden), who was among Ieyasu's most important advisers on matters of statecraft. Sūden's expertise was not restricted to matters of religion: he had negotiated the difficult relationship with China, charting a diplomatic protocol that would please the Chinese, without portraying Japan as a subservient tribute state.[12] Sūden combed the long expanse of Japanese Buddhist law (a history reaching back to the Nara codes of the seventh century), eventually emerging with the Ordinances Regarding the Various Sects and Temples (*Shoshū jiin hatto*). Much of this new set of laws, promulgated between 1610 and 1615, was based on precedent, but some areas, such as the regulations on temples, were entirely new.

At their core, these new regulations were aimed at ordering and structuring the Buddhist institution. Earlier regimes had enacted laws regulating Buddhism, but the Tokugawa system was more ambitious and enforced with a far greater energy. It maintained the existing practice of extending legal recognition to only a certain number of Buddhist schools and surpassed it by further strengthening the exercise of authority within these schools. There were to be no more independent Buddhist institutions: every temple would now belong to a school and find a place within an intricate hierarchical network. The very top of each school was capped by a single temple, which in turn reported to the Commissioner for Temples and Shrines (*jisha bugyō*), a secular authority that was appointed at both national and domain levels. Only the small number of temples connected with the imperial court were excluded from these networks, and these were under the direct authority of the shōgun.

Within the temples, the state upheld the authority of monastic superiors but also gave legal weight to the *vinaya*, the monks' own code of conduct. The collection of alms, performance of ritual, and other matters that had once been internally regulated by the Buddhist schools now became matters of overt state concern. As in Ming dynasty China, one of the key choke points was training and ordination. Tokugawa laws made it more difficult to gain entry into the priesthood and restricted the flow of ideas by demanding that only the oldest and most accomplished monks would be allowed to publish their interpretation of Buddhist sutras. A monk of the Sōtō branch of Zen, for example, would be required to have studied for thirty years before ever being allowed to put brush to paper with his own thoughts. And anyone could be punished for transgression. Although the new laws enforced hierarchy within the monasteries, they also promised collective punishment for

[12] Ronald P. Toby, *State and Diplomacy in Early Modern Japan: Asia in the Development of the Tokugawa Bakufu* (Stanford, CA: Stanford University Press, 1991), 59.

certain offenses and encouraged monks to report on anyone in their groups – even a superior – who was caught flouting the laws.

But the greatest innovation was not simply to clamp down on the monks themselves, but to use Buddhism to extend shogunal authority *outside* the temple walls. As the ban on Christianity was enforced with ever-increasing severity during the early seventeenth century, monasteries began issuing "temple guarantees" (*terauke*), documents certifying that the holder and his household were indeed faithful Buddhists. Over the next few decades, the practice spread. It was gradually adopted first by individual domains, and eventually by the shogunate, which even standardized the wording on the certificate itself:

> With regard to the one said here of ____ village, it is true that the person indicated is a patron of our [Buddhist] sect. In case someone comes out and accuses [the person] of being a Kirishitan, this humble monk will come [to your office] and testify [to the truth].[13]

During the latter half of the seventeenth century, temple certification was gradually institutionalized. Eventually, every Japanese would be required to affiliate with a Buddhist temple, to become its *danka*, or what we might for the moment think of as a parishioner. (As we shall see presently, there are important differences between the two concepts, such as the fact that geographic proximity often had little to do with the choice of temple.) In his exhaustive study of the topic, the historian Nam-lin Hur describes the reach of the *danka* system into Tokugawa society. "The social life of the Tokugawa Japanese was absolutely dependent on temple certification. If one were severed from it, then not only would one be deprived of one's citizenship, but one would also jeopardize the lives of one's family and relatives."[14] With a very few exceptions, even Shintō priests were obliged to participate.

But if the ostensible reason behind the *danka* system was to root out any remaining Christians, why did it take so long to take shape and continue for so long after the Christians were effectively gone? On the one hand, the fear that a Christian fifth column was biding its time and waiting for the government to let its guard down was surprisingly durable. Centuries after the last Jesuits had left Japan, many Tokugawa officials and intellectuals still saw Christians lurking around every corner. Perhaps more important were its many practical advantages. The *danka* system was effectively an annual national census. Using surviving

---

[13] Nam-lin Hur, *Death and Social Order in Tokugawa Japan: Buddhism, Anti-Christianity, and the Danka System* (Cambridge: Harvard University Asia Center, 2007), 67.

[14] Hur, *Death and Social Order*, 104.

danka records, scholars of Japanese history can say with pinpoint precision who lived where, when the population rose or fell, and how many
people lived in each household. Temple registration sometimes even
included such useful information as the size of landholdings. More
importantly, all levels of the Tokugawa government knew it, as well. In
contrast, historians can at best estimate the population of Qing dynasty
China to the nearest million.

Many different groups of people became invested in the *danka* system,
but the most obvious beneficiaries were the Buddhists themselves. The
temples may have lost their freedom and carried the burden of serving the
state, but they were well compensated. For one thing, the *danka* system
required a vast expansion of the Buddhist institution: from an estimated
thirteen thousand Buddhist temples during the Kamakura period, the
number grew to at least a hundred thousand (possibly twice as many)
under the Tokugawa.[15] Temples grew wealthy, not on landholdings, but
on donations and services. When a temple wrote or renewed a *terauke*
certification, it charged a fee. Most important of all, when any temple
parishioner, which is to say anyone in Japan, died, he or she received
Buddhist mortuary and commemorative rituals. Buddhist funerals were
the heart of the *danka* system. For this reason, Hur makes a point of
describing *danka* not as parishioners, but as "funerary patrons." Like
temple registration, the funeral requirement extended also to Shintō
priests. (There was an attempt to institute a custom of Shintō funerals, but because this would have involved the repulsive and polluting
practice of handling dead bodies, the priests themselves were less than
enthusiastic.) The monopoly on funerals was truly the gift that kept on
giving – the more *danka* a temple could gather, the more services and
income it could guarantee. Over the course of two and a half centuries,
this would prove phenomenally lucrative.

But beyond financial gain, how did Buddhism fare in its Faustian
bargain with the Tokugawa? First, it is important to remember that the
relationship between the two might not have been quite so crass and self-
serving as the preceding description alone might suggest. Many of the
Tokugawa shōguns were themselves sincere Buddhists. Tokugawa Ieyasu
was reportedly a devout believer of Pure Land Buddhism and died chanting the name of the Buddha. After his death, a popular belief arose that
Ieyasu would return as a living Buddha to protect the nation in times of
need. (A similar belief also surrounded Kūkai, the founder of Shingon.)

---

[15] Nam-lin Hur notes that other estimates range from 200,000 to 250,000 but dis-
counts the often-cited figure of 470,000 temples; Hur, *Death and Social Order*, 373–4,
note 1.

His great-grandson, Tokugawa Tsunayoshi (1646–1709), was so concerned with the welfare of animals that he made it a crime to kill wolves
wantonly or harm Edo's rapidly growing population of street dogs.[16] Even
then, Tokugawa support for Buddhism was hardly unified or unequivo-
cal. Many within the shōgun court, as well as at the level of individual
domains, remained mistrustful of Buddhism and took active steps to prevent the temples from becoming too strong or from exploiting *danka*.

But on the whole, the support was certainly present and, over time,
proved to be something of a mixed blessing. The commonly levied
charge is that Buddhism in Tokugawa Japan grew lazy, corrupt, and
stagnant. Monks continued to produce volumes of new scholarship,
but few new ideas. Within the monasteries, true devotion was replaced
by formulaic rules and empty ritual. Outside, the monks spun their
monopoly on death rites into new and more elaborate ceremonies, to
the point that funerals took center stage. Even if these images have
been somewhat exaggerated by time, and by the years of anti-Buddhist
sentiment that followed, few would think of the Tokugawa as a time of
particular energy or innovation.[17]

The wealth and prestige of the monasteries generated new problems
of corruption, and especially of sexual license. The image of debauchery
within the monasteries was described in the novel *A Life of an Amorous
Woman* (*Kōshoku Ichidai Onna*), by Ihara Saikaku (1642–93). At one
point in her long chain of amorous adventures, the heroine of the novel
is contracted to be the consort of a high-ranking monk, who clearly had
much on his mind other than salvation:

> The priest to whom I had entrusted myself was a disagreeable man.
> He indulged ceaselessly in fornication, until all my interest in these
> matters stopped and all my pleasure died away. Gradually I became
> wasted and thin from overmuch indulgence. Yet the bonze had not
> the slightest mercy on me, and would regard me with a baleful look,
> as though to say, "If you die, I shall simply bury you in the precincts
> of this temple."
>
> But in the end I forgot my forlorn feelings; even the sound of the
> gong and cymbals, at which formerly I had stopped my ears, now
> became familiar and served to beguile the hours; no longer was I
> conscious of the reek of burning bodies; and, when people died one
> after another in the neighborhood, I thought happily of the profit that
> would accrue to the temple.

[16] Brett L. Walker, *The Lost Wolves of Japan* (Seattle: University of Washington Press,
2005), 80–3.

[17] Steven Heine and Dale Stuart Wright, for example, dispute this view. *Zen Ritual: Studies
of Zen Buddhist Theory in Practice* (New York: Oxford University Press, 2008), 34.

In due course I learned of the temple's slovenly ways, and found that even the acolytes would wrap dried sardines in old scraps of paper, on which they had scribbled the Sutra of the Names; they would hide these packages in the sleeves of their vestments and later bake the fish.[18]

Even if we dismiss such accounts as fiction, there clearly was a problem keeping the monks to their vows of celibacy. In 1685, a priest was banished for romancing women in the Shōgun court. In 1718, a new law prohibited monks from keeping women in their quarters. In 1796, the government made a show of punishing more than seventy priests who were frequent visitors to the pleasure district in Edo.

How did believers react to the perceived depravity of the Buddhist clergy? One popular belief suggested that the Buddha had already abandoned the monks. According to this thinking, the monks might once have been the vessels of the Buddha's teaching, but in the current degenerate age, the Buddha only entrusted them with part of the dharma. The *real* truth was now revealed only to the lay faithful, who communicated it to each other through underground networks. This idea of secret dharma transmission (*hiji-hōmon*) remained marginal within Buddhist institutions. Even teachings such as True Pure Land, with its anticlerical bias, officially disowned this sort of claim. But among many of this movement's supporters, it carried on as an undercurrent of discontent with the state of the clergy.

A slightly different reaction arose from those loyal to what they saw as true Japanese culture. We have already seen a suggestion of how some had tried to create Shintō alternatives to the Buddhist funeral monopoly – there was also a Shintō version of the *terauke*. At the same time, the Tokugawa period also saw a growing interest in recovering the "true" Japanese tradition from within a sea of foreign influences. And for many of its supporters, nothing felt more foreign than Buddhism. It was Buddhism that had opened the massive tide of continental influences that flooded Japan during the Nara period. Despite the fact that Buddhism had by now been in Japan for more than a millennium, and that the schools that now flourished under Tokugawa rule were thoroughly Japanese, it was still seen, at least by some, as quintessentially foreign. We shall be hearing more about this movement in a later chapter, but for now, it is worth remembering that frustration with Buddhism fit into a larger picture and was frequently expressed in nationalist terms.

---

[18] Ihara Saikaku, *The Life of an Amorous Woman: And Other Writings* (New York: New Directions, 1969), 437–9.

The relationship between Buddhism and the native tradition, meaning Shintō, revolved around one simple question: which of the two is the truer teaching? Of course, the nativist scholars of the Tokugawa were not the first ones to ask this question: when the first Buddhist statue and sutras were carried over from Paekche in 538, the first concern that everyone had was whether the native *kami* would welcome the arrival of a new deity. Over many centuries, Buddhism and Shintō had learned to coexist. They shared the same temple space and just like the "Three Religions" in China even found ways to carve out ritual specializations. Whereas the Buddhists gained a monopoly on funerals, local festivals, especially those concerned with agriculture, were generally celebrated with Shintō rites.

But more fundamentally, the relationship between the two religions was shaped by a concept taken from Mahāyāna Buddhism: that of contingent truth. Remember that in Mahāyāna, the teaching of the Buddha is continuously being revealed as mankind proves himself ready to learn deeper and greater truths. Earlier teachings are not false, although they may be unsophisticated versions tailored to fit the limitations of the audience – in the same way that one might use stories, half-truths, and oversimplifications to explain complicated ideas to a child. As mentioned earlier, this conception was used to account for the coexistence of Buddhism and Shintō. Both teachings, it was explained, are true and both are divine. The only difference is that one is the full story, and one is the simplified version, a formulation captured by the name *honji suijaku*, or "true substance and visible traces." The question, however, is which is the *honji*, and which is the *suijaku*.

For most of the time, people regarded Buddhism as the superior teaching, for which Shintō had been sent to prepare the way. But there had always been a group of people who claimed that it was the other way around. During the early fourteenth century, Kitabatake Chikafusa (1293–1354) expressed the idea that Japan must be the center of the world, because its imperial line descended from *kami*. Even if they occasionally emerge as bodhisattvas elsewhere, it is only in Japan that *kami* reveal their true essence. A century later, Yoshida Kanetomo (1435–1511) reversed the *honji suijaku* formula entirely by advancing the idea of "Prime Shintō" (*yuiitsu shintō*). In a 1485 exposition, Yoshida argued that Shintō was the core of all religions, whereas Buddhism, which had arrived only recently on Japan's shores, was a mere branch. Continuing the tree metaphor, he quoted Suiko as saying:

> Japan produced the seed, China produced the branches and leaves, India produced the flowers and fruit. Buddhism is the fruit, Confucianism is the leaves, and Shintō is the trunk and roots.

Buddhism and Confucianism are only secondary products of Shintō. Leaves and fruit merely indicate the presence of the trunk and roots; flowers and fruit fall and return to the roots. Buddhism came east only to reveal clearly that our nation is the trunk and roots of these three nations.[19]

Just to drive his point home, he even added a particular insult of claiming that the Buddhist patriarchs Saichō and Kūkai (founders of Tendai and Shingon) had only pursued Buddhism in order to gain a better understanding of the secret meaning of Shintō.

So while Buddhism did not exactly grow fat on the patronage of the Tokugawa shōgun, it did indeed make more than a few enemies. Monks were lampooned for their corruption and venality, political support for temples was matched by close surveillance by secular authorities, and some among the faithful suggested that the Buddha had abandoned the clergy altogether. Those who tired of the teaching even found ways of turning its own theological claims against it. For the moment, however, these were mere murmurs of discontent. But the very success that the monasteries enjoyed also tied them to the political fate of the shōgun and sowed the seeds for the violent backlash that was bound to occur. And when the Tokugawa government finally did fall in 1868, it would appear for a time that Japanese Buddhism might go down with it.

III. Samurai and nothingness: Zen and the Japanese warrior elite

What is Zen?

If you look at how it is portrayed in contemporary popular culture, Zen appears to be just about everything. The word is used to market almost any kind of product you can imagine: restaurants, MP3 players, tea, body lotion, clothing, home decoration, and pornography. An article in the fashion magazine sitting on my coffee table encourages its readers to "Zen out," whatever that means. Many thousands of books with *zen* in the title promise not only to calm your spirit, but also to teach you how to use zen in marketing, war, microwave cooking, and of course, dating. (But not vehicle repair. The well-known title *Zen and the Art of Motorcycle Maintenance* is a novel, not a how-to book.)

Not surprisingly, many of these images center on traditional Japanese arts: tea ceremony, painting, flower arrangement, and especially military

---

[19] Wm. Theodore de Bary et al., eds., *Sources of Japanese Tradition*, 2nd ed. (New York: Columbia University Press, 2001–2005), 1:355.

arts, such as archery, swordsmanship, and various schools of unarmed fighting. This may seem to be a rather mysterious pairing. If Buddhism is a religion of peace, how is it applied to the battlefield? More fundamentally, is this association based in fact, or is it another popular culture myth? Is Zen the provenance of samurai, or just of samurai movies?

So again, what is Zen?

The name is a Japanese pronunciation of the Chinese *chan*, which in turn is an approximation of the Sanskrit term *dhyāna*, which can be loosely translated as "meditation." It is, in short, a tradition of Buddhism that seeks enlightenment not through divine mercy or ritual, but through turning inward. A story often recounted in Chinese and Japanese scriptures is that the school was founded by the Buddha himself, who communicated the idea of Zen by holding up a single flower.[20] Of all the disciples who saw this gesture, only one understood its profound meaning and passed his wisdom down through a series of patriarchs. From India, the school was reputedly introduced to China during the fifth century by the Indian monk Bodhidharma (who is also credited with introducing martial arts and tea) and developed by Huineng (638–713), who is regarded as its sixth patriarch. By the time the school was imported to Japan, it had already been developing for five centuries in China and Korea. It reached Japan just as the third wave, schools like Nichiren, Pure Land, and True Pure Land, were forming. Despite the many differences among them, these schools do share a common rejection of the artificial intellectualism of Tendai and the exclusive secrecy of Shingon. In different ways, the new schools were all a return to fundamentals, to simplicity and sincerity. Zen was very much part of this trend.

All schools of Buddhism seek enlightenment – the difference lies in how they define enlightenment, and the path they take to achieve it. Is enlightenment *external*: a way to tap into the wisdom, mercy, and power of a divine realm? Or is it an *internal* transformation of consciousness? If it is the former, does one reach the Buddhas and bodhisattvas through ritual or through piety? If the latter, do you change your consciousness through meditation, through deprivation of the flesh, or through the

---

[20] But not in India. This well-known story of the Buddha's "flower sermon" was probably an invention of medieval Chinese monks. See Ishii Shudo, "The Wu-men kuan (J. Mumonkan): The Formation, Propagation, and Characteristics of a Classic Zen Kōan Text," in Steven Heine and Dale S. Wright, eds., *The Zen Canon: Understanding the Classic Texts* (New York: Oxford University Press, 2004).

harsh discipline of monastic life? Like every school of Buddhism, Zen
defines itself by means of these fundamental questions, and to understand their answers, we have to go back deeper into the long tradition of
Buddhist philosophy, beginning with questions of existence.

Existence is a natural problem for Buddhism. If existence is suffering,
suffering is desire, and desire is caused by illusion, then by simple logic,
everything is illusion. What then *does* exist? These were the questions debated by the intellectual traditions of Nara Buddhism, ones that in an
earlier chapter we compared to medieval Catholic theologians' counting the number of angels on the head of a pin. And like the medieval
Catholics and their angels, the Buddhist monks of Nara Japan hotly
debated the questions of existence not simply as an intellectual exercise,
but because the answers had profound theological significance. One
school, aptly named Consciousness Only (Yuishiki, also known as the
"Dharma characteristics" school), said that all existence is a dream, in
other words, a function of consciousness. Even the Buddha exists only
because we imagine him to exist.

Other schools claimed that there is a fundamental existence that is
shared by all things. As a shorthand, this fundamental, larger existence was sometimes referred to by terms such as *Buddha existence*, but
what was really meant was existence of the universe as a whole. This
is different from individual existence, the idea that the things around
you – the book in your hands or the chair you are sitting on – have a distinct nature, form, or existence. For example, the book may seem solid
enough, but from second to second, it is transforming on a molecular
level (and yes, medieval Buddhists did have an idea of atoms, although
not quite the one that we have today). Before it was a book, it was a tree,
and someday it will become garbage, then compost, soil, and perhaps
eventually, another tree and even another book. We believe that things
exist only because we lack the perspective to see them cycle in and out
of different forms. Of course, the same applies to people, as well. Trying
to hold on to your own existence, your own individual consciousness, is
like going to the ocean and trying to capture a wave in a jar. You may
catch water, but no wave.[21]

Attaining enlightenment, then, is a matter of changing perception. In
daily life, most people see only the temporary, illusory nature of things
around them, but an *enlightened* consciousness sees beyond this. To
change from an ordinary consciousness to an enlightened one means

---

[21] For a detailed but wonderfully clear explanation of such debates within Nara
Buddhism, see Daigan Matsunaga and Alicia Matsunaga, *Foundation of Japanese
Buddhism* (Los Angeles: Buddhist Books International, 1974–1976), 26–137.

breaking the existing patterns of thought and understanding that keep you trapped in the maze of illusions most people call life. And the hardest illusion to destroy is that of one's *own* existence. How do you look yourself in the mirror and tell yourself that you do not exist, at least not as an individual? What is even harder to imagine is someone's embarking on a quest for enlightenment, which is necessarily a selfish, or at least a very self-conscious, task, knowing that the final destination is the abnegation of one's own self.

This conundrum, and its solution, are the subject of a series of ten pictures (see Figure 5.4) and short poems composed by a Chinese Chan teacher during the 1200s. They begin with a young farm boy going out in search of his lost ox. In the next few pictures, he finds the ox, which after a battle of wills becomes so tame that the boy is able to relax, safe in the knowledge that the ox no longer has the desire to wander away. So far, the story is a pretty obvious metaphor: the boy is the seeker of knowledge, and the ox is his conscious mind, the ego, and the distractions that need to be brought to heel before one can set out on the road to enlightenment. It is in the final few frames that the story becomes a bit surreal. The boy is so accustomed to allowing the tame ox to roam free that he completely forgets about it. Gradually the ox blends into the mist and finally disappears into nothingness. In the eighth picture, which is simply an empty circle, the ox and the boy have both disappeared:

> Whip, rope, person, and bull – all merge in No-Thing.
> This heaven is so vast no message can stain it.
> How may a snowflake exist in a raging fire?
> Here are the footprints of the patriarchs.

The untamed mind has been tamed, and the boy, representing the seeker of enlightenment, has forgotten himself. He has, in the metaphor introduced earlier, ceased to exist as a wave and begun to exist as the ocean. In the final picture, the boy – now enlightened – reappears setting out on a life of wandering.

The two branches of Japanese Zen follow two paths to this same goal. Sōtō Zen, which was introduced from China by the monk Dōgen (1200–53), begins by asking why we are looking for enlightenment at all. If all things already possess universal existence, or Buddha nature, then why does anyone need to go in search of it? The problem is that although all people have this Buddha nature, most of us are too distracted to see it. Instead, we live in a world of our own illusions: we become so busy with ghosts of the past and dreams of the future that we cannot be conscious of our actual existence in the present. Intellectual

Figure 5.4 Scenes from the Ten Oxherding Pictures. In these four images, the boy catches the wild ox and gradually tames and forgets it. Note how the color of the ox grows lighter. These anonymous woodcuts first appeared in a 1585 compilation of Chinese texts entitled "A Whip to Push through the Zen Gate" (*Chan guan ce jin*).

Figure 5.4 *(continued)*

quests, such as the scholarly study of the sutras, are an especially seduc-
tive and dangerous trap. So instead of study, prayer, or ritual, what
does Sōtō Zen advise you to do? For the most part, nothing. The most
famous Sōtō activity (but by no means the only one) was simply to
sit. Monks would line up on platforms facing a wall, close their eyes

slightly, and sit. The idea was to clear the mind, not by forcing thoughts out, but by allowing them to float away naturally, like bubbles in a glass of water. This kind of meditation is called "dropping body and mind," or more simply "sitting in Zen" (*zazen*).

The other branch of Zen, called Rinzai, was also taken back to Japan by a monk traveling in China. Like Sōtō Zen, this school aims to banish those thoughts that distract us from higher consciousness, but instead of stillness, Rinzai seeks emptiness in activity. This is why Rinzai is associated with arts that seem simple but are in reality exceedingly subtle and absorbing. Tea ceremony, for example, appears to the outsider to be a rather basic sequence of events: one person prepares a bowl of powdered green tea and passes it to his or her guests. But if you know what to look for, you can see the painstaking precision of each movement: how quickly or slowly the host stirs the tea, or how the guests hold the bowl when they drink, not to mention the aesthetic setting, such as the choice of porcelain and paintings in the room. But tea ceremony is not merely an extremely refined aesthetic: it is also an activity that absorbs all of the conscious thought of the guests and host. And where distracted thoughts are replaced by mindful concentration, that is enlightenment. Other arts such as painting have a similar function. Some would place certain athletic activities in this category, as well. The so-called marathon monks of Japan (who belong, in fact, to a sect of Tendai) run enormous distances not as proof of devotion or punishment for misdeeds, but as a way of training and focusing the mind. (Even less extreme athletes might find something familiar in this.)

Perhaps the best known Rinzai activity is solving *kōan*. Well, not really solving: a *kōan* is a question or story that defies solution, possibly even logic itself. As part of their training, novice monks would be assigned *kōan* to meditate on for years at a time, the goal not being to find a solution, but rather to break the mind of the habit of logical, linear thought. The most famous collection of *kōan*, called the *Gateless Gate*, a collection of forty-nine of the most famous *kōan*, includes puzzles such as the following:

- A monk asked Ummon, "What is Buddha?" Ummon answered him, "Dried dung."
- Goso said, "When you meet a Man of the Way on the road, greet him neither with words, nor with silence. Tell me, how will you greet him?"
- Master Shuzan held out a bamboo spatula and asked, "If you call this a bamboo spatula, you offend the principle of Zen. If you call this no bamboo spatula, you violate the law of common-sense. What will you call this?"

Although the point of such exercises was not to find an answer, the master would occasionally quiz the novices to see whether they had indeed made any progress. Since the questions themselves had been around for ages (*Gateless Gate* was being used by Chan monks in China hundreds of years before it reached Japan), some of the craftier novices even found ways to circulate cheat books containing model responses.

So what, if anything, does any of this have to do with samurai?

There are certainly many reasons why a professional warrior class would be interested in Buddhism. Religion has at its heart the questions of life and death, which are themselves the stock and trade of the soldier. Among Asian traditions, Buddhism is particularly concerned with salvation. The *ikkō* faithful fought the armies of Oda Nobunaga with the unique fervor of the zealot precisely because they knew that death in the service of a righteous cause all but guaranteed them rebirth in the Pure Land of the Buddha. Salvation was a concern not merely for those facing death, but also for those who kill for a living. Technically, Buddhism absolutely forbids the taking of any life – this is why Buddhists should be vegetarian. In reality, many branches of Buddhism both inside and outside Japan have found ways around this prohibition. For example, one can kill in defense of the dharma. One can even kill as an act of compassion, such as killing someone who is on the verge of committing a heinous crime. Being less doctrinal than perhaps any other school of Buddhism, Zen was also less bound to this sort of prohibition, or, at least, more creative in how it interpreted it.

As a school, Zen was particularly attractive to the warrior class. In a classic article, Martin Collcutt describes just some of this spiritual appeal: "The practice of meditation (*zazen*), the vigorous give-and-take during encounters with Zen masters, the emphasis on unflinching self-awareness – all were novel and challenging experiences, entirely in keeping with the lifestyle of the medieval warrior."[22] As men on a mission, samurai and Buddhist monks had much in common. The *Hagakure* (Hidden amongst the Leaves), an eighteenth-century book of samurai maxims, cautions readers that "it is a great mistake for a young samurai to learn about Buddhism," not because it objects to the teaching per se, but because no man can serve two masters. Instead, it uses the example of Buddhist monks to illustrate the need for bravery in all endeavors:

> I have learned clearly that these stories of the Way of the Samurai have
> been an aid on the road to Buddhism. Now a warrior with his armor

---

[22] Martin Collcutt, "The Zen Monastery in Kamakura Society," in Jeffrey P. Mass, ed., *Court and Bakufu in Japan: Essays in Kamakura History* (New Haven, CT: Yale University Press, 1982), 192–3.

will rush into the enemy camp, making that armor his strength. Do you suppose that a monk with a single rosary can dash into the midst of spears and long swords, armed with only meekness and compassion? If he does not have great courage, he will do no dashing at all. As proof of this, the priest offering the incense at a great Buddhist memorial service may tremble, and this is because he has no courage. Things like kicking a man back from the dead, or pulling all living creatures out of hell, are all matters of courage.[23]

But despite this spiritual affinity, it would be a great exaggeration to equate Zen and the warrior class. For one thing, allegiance to Zen was not exclusive. Both ordinary warriors and the emerging military elite gave their support to many schools and temples – often at the same time. The difference is that supporters of Zen were primarily from this class, as opposed to nobles, merchants, or townsfolk. Collcutt makes the point succinctly. "Zen," he says, "can properly be described as the religion of the samurai in the Kamakura period only in the sense that most of the patrons of Zen were *bushi* [warriors], not that most *bushi* were patrons of Zen."[24]

But the real support for Zen arose from the emerging military elite. Powerful military families of the Kamakura and Ashikaga eras, including several of the shōguns themselves, were generous patrons of Zen and supported the monasteries financially and politically. Beyond theological concerns, Zen was attractive to this emerging elite because it was not as well entrenched as the other schools. It did not have their court influence, landed wealth, or private armies.

Another attraction was cultural: Zen opened the door to an entire world of culture, scholarship, and beauty. Just like the Confucian gentry in China, the new warrior elite in Japan were drawn to Zen for reasons that were at least as much aesthetic and social as they were religious – perhaps even more so. At the time it was introduced to Japan, Chan was the most flourishing and vigorous school of Buddhism in China. The wave of Chan monks who crossed the sea also took with them the newest artistic and intellectual trends (as well as vital intelligence on the state of the Mongol advance). As Chan became Zen, it profoundly influenced the direction of Japanese arts, from physical arts such as ceramics and painting to performance arts like Noh theater. As their status grew, the warrior elite became ever more drawn to this world of refined beauty – one that they could claim as their own. These activities were more than mere pastimes. During the years of civil war that

23 Tsunetomo Yamamoto, *Hagakure* (Tokyo: Kodansha International, 1979), chap. 6.
24 Collcutt, "Zen Monastery," 199.

preceded the Tokugawa unification, tea ceremony became a national craze. Oda Nobunaga himself was an avid collector of the fine articles used in tea ceremony: after taking the city of Kyoto in 1568, he scoured the city for items of particular age and value. Tea ceremony became a vital political and social tool. It was used to seal alliances, to display culture, refinement, and, of course, power. In 1587, Toyotomi Hideyoshi held a "Great Tea Party," at which his massive collection of artistic treasures was displayed. Until the day Hideyoshi ordered him to commit suicide, the most powerful person in the general's retinue was the tea master Sen no Rikyū (1522–91).[25]

As we shall see, this image of warrior Zen became increasingly romanticized toward the beginning of the twentieth century. Writing in 1913, the Zen scholar Kaiten Nukariya even went as far as saying that Zen monks and samurai were two sides of the same coin. Both lived with the same rules of discipline, the same spartan dignity, and the same ethos of mindful action. If Zen monks or samurai appear rude, it is only because both have cultivated a sense of detachment from the meaningless conventions of daily life and prefer to dwell in a world of unvarnished simplicity.[26] Romantic or not, this image certainly had historical resonance. A proverb from the Kamakura period summed it up: "Tendai is for the imperial court, Shingon for the nobility, Zen for the warrior class, and Pure Land for the masses."[27]

[25] H. Paul Varley and George Elison, "The Culture of Tea: From Its Origins to Sen no Rikyū," in Elison Smith and Bardwell L. Smith, eds., *Warlords, Commoners and Artists: Japan in the Sixteenth Century* (Honolulu: University of Hawaii Press, 1981), 187–222.

[26] Kaiten Nukariya, *The Religion of the Samurai: A Study of Zen Philosophy and Discipline in China and Japan* (1913; repr., Totowa, NJ: Rowman & Littlefield, 1973).

[27] Winston L. King, *Zen and the Way of the Sword: Arming the Samurai Psyche* (New York: Oxford University Press, 1993), 30.

6   Apocalypse now

I. Why the world keeps ending

If you want a happy ending, that depends, of course, on where you stop your story.

– Orson Welles

Seen from a global perspective, October 23, 1844, was not an especially eventful day. The world was remarkably, if atypically peaceful. England was beginning what would be the long reign of Queen Victoria, and the United States just ending the profoundly uneventful presidency of John Tyler. No wars were fought: the only shadow of conflict was that looming between Mexico and what was for not much longer to be the independent Republic of Texas. Karl Marx had just met Friedrich Engels and completed one of his minor works. Charles Dickens had recently published the final installment of the serial novel *Martin Chuzzlewit*. Although not newsworthy at the time, the actress Sarah Bernhardt was born in Paris on this day. The lead story in the London daily *Times* concerned the upcoming visit of the Queen to the city, including helpful hints of where to stand for the best view of the royal procession. Nearly one whole page was devoted to a long, indignant letter from one member of the public who questioned the wisdom of forcing women in workhouses to break stones for a living. It was something of a slow news day.

But for a hundred thousand followers of the preacher William Miller, October 23 presented a very serious problem – it should not have arrived at all. When the sun did rise over that day, it marked the beginning of what they would call their Great Disappointment.

William Miller (1742–1849) was a prosperous farmer from upstate New York. He was a well-read and highly respected member of his community. His father had fought in the American Revolution. Miller himself was commissioned as a lieutenant in the army and had personally raised a company of men to fight the British in the War of 1812. In a pursuit typical of his times, Miller had spent decades combing the

123

Bible, not for inspiration, but for clues. He closely read the story of the creation, and the prophetic books of Daniel and Revelation to determine a literal chronology of past and future events. Using a complex series of numerological gymnastics, in which he computed biblical days to equal certain numbers of years, Miller produced a series of dates, finally deciding on October 22 as the preordained date for the return of Jesus Christ and final cleansing of the world, which he styled the seventh day of creation. He spread word through conferences and publications and quickly gathered a large and devoted following.

It hardly needs saying that the presaged events did not transpire as predicted. This was of course profoundly traumatic for Miller's followers but, significantly, did not mark the demise of the movement. Miller himself remained highly revered and died a few years later still convinced that the eve of the Second Coming was nigh. His movement continued to develop without him. Today we know the main branch as the Seventh-Day Adventists, a church with fourteen million followers worldwide.

I mention this event because it so grates against our instinctive modern sensibilities. The problem is less the centrality of the Second Coming itself (Miller was hardly alone in his preoccupation with the literal interpretation of biblical events) than the willingness of people to remain faithful to the movement after its predictions had proven so spectacularly false. Miller had built his reputation on the promise of an apocalyptic event, and that event did not transpire. How could his movement possibly recover from such a decisive and humiliating blow?

The fact is, however, that the movement not only recovered, it thrived. So have others. This, according to Stephen O'Leary, a scholar of religion at the University of Southern California, is proof that we need to understand the attraction of apocalyptic belief in a manner other than the "scientific paradigm" of hypothesis and experimentation. One may be logically won over to the immanence of the apocalypse, but nothing resembling conclusive *proof* appears until it is too late. In a literal sense, conversion to the idea of the coming apocalypse involves a personal moral transformation – a leap of faith.

This same caution applies equally to all religious belief. Religious faithful are rarely swayed by attempts to disprove their beliefs on supposedly evidential grounds. We know that the sky is blue and the trees are green because we can see them plainly before us. We assume that the sun will rise in the morning because experience has taught us that it always has. Yet everyone must also believe something more than what our senses tell us – that these glories evolved naturally, that they were created, or some combination of the two. In a book title obviously intended to provoke, the biologist and popular author Richard Dawkins dismisses religious belief in the face of empirical disproof as the "God delusion." The idea, hardly a novel one, is that scientific and religious thought are fundamentally incompatible, and that anyone who chooses the latter over the former is simply lacking either in education or in the courage to wake up and face rational reality. Yet, catchy book titles aside, the two types of thought are so different as to be largely incomparable – epistemological apples and oranges. Put simply, knowledge is a function of the rational mind, whereas belief belongs to the heart. Belief does not only describe the world we see; it explains something deeper and more fundamental about its reasons and underlying logic.

Although some scholars would no doubt disagree with me on this, I have always felt that in order to begin to understand a religion that is not your own, it is important, vital, to develop a sympathy for its beliefs, ethics, rituals, and aesthetics. You can study birds from a distance, but not religion. That means participating physically and spiritually, and trying, as much as is ever possible, to truly enter the heart of the devotee. This is relatively easy in terms of religious ethics. It is not difficult to reconcile yourself to the call to be good, kind, and mindful, even if these ideas are enshrined in the doctrine of another faith. As we will discuss in the final chapter, when interfaith dialogue succeeds, it is often precisely because it restricts itself to this relatively shallow level of interaction.

Accepting other beliefs, especially those that fall into the realm of the mystical, salvationist, and prophetic, presents something more of a challenge. We may admire certain aspects of another religion, but can we really say that we believe in their miracles, their idea of the afterlife, their gods? Yet we *must* take these beliefs seriously. The alternative is to dismiss them as quaint and misguided – the refuge of a primitive people. Such an attitude is not just deeply condescending; it is also very sloppy thinking. It allows us to avoid thinking seriously about other people's beliefs, about what makes them attractive and compelling. This is why the example of groups such as the Millerites is important; it shows us the power of these beliefs: that the value and significance of an apocalyptic prediction are somehow greater than the literal truth or falsity of the event itself. This is why the movement faced a Great Disappointment, but not a lethal one.

Every religion – every belief system – has some idea of how, when, and why the world will end. It is a natural question that demands answering, as often by science as by scripture. This author spent a good part of his early childhood terrorized by one such image as presented in a *National Geographic* atlas of the world. The book began with a section of color plates introducing some fundamentals of geological and astronomical science, briefly covering such topics as plate tectonics, weather systems, and the place of the Earth in the cosmos. One depicted the evolution of the Solar System, complete with the birth and eventual death of the Sun, the largest image being that of a future Earth, scorched and lifeless, on the eve of being devoured by the dying star. Goodness knows how long I lived in abject terror of the immanence of this event. (I must have been very young at the time, since my subsequent nightmares of global catastrophe all featured the image of my crayons melting into a colorful swirl.) The point is that speculation about the end of the world is hardly the exclusive realm of theologians. Even among those who might wish to do so, these questions are simply too important to ignore.

For many readers, the most familiar image of the apocalypse will be the Christian one, that which is portrayed in the biblical Book of Revelation. Even the word *apocalypse* alludes vaguely to this version; it originates in the Greek *apokalupsis*, which refers not to destruction, but to the *revelation* of a divine mystery. The Christian apocalypse begins with the prophesied return of the Christ Triumphant, who not only ends the current world, but also closes the book on it in the Final Judgment. The blessed are then invited into a new, perfected thousand-year kingdom, the Christian millennium, after which will follow the resurrection of the Christian dead and eternal reign of Christ. (This imagery of the millennium gives us the term *millenarian* as a synonym for hopefully apocalyptic and produced a mass panic as Europe approached the year 1000. It no doubt also played at some level into the fears of the Y2K computer glitch, when more than a few people expected all of the airplanes to fall out of the sky after the last seconds of 1999 had ticked away.)

Interestingly, the Christian apocalypse contains elements that recur in other versions, as well. The first is a particular understanding of time. In most images, the apocalypse is not the end of the world, but merely the end of the world *that we know*. After this, another world will follow. Moreover, our world is not the first; one occurred before it, as well. This division of time into three parts – the mythical past, the present age, and the distant future – should, I believe, make a certain instinctive sense. Most readers, regardless of religious beliefs, will accept the idea that the world existed before us, meaning humanity, and it will continue to exist after we are gone. The two ages that bookend our own are shrouded in mystery and are separated from ours by concrete events of cosmic significance.

A second is the appearance of a Messiah. The term comes, of course, from the Hebrew *moshiach*, meaning "anointed one," and has been interpreted in Judaism in many different ways, alternately as divine king or harbinger of a divine age, in either case sharing the common feature of being a hopeful and long-awaited figure. The Jewish image of the Messiah is obviously different from the Christian interpretation but shares the element of inevitability. In both cases, the Messiah is not a possibility, but a promise; his arrival is necessary and portended in scripture. In these and other versions, it is the Messiah, or else someone who arrives on the scene soon thereafter, who initiates the third element, the Final Judgment, and presides over the age that follows.

You will no doubt be struck by certain attractive symmetries within this scheme. In the Christian idiom, the age of man begins with the creation of Adam, is punctuated with the historical arrival of Jesus, and ends with the return of Christ Triumphant. The whole story is one of man's progress, from flawed refugee of Eden to his redemption through Christ, and finally his ascent to perfection following the Final Judgment. The arrival of the Messiah not only proves scriptural predictions correct, but brings them to fruition. In fact, it brings everything, all of human history, to fruition. An apocalypse may end the world, but it also gives it a reason for having existed in the first place. This is why the motif of the judgment, of sifting and reordering, is so durable. This final hour is the point when all injustices are righted, when all loose ends are tied up, and when all questions are answered. The end of the world is like the end of a movie – that is when you find out what everything has been leading up to, what it all has been for.

The significance of the apocalypse as the great answer to human questions is also seen in nonreligious visions of the end. Some of these are strikingly bleak. Anyone who grew up before the breakup of the Soviet Union knows how chillingly present was the specter of global nuclear war. This is only one of many scenarios in which mankind perishes by his own hand; in fact, we have been predicting such an end since the advance of technologies of war made it an imaginable outcome. Reacting to the horrific carnage of the First World War, and anticipating much more ahead, animators at MGM produced the 1939 short feature *Peace on Earth*, in which an old squirrel regaled his grandchildren with tales of a monstrous race of beings called man, which once dominated the land but since then had fought themselves out of existence. As the cherubic woodland creatures gathered around to hear the tale, viewers were greeted by the images of war, gruesome in their familiarity: of faceless men marching in the rain, bayonets and barbed wire, the skeletal remains of bombed out cathedrals. Finally, we see the fate of the anonymous last man, his humanity and nationality masked by goggles, a helmet, and a respirator, as he is fatally wounded and sinks slowly into the mud. What an ending, but the meaning is clear: mankind's story is fundamentally one of greed, hubris, and violence, and, sooner or later, he will be the agent of his own destruction.

Even if it does not include the ultimate end, political messianism performs the same function of giving meaning and purpose to history. Certain political figures were, even in their own lifetimes, portrayed as larger than life, as the embodiment of an ideal, a people, or a universal truth. Not surprisingly, these tend to be demagogic figures. In Nazi propaganda, Adolf Hitler was not just a political leader: he was the savior of the Aryan race, the one who would lead it to its true destiny as masters of the world and initiate its thousand-year reign. During the height of his cult of personality in the 1960s and 1970s, Mao Zedong was perceived as no mere leader; he was the Red Sun of the East. His brand of communism was more than just a good idea; it was nothing less than the culmination of thousands of years of class struggle and national aspiration.[1] All of China's history, the history of all oppressed people, every insult suffered, aspiration crushed, and dream deferred, led inexorably to Mao and was made meaningful through his revolution. This level of hyperbole is not my own. Figure 6.1 shows Mao as he was often depicted: beaming out over humanity in a manner reminiscent of a benign deity. A song from the height of the Cultural Revolution reveals what could only be called a *religious* devotion to Mao Zedong:

> Piercingly staring at the clouds and the sky,
> Our longing hearts burning with anxiety.
> When Chairman Mao enters Tian'anmen Square,
> Even mountains and rivers rejoice.
> To have seen the Great Teacher Chairman Mao is the fulfillment of
> our brightest wish.
> Ah!
> How many nights did we dream of you, ah!
> Burning tears of happiness keep running down ...
> Longed for day by day,

---

[1] Here Marxist theory provided more than a little inspiration. As we shall see in a later chapter, Marxism sees the progress of human history in a strict linear fashion. Societies that are more fair are also more advanced and productive, and will thus naturally replace older, more exploitative ones. This is why communist propaganda so frequently employs metaphors of forward, backward, or lateral motion (such as when it speaks of the dangers of reaction or deviation to the Left or Right). What Mao was promising was the immediate institution of utopian communism – the final, and for most, distant destination of Marxist history. From a Marxist perspective, he was ending the history of the world we know and ushering in a new age.

全世界无产阶级联合起来打倒美帝国主义

北京市工艺美院革委会制

Figure 6.1 "Proletarians of the World Unite to Overthrow American Imperialism!" This 1967 poster by the Beijing Academy of Arts alludes to Mao Zedong's nickname as the "Red Sun of the East."

Hoped for year by year, ah!
Today we're at your side.[2]

In this case, one could not help but be caught up in the movement – exhibiting anything less than fanatic enthusiasm could have very serious political consequences – but what about those times when a vision of the apocalypse separates people from society, when movements become what we might commonly call cults? (Now that I have used the term, somewhat incorrectly, in fact, I should explain that for scholars of religion, the word *cult* refers broadly to any coherent system of belief and worship. Here, I am speaking of the more popular sense of the term as a dangerous, shadowy sect that preys on the lonely and impressionable.) The basic elements are the same. We are surrounded by visions of the apocalypse, scientific or religious, immanent or distant. Spend ten minutes on the Internet and you will find ten times that many explanations of when, why, and how the world will end. Some of these will be more mainstream than others, based on how well they resonate with what

[2] Vivian Wagner, "Songs of the Red Guards: Keywords Set to Music," Indiana University East Asian Working Paper Series on Language and Politics in Modern China, 1996. Available online at http://www.wellesley.edu/Polisci/wj/China/CRSongs/wagner-red-guards_songs.html.

we see around us. On September 10, 2001, few Americans would have given much thought to the immanence of a manmade apocalypse. One day later, the idea suddenly felt much more plausible.

Adherents of a teaching will work to make their vision fit the expectations of their audience – buttressing their claims with scripture, science, whatever works. At this state, their message is aimed at the rational mind. It creates an argument designed to convince outsiders of the veracity of certain facts and to demonstrate that, taken together, these facts point toward a coming event. Think of the proponents (or the detractors) of the theory of global warming. A good argument in support of the reality of global warming will incorporate a variety of scientific data – time lapse photos of melting ice caps, reports of erratic weather and poor harvests, and supportive statements from high-profile personalities – to accomplish the relatively limited goal of winning over skeptics to the idea that human behavior is leading to catastrophic consequences. But this kind of message is not intended to make true believers of everyone. Campaigns aimed at a mass audience at best hope to win the majority over to a nodding acceptance, and within this majority, to entice a few to step forward and take a more active interest. These are the ones who will join the ranks of the movement itself.

At some point, however, something changes: the movement tightens, closes ranks, and, as one scholar describes it, "ups the ante."[3] This is when a mass movement transforms from a large casual following to a small, devoted, and often secretive one. Usually what prompts the change in the movement is a transformation within the teaching itself – the apocalypse moves from a distant event to something more immanent. Sometimes, as with the Millerites, the new urgency arises when the apocalypse is predicted for a specific date. It is at this point that members are forced to make their leap of faith, to choose either to remain with the movement or to leave. Most choose the latter, but for the few who stay on, the risks and demands increase accordingly. This event completely transforms the dynamic of the movement. It is the point when members of the devoted core might surrender a share of their individuality and make their break with the world they are leaving behind – severing ties with family, selling property, breaking laws. The immanent apocalypse is not the only reason for typically "cultish" behavior, but it does explain the extreme disregard that many such movements have for society. Even when the predictions are inevitably discredited, members are by this point often so deeply committed to

---

[3] See the introduction to Albert I. Baumgarten, ed., *Apocalyptic Time* (Leiden: E.J. Brill, 2000).

the movement that many can be swayed by any number of explanations for why the prophecy was not fulfilled: that the time was not right, the event will occur in gradual stages, the prophecy was a divine test of faith, and so on.

In any case, even these seemingly inexplicable extremes of belief correspond to the basic functions of how and why people think about the apocalypse. At a practical level, knowledge of how and why the world will end is vital for how we prepare for the event, if and when it is coming. More fundamentally, however, an image of how the world will end also provides structure and meaning for the world we live in. In this sense, belief in the apocalypse is no different from ideas of the afterlife, in that it presents a code of actions that one may follow in order to ensure salvation, the one being postmortem, the other posteverything. In addition, the idea of an ultimate judgment, of heaven and hell, provides the believer with a sense of divine justice, a comforting knowledge that good or evil deeds committed in this lifetime will all be tallied up in the next.

The point of all of this is to try to make some sense of apocalyptic beliefs, to show that they are neither primitive nor necessarily fanatical. They always exist, like music playing in the background, only at certain times rising to the surface and grabbing our attention. As we will see, China developed over the course of many centuries a number of elaborate beliefs about the apocalypse, who would initiate it, and which steps one should take once it arrived. And when conditions were right, these ideas could move millions.

II. The White Lotus: Six centuries of Chinese heresy, 1360–1860

The end of the world has a long history in China. We have already mentioned how millenarian longing hastened the end of the Mongol dynasty, and how the first Ming emperor, Zhu Yuanzhang, took every precaution to make sure that groups such as the Red Turbans and the Incense Army could never rise again. But Zhu was fighting a losing battle. The type of millenarian thought on which he had ridden to power already had very deep roots in Chinese society and was inspired by a number of different sources.

We are not speaking here simply of political change, the rise and fall of dynasties that the Confucians associated with the Mandate of Heaven, but rather of something more fundamental. Political millenarianism means the foundation of a completely new form of government and society, the sort of change that relies on a reordering of the cosmos or the arrival of a divine figure. As early as the second century, a kingdom rose up in the mountainous Southwest (now the province of Sichuan) in anticipation of a divine ruler: none other than the deified manifestation of Laozi called the Most Supreme Lord Lao (*Taishang laojun*). The founders of this kingdom followed a teaching called the Way of Great Peace, and relied on calculations of the sexagesimal (cycles of sixty years) calendar to determine the date of the apocalypse, following which eighteen thousand of its members would live on as the "seed people" (*zhongmin*) who would repopulate the world.[4]

Daoist predictions of divine kingship and the science of counting the cycles of creation and destruction intermingled with similar ideas from Buddhism. Long before it reached China, Buddhism had developed its own metaphysics, including the idea that the cosmos oscillates between periods of rise and decline. The top of the cycle resembles a paradise on earth – all beings are enlightened, society is peaceful and benevolent, and the human life span lasts for thousands of years. Conditions are correspondingly grim at the bottom of the cycle, a time when human existence would at best be (to quote Thomas Hobbes) "nasty, brutish, and short." Most accounts placed our current age within a cycle of decline that was near, but had not yet reached, the bottom. (This is what Buddhists refer to as the Decline of the Dharma and underlies the Mahāyāna idea that humans must rely on the aid of bodhisattvas to clear their karmic debt.) These cycles, each lasting thousands of centuries, will continue to repeat until some point in the very distant future, when a Divine King will appear to unite the world. This king, unique even among *cakravartin*, will appear at the top of one of these cycles, purge the world of guilt and suffering, and establish an immortal paradise, presided over by the Maitreya Buddha, successor to Śākyamuni.

These ideas changed once they reached China. For one thing, the Divine King and the Maitreya Buddha were combined, so that now it is the new Buddha himself who initiates the change. More importantly, the arrival of the Buddha moved from the apex of the cycle to the nadir, so that the Buddha arrives when matters have reached their lowest point. The result is easy to predict: in times of war and famine, when people are most desperate for hope, someone will arrive on the scene claiming to be the Maitreya Buddha and calling on the suffering populace to join his army and destroy the remnants of the old world in order to usher in the new millennium. These images were remarkably

---

[4] Terry F. Kleeman, *Great Perfection: Religion and Ethnicity in a Chinese Millennial Kingdom* (Honolulu: University of Hawaii Press, 1998), 61–85.

durable and proved attractive enough to mobilize peasants again and again over the course of many centuries.

One reason that even Zhu Yuanzhang was unable to destroy these beliefs was that they were deeply rooted in the everyday religious beliefs of rural China. Unlike Tokugawa Japan, where the *danka* system had vastly expanded the number of Buddhist temples, the number of formally ordained clergy in the Chinese countryside was relatively small. This was particularly true in the northern part of the country. During the nineteenth century, large northern cities such as Beijing or Tianjin had dozens of monasteries, but in the surrounding countryside only a handful were scattered over a large area. There are limited hard data for the rural areas, but one district south of Tianjin, in which there were only two Buddhist temples for nearly twenty thousand people, was probably typical of much of the area. It would not be hard to imagine many country people living their whole lives without ever meeting a formally ordained Buddhist monk face to face.[5]

So if Buddhist monks were not the central figures in village religious life, then who were? Generally, it was lay religious leaders of what official sources call the White Lotus Teaching (*bailian jiao*), or more broadly, heresy (*xie jiao*). The former name is a bit deceptive: there never was a single religious teaching actually called White Lotus. What the Chinese government called White Lotus was in fact a whole tradition of different teachings: the Eight Trigrams (*ba gua*), Green Lotus (*qing lian*), Single Incense (*yi zhu xiang*), Primordial Chaos (*hunyuan*), Golden Elixir (*jindan*), Lord Lao (*laojun*), Li Trigram (*li gua*) teachings, among many others. When Ming law banned the "White Lotus Society of Maitreya," this was the type of religion it had in mind. Official sources and polemic texts such as the *Detailed Argument against Heresy* (*poxie xiangbian*, written by a Confucian official during the early nineteenth century), accuse these teachings of a variety of crimes: fraud, debauchery, and, of course, sorcery.

Because these groups inspired peasants to take up arms, scholars often associate them with violence. But this is not an entirely accurate picture. The problem is that these groups only appear in historical records when they were caught breaking the law. The rest of the time, which was most of it, they were invisible. For this reason, official records alone never paint an accurate picture of religion, especially the religious life

---

[5] Thomas David DuBois, *The Sacred Village: Social Change and Religious Life in Rural North China* (Honolulu: University of Hawaii Press, 2005), 88–102; Vincent Goosaert, "Counting the Monks: The 1736–1739 Census of the Chinese Clergy," *Late Imperial China* 21, no. 2 (2000), 40–85.

Figure 6.2 The Heaven and Earth Teaching. The Heaven and Earth is a lay teaching that has thrived in northern China for about four centuries, and would have once been labeled as White Lotus. Such teachings remain officially illegal, although their activities are largely tolerated. Photo by author.

of ordinary people. (In his classic study of local Catholicism in Spain, William Christian compares using official sources to understand religion to "trying to get a sense of everyday American political life from FBI files.")[6] In fact, the religious teachings known as White Lotus pervaded the countryside. Many were permanent and stable fixtures in village religious life. Particularly in northern China, when villagers needed religion – for a funeral, an exorcism, a blessing, or simply advice – they did not go in search of a Buddhist monk; they went instead to the lay teachings that flourished in their midst.[7] Some of these teachings, such as the Heaven and Earth Teaching (*Tiandimen jiao*) shown in Figure 6.2, continue to play a similar role today.

While each of these various teachings had its own characteristic scriptures (often these were memorized and recited orally, rather than written down), they tended to share certain basic ideas in common. One was

[6] William A. Christian, *Local Religion in Sixteenth-Century Spain* (Princeton, NJ: Princeton University Press, 1981), 4.
[7] The classic work on these groups in English is Johann Jacob Maria de Groot, *Sectarianism and Religious Persecution in China, a Page in the History of Religions* (Amsterdam: J. Müller, 1903); see also DuBois, *Sacred Village*, 152–85.

belief in a deity called the Eternal Venerable Mother (*wusheng laomu*). As her name suggests, the Eternal Venerable Mother is the source and creator of all things. This includes human beings, who were originally divine but over time have become blinded by the greed and desires of the mortal world and have forgotten their true nature. Desiring to recuse men from their wicked ways, the Eternal Venerable Mother has over the ages sent her children down from heaven as teachers. We know these teachers as the founders of the "three teachings," Confucius, Laozi, and the Buddha. (The list would later be expanded to include Jesus Christ and Muhammad.) In typical Mahāyāna tradition, it was said that each of these teachers delivered only a piece of the True Teaching, the culmination of which would only be revealed on the eve of an event called the Dragon Flower Assembly.[8] At this point, all of the deities will assemble in heaven to witness the Buddha Śākyamuni hand a white lotus to Maitreya, marking the change of the epoch. Here on Earth, we will know this moment as the apocalypse. A certain number of humanity (various scriptures calculated the exact number differently) will ascend to a paradise presided over by the newly crowned Maitreya Buddha. These are, of course, the ones who have recognized and accepted the True Teaching. The unsaved will suffer an eternity of torment.

   The White Lotus tradition, in other words, had an inherent mille-narian streak, but then again so do most religions. The great majority of the time, talk of the apocalypse was no more immediately relevant to Chinese villagers than Revelation is to most Christians. But when conditions turned bad, as they did during the nineteenth century, these ideas suddenly took on a new meaning. And because the teachings and ideas of the White Lotus tradition were so pervasive, an outbreak of apocalyptic panic or millenarian violence in one place was soon succeeded by another and another.

   In a way, the problems of the nineteenth century were the price of success in the eighteenth. The first half of the Qing dynasty was stable and prosperous. As a result, the population grew steadily by about 1 percent per year, which may not sound like much but adds up quickly. In 1750, the population of the Qing Empire was about 179 million – by 1800, it was nearly 300 million. Much of this new population moved to new lands that had been opened by conquest, or by new crops, such as maize and peanuts, which allowed people to grow food on poor or

---

[8] The term *dragon flower* also signifies the bodhi tree under which the Buddha was enlightened. Ma Xisha, "Lishi shang de Milejiao [Manicheism in history]" in Ma Xisha, ed., *Dangdai Zhongguo zongjiao jingxuan congshu: Minjian zongjiao juan* (Beijing: Minzu chubanshe, 2008), 4.

sloping soil. But by about 1800, the amount of arable land had more or less topped out, and any new population growth would have to use the same amount of land more intensively. This is not a matter of personal space. Overpopulation eventually forced many to live at the edge of sustenance, and even the smallest setback – a poor harvest, an untimely rain – could spell starvation. In 1932, the economic historian R. H. Tawney famously compared the state of the Chinese peasant to a man standing up to his neck in water, so that even the slightest ripple will cause him to drown.[9]

One of the most common and tragic responses to poverty was to kill unwanted daughters. Because the name of the family (and, more critically, the task of caring for the graves and spirits of ancestors) would fall only to sons, a family at the edge of starvation could not afford to care for daughters. Some baby girls were married young, sold, or (as in Figure 6.3) adopted out, but many were simply left to die. In areas of endemic poverty, this practice could produce a severe imbalance in gender: as early as 1775, one county in Zhejiang province reported having 131 males for every 100 females. In the poor province of Shanxi, this number soon grew as high as 156. The extra men, known colloquially as "bare branches" or "bare sticks" (*gu gun*), had nothing to lose. With no hope of ever finding a wife, these men had no future to look forward to but a life of toil, an early death, and, with no descendants to care for their soul, an afterlife as a wandering ghost. They were, not surprisingly, very eager for any chance to change their fate.

It would not be long before the tensions brewing in the countryside found a violent outlet. One of the earliest began in the late eighteenth century, when a martial artist named Wang Lun (d. 1774) started making the rounds of rural markets in a poor area of Shandong province, displaying his prowess at healing and meditation and spreading his Clear Water Teaching (*qingshui jiao*).[10] By 1774, he had gathered enough followers to rise up and capture a handful of fortified county towns. It may be difficult to imagine what Wang and his followers were hoping to achieve – at this point, the Qing military was still easily strong enough to crush a small, local rebellion. Wang was quickly captured, tortured, and put to death. But Wang had foreseen a more even fight. Wang promised to fend

---

[9] R. H. Tawney, *Land and Labor in China* (Boston: Beacon Press, 1966).

[10] Susan Naquin, *Shantung Rebellion: The Wang Lun Uprising of 1774* (New Haven, CT: Yale University Press, 1981). Some scholars will point out that the Clear Water Teaching is an offshoot of the Eight Trigrams Teaching, which in turn is a branch of the Green Lotus Teaching. Because these many teachings all borrowed ideas and even scriptures from each other, the actual relationship among them is rather difficult to trace.

Figure 6.3 Scenes of Chinese famine. These woodblock images are from a set commissioned to raise relief funds during the famine of 1876–9. **A**. Parents are shown either giving or selling their son to a wealthy family.

off Qing weapons with his magical arts (a tradition known as "knives and bullets do not enter," *qian dao bu ru*), and, once the rebels had proven themselves by joining the battle, that divine soldiers would arrive from heaven to finish the job. Although Wang Lun did not specifically prophesy the apocalypse, his short-lived rebellion revealed how willingly people in distress would join a movement that looked promising.

One generation later, the Lin Qing Rebellion picked up many of these same themes. Lin Qing (1770–1813) was a peasant from the outskirts of

B

Figure 6.3 **B**. Other images depict people resorting to more desperate measures, such as suicide or, as shown here, cannibalism. Committee of the China Relief Fund, *The Famine in China*, illustrations by a native artist with a translation of the Chinese text (London: C. Kegan Paul, 1878).

Beijing who found work as a barge puller on the Grand Canal. This work gave him opportunities to see a bit of the country and to be introduced to White Lotus teachings that flourished among his fellow laborers. Lin joined a teaching called the Eight Trigrams and established himself at the center of a wide network of teachers and disciples in the Beijing suburbs. In 1808, he declared himself to be the Maitreya Buddha, which was tantamount to announcing the end of the world. He called on his followers to overthrow the Manchu Qing and place a Han emperor on the throne, going as far as handing out titles for the coming kingdom. In 1813, a small group of rebels even reached the Forbidden City. Although they never accomplished more than firing a few arrows over the massive red walls when the rebellion was quickly crushed, the fact that such a group could organize in the shadow of the capital was a profound shock to the Jiaqing emperor (1760–1820), and a portent of much larger problems to come.

The greatest of all of these rebellions, the one that broke the back of the mighty Qing dynasty, was the Heavenly Kingdom of Great Peace (*taiping tianguo*), better known as the Taiping rebellion. It began in the far south, in the poor, mountainous province of Guangxi, with a failed scholar named Hong Xiuquan (1813–64). Hong was an ethnic Hakka who had prepared since childhood to take the Confucian civil service exams but, even after repeated attempts, was never able to gain his coveted degree. Over the years, frustration and disappointment took a heavy toll. After his third failed attempt, Hong fell into a fever and began to experience visions. In one of these, an old woman bathed him and talked about his "descent to Earth." In another, an old man clad in black gave him a sword with which to kill demons. (Destroying evil forces, you may remember, is one of the basic functions of territorial Daoism.) He also saw a younger man with golden hair, whom he referred to as "older brother." As he sought to understand these visions, Hong uncovered a Christian pamphlet that a missionary had handed him years before and began to realize that the old man was in fact God the Father, the younger man was Jesus Christ, and he himself must be none other than God's second son, the third member of the Holy Trinity.

Hong was quick to act. The 1840s were a time of crisis in Guangxi, with increased ethnic tensions between the Han and the Hakka minority. The Hakka had migrated many centuries earlier from northern China. They had always remained distinct and as a result had been more receptive to Christianity. As agrarian pressures intensified ethnic tensions to the point of violence, many of the besieged Hakkas welcomed the revelation of one of their own as a Christian deity. And as the movement gathered speed, others soon joined in. Throughout the 1840s (just as the Millerites were facing their Great Disappointment), Hong gathered disciples, baptizing them in Christian fashion and destroying the temples of local deities, which he perceived to be the demons God had asked him to slay.

In 1850, he commanded his ten thousand or so followers to sell their possessions and move with him to remote Zijin Mountain, and from there Hong declared himself Heavenly King (*tian wang*). His ambition was now clear: the brother of Jesus would not only destroy China's spiritual demons; he would also overthrow the Qing dynasty and recover the Mandate of Heaven. As Map 6.1 shows, Hong's forces moved north, growing in strength along the way. In only three years, his "long-haired"

Map 6.1 Route of Taiping advance.

army (since they were in rebellion, his troops stopped shaving their hair in front as demanded by Qing law) reached and conquered the city of Nanjing, which Hong renamed *Tianjing*, or "Heavenly Capital." Now in control of much of southern China, Hong created a kingdom that was ruled by a combination of religious Puritanism and peasant egalitarianism. He and his ministers drew heavily on ancient customs, using elaborate titles and rituals from as far back as the Zhou and outlawing such vices as prostitution, gambling, and opium use. They created a new calendar and published a seemingly endless series of theological proclamations, including versions of the Old and New Testaments that were annotated and "corrected" by Hong himself. All property was to be shared communally, including land, which would be distributed evenly according to population.

For a while, it appeared that Hong's kingdom might even overthrow the doddering Qing. At its height, the Taiping kingdom included all or part of seven southern provinces. From there Hong's generals sent out two major expeditions: one that went west into the mountains of Sichuan, and another that reached north all the way to Tianjin, just a few days' march away from Beijing itself. Foreign observers, many of them missionaries, were at first thrilled with reports of a Christian emperor taking the Chinese throne, but their enthusiasm quickly cooled. In contrast to the their promise to build a peasant utopia, one English visitor to Tianjing said of the Taiping that "they do nothing but burn, murder and destroy.... They are detested by the country people ... they have held Nanjing for eight years and there is no sign of rebuilding it." More to the point was the reaction of an American missionary: "As to the religious opinions of Hong ... I believe them to be abominable in the sight of God ... in fact, I believe he is crazy." Long disabused of their earlier egalitarianism, the top leadership amassed vast wealth, and Hong himself began spending more and more time with his harem. Dissent among the leaders weakened the movement, and eventually a number of Qing provincial officials managed to raise and train an army that pushed the Taiping forces back, finally retaking their capital in 1862. Hong himself committed suicide in his palace, one of an estimated twenty million Chinese lives lost.

The Taiping Rebellion was by far the greatest military disaster of the Qing dynasty. It was followed by a number of aftershocks, but the greatest damage had already been done. The lightning advance of Taiping armies through the southern provinces had revealed both the sorry state of Qing military garrisons and the desperation of millions of peasants, who were willing to pick up arms and follow the movement on its march to Nanjing.

7   Out of the twilight: Religion and the late nineteenth century

I. Fists of Justice and Harmony: Christian mission and the last stand of Chinese traditionalism

Over the nineteenth century, the Qing gradually lost the upper hand in dealing with the Western powers. The change resulted not from religion, but from commerce. As the Iberian powers went into decline during the late 1700s, Britain emerged as China's greatest European trading partner. Initially, this trade was conducted entirely on Chinese terms: it was bottlenecked through the single port of Canton and consisted almost entirely of an exchange of Chinese tea for British silver. The tea trade was so massive and so valuable that even a low import duty of 12.5 percent provided a tenth of all British government revenue. But it was not sustainable. After a long series of behind-the-scenes negotiations over court protocol, British envoys finally met the aging Qianlong emperor in 1793. To the request for more equal terms of trade came the emperor's famously dismissive response: "We possess all things. I set no value on strange or ingenious objects, and have no use for your country's manufactures."[1]

By the early 1800s, British firms (including such august names as Jardine Matheson) were making up their losses by illegally trading opium up and down the coast, and by 1840 the tension between the two countries reached the point of war. There was relatively little actual fighting – most of the two Opium Wars (1839–42, 1856–60; the second of these is sometimes called the Arrow War) consisted of British gunboats shelling Chinese coastal defenses – but they marked the beginning of a series of military encounters with foreign powers, each of which would prove more disastrous than the last. These wars, and the reparations China had to pay after each defeat, combined with the high cost of suppressing the Taiping Rebellion, sent the country

---

[1] Immanuel Chung-yueh Hsü, *The Rise of Modern China* (New York: Oxford University Press, 1970), 149, 161.

into a spiraling decline that eventually spelled the end, not just of the Qing dynasty, but of the entire imperial system.

The shifting balance of power immediately affected the fate of Christianity in China. Not counting Hong Xiuquan's claim to be the younger brother of Jesus, the last time we saw Christianity in China was in the early 1700s, when the Yongzheng emperor expelled the foreign missionaries and the Qianlong emperor banned the propagation of Christianity altogether. Of course, the fact that Hong had been able to learn about Christianity at all, even if only enough to inspire his delusions, suggests that the ban was not especially well enforced. Early Qing emperors may have evicted the missionaries, but they never instituted anything comparable to the door-to-door purge of native Christians seen in Tokugawa Japan. One reason was that the Qing, larger and more confident, had perceived the foreign religion as an irritation, but never really as a threat. They certainly did not imagine, as did the Tokugawa, that the missionaries were the vanguard of a foreign invasion force. Moreover, they could not have enforced such a policy even if they had wanted to do so. At best, the Qing had only a very tenuous grip on local society, and as the government went into decline during the nineteenth century, this hold would grow ever looser.

When the Christian missionaries began trickling back into China in the mid-1800s, they returned to a very different place. Beginning with the treaties that ended the two Opium Wars, every Chinese defeat had opened up new cities, particularly along the coast, to foreign trade and residence. Large areas of these "treaty ports" were directly administered by different foreign powers: that is why you could go to Shanghai and see British racing clubs, Italianate villas, onion-domed Russian churches, and French war monuments. Before it was renamed, the lovely round garden in the middle of Tianjin was known as Victoria Park. European power and culture were firmly entrenched along the coast and began rapidly reaching inland. The Qing court was at a loss for how to respond. Some called for China to strengthen itself by learning Western science and possibly even some of its culture, while others, far less realistically, wanted to call in the army and push the foreign devils back into the sea.

The missionaries, as well, were different. The original Catholic missions had never completely left and began to return in larger numbers as early as the 1840s, but Iberian Jesuits were now replaced by priests of different countries and different orders, most notably the French Missions Étrangères de Paris. These were joined (and eventually outnumbered) by Protestants, lay men and women from Scandinavia, Germany, and especially the English-speaking countries of Europe and

North America. Many well-known colleges in the United States were founded as mission institutions and over the years sent hundreds of alumni to China.

Initially, the Christian influence was limited to the treaty ports, but after the 1858 Treaty of Tianjin legalized mission in the interior, different groups began to spread throughout the country. There was some overlap of effort, and occasional conflict between missions. As before, the Vatican allocated Catholic mission territories to specific orders. If another order wished to enter the China field, they had to petition the Vatican or ask an existing mission to cede part of its territory. The Protestants tended to make the same sort of agreements among themselves. Irish and Scottish Presbyterians, the Danish Missionary Society, and American Baptists working in Manchuria divided up the areas each would work in and met regularly to ensure that their different missions were in fact putting forward their best coordinated effort. On the whole, Protestant and Catholic missions were at least cordial, if not friendly. When conflict between them did occur, it was often because one side felt the other was taking a shortcut to win converts. Protestants accused the Catholics of caring more about baptisms than faith and especially disliked the Catholic practice of baptizing the dying. The Catholics felt that Protestant evangelization was too aggressive and thus produced shallow Christians.

The new missionaries built a variety of social institutions. Both Catholics and Protestants built schools, again with a very slight difference in emphasis. Most Catholic education was elementary, as part of a strategy of raising children as members of tight-knit Catholic communities. Protestants saw a broader mission of "enlightening" China with the best of Western science and civilization, hoping that these would make people more receptive to Christianity. Both types of education had an enormous impact on generations of Chinese students. By 1889, some sixteen thousand of them had passed through mission schools. Missionaries also built institutions devoted to social welfare, such as orphanages, hospitals, and homes for the poor. Such institutions were not new to China: many Confucian elites of the Ming and Qing dynasties had funded "Halls of Benevolence" (*shantang*) that performed a similar role. But the Christian institutions were bigger and more permanent. Even if they did not care for the Christian religion, many prominent Chinese expressed admiration, and even a tinge of jealousy, at the scale and influence of the foreign charities.

But for all their good works, were the foreign missions *imperialists* in the pejorative sense in which we use the word today? It is, of course, impossible to generalize, but it is worth noting that some missionaries themselves were aware of the tendency to resort to methods that were not exactly Christian. They noted, for example, that many missionaries used the promise of economic aid to win converts or conflated the universalism of the Christian message with the superiority of Western culture. Some reacted against this tendency by calling for a new kind of mission, one expressed by the American missionary Rufus Anderson (1796–1880), who urged Christians to spread only the gospel and absolutely nothing else. Anderson wanted to create what he called "three-self" churches, which would be self-governing, self-funded, and self-propagating. In a word, they would be independent. Others shared his vision. In 1865, James Hudson Taylor (1832–1905) founded the China Inland Mission (CIM), a nondenominational organization of Protestant missionaries, primarily from the United Kingdom, and later Canada and the United States. The CIM wanted to leave the safety of the treaty ports and reach directly into village society, and, to do that, it needed to adapt. Before being sent into the field, missionaries of the CIM spent years learning Chinese, and once they were there, they were expected to eat, live, and dress not as foreigners, but as Chinese. Men even had to grow a queue, as the Qing demanded of their own subjects.

But many Chinese felt that the missionaries were up to something much more sinister and took action to keep them out. Anti-Christian tracts, some composed by high-ranking officials, began to appear during the early 1860s. The first headquarters of the CIM in Yangzhou was attacked and burned in 1868. Two years later, an angry mob burned down the Notre Dame church in the northern city of Tianjin. The sign at the rebuilt church now declares that this was a patriotic act of Chinese defending their motherland against spiritual pollution by foreigners; the reality is a bit less picturesque. With frequent droughts, famines, and overpopulation, life in this part of China was often precarious, especially for children. Catholic missions often responded to this problem in two ways: those children who could be saved were accepted into an orphanage, and those who could not were baptized so that they could die in a state of grace. Priests of the Notre Dame mission were so keen to baptize these dying children that they offered a cash reward for anyone who brought in a child who was *articulo mortis*, that is, on the point of death. Whatever their intentions, this was fairly awful public relations. Word spread quickly about the strange foreigners keeping children behind the big stone walls, including the rumor that the nuns were using the children's eyes and organs for magic spells. It would not be long before matters reached the point of violence. Even under less dramatic conditions, it was common to think of the foreign missionaries as wizards with evil intentions. The English missionary Arthur Peill described one such encounter during a long drought in Cangzhou, near Tianjin: "I remember one day an old woman looking daggers at me as I passed, and snapping out the suspicious question: 'Why doesn't it rain?' as if I knew quite well, and could send it if I liked."[2]

A student of history might recall that during these same years, crowds of angry Chinese were attacking not only churches, but other signs of the Western presence, such as telegraph lines and railroads, as well. Certainly superstition played a part in this: some felt that the wires and rails snaking across the countryside blocked the flow of feng shui, thus causing droughts and ruining crops. Similarly, when the Christian missions began building churches in the Chinese countryside, many peasants objected to the shape, claiming that the tall spires offended the heavens and bottled up the rains.

But if you look closely, some of what at first appears to be simple, blind superstition does begin to make more sense. At least some of those people who went out and tore up train tracks and telegraph wires must have understood that these new inventions could carry the power of the foreigners, now concentrated largely along the coast, into the interior. Similarly, the introduction of Christianity was not necessarily a good thing, especially when it proved disruptive to village life. If only one member of a family or certain families within a village chose to become Christian, it could create great tensions within the community. A rural village often manages its affairs as a collective. It will band together to do things as a community: building bridges, repairing irrigation canals, or hiring a watchman for the fields. This includes religion. Even now, villages will hold festivals to address collective religious concerns: rituals to pray for good fortune, to keep out evil spirits. One of the most important of these rituals in northern China was to pray for rain (qiu yu) during the dry summer months. Rain is the epitome of a collective good: everyone needs it, and, as the saying goes, "rain falls on the good and bad alike." When a village gathered to perform a religious ritual such as a prayer for rain, each family would make some contribution; one could not simply decide to opt out. But either as a matter of conscience or simply because they did not want to pay, Chinese Christians often did just that. Many Christians also refused to perform traditional funeral rituals for their own ancestors. This was more than just an offense against morals and customs: without proper funeral and burial rituals, the dead become vengeful ghosts who pose a threat to the whole village.

---

[2] Arthur D. Peill and J. Peill, *The Beloved Physician of Tsang Chou: Life-Work and Letters of Dr. Arthur D. Peill, F.R.C.S.E.* (London: Headley Bros, 1907), 48.

The presence of foreign missionaries often made a bad situation worse. By the close of the nineteenth century, the foreign powers were carving out heavy concessions from China and used violence against their own citizens as a pretext to demand more. The court was thus extremely anxious to avoid any sort of conflict with the foreigners, a situation that some missionaries were ready to exploit. Missionaries often intervened on behalf of Chinese Christians, for example, in legal conflicts with their non-Christian neighbors. This was not entirely unjustified: the missionaries themselves thought that they were simply balancing out the anti-Christian sentiment among the influential scholarly elite. But the perception was that the Chinese Christians, in league with the foreigners, were abusing their positions and that the government was either unwilling or or unable to stop them. Across China, the tension began to grow.

The summer of 1899 was hot and dry. After years of poor weather, many farmers had no food left in reserve. Some starved, and many others left their homes to join wave after wave of migrants looking for food. During these stressful years, a new set of beliefs had been circulating through the countryside of northern China. Throughout the provinces of Shandong and Zhili, young men had begun learning a style of martial arts called Fist of Justice and Harmony (*yihe quan*). As the style spread from village to village, familiar ideas about magical resistance to knives and bullets followed in its wake. But with one change: Instead of spending years mastering Daoist and martial arts, the idea was that one could become invulnerable simply by being pure of heart and allowing the Chinese gods – Guandi, Yue Fei, and the Monkey King (Sun Wukong) – to enter one's body directly. The fighting style, and the stories behind it, spread as groups of young men traveled the countryside exhibiting their new powers at markets and fairs. Their martial arts and possession rituals always drew a crowd, sometimes with mixed results. Peill observed one such display in Cangzhou, but unfortunately, the men were possessed not by one of the more heroic deities, but by Zhu Bazhen, the pig deity from the novel *Journey to the West*. The crowd was distinctly unimpressed. As Peill describes the scene, "so successful were their invocations that, when possessed, they groveled nose down in the soil, so much to the disgust of their fellow-villagers."[3] But even with such occasional mishaps, the new ideas spread like wildfire through the drought-stricken North China Plain. The movement soon had a name: the Society of Justice and Harmony Society (Yihetuan). Seeing their martial arts, foreign observers simply called them Boxers.

[3] Peill and Peill, *Beloved Physician*, 46.

Figure 7.1 Boxers in Tianjin. A rare photograph of Boxers on the march. Most foreign images of the Boxers show either prisoners or executed corpses. Image supplied by Digital Collections, Library of Congress.

Strictly speaking, their movement should not be called the Boxer Rebellion because they were not rebelling *against* the government – they were rising up to defend it.[4] Even though the movement never had any real leadership, it did have a mission: to rid China of the foreign devils and their religion. During the summer of 1900, bands of Boxers began to converge from all directions on the foreign enclaves of Beijing and Tianjin (see Figure 7.1). The Qing court (and especially the infamous Empress Dowager Cixi, 1835–1908, who held the real power) at first did not know how to respond but eventually threw its support behind the Boxers. It might have had good reason for doing so. In their defense, the Qing were certainly aware that even after ruling China for nearly three centuries, they were *also* perceived as foreigners, and that the Boxer slogan "Support the Qing; destroy the foreigners!" (*fu Qing mie yang*) was only a slight variation of the ones that had been raised in rebellion against them (e.g., "support the Ming; destroy the Qing!"). Nevertheless, the court was so confident in the movement that it declared war on all of the powers at once. Of course, by this point, the real power of the court to enforce its decrees was not what it once was, and in reality local and provincial leaders were free to do as they

---

[4] Joseph Esherick makes this point emphatically in *The Origins of the Boxer Uprising* (Berkeley: University of California Press, 1987).

Box 7.a. Two views of the Boxer siege

From the diary of an American inside the foreign legations:

> Every one realized when we became besieged that we were in a position that only divine help and a speedy rescue could avail us. Surrender under any circumstances could now only mean butchery. We had seen the survivors of the massacre at the south cathedral come among us with children almost hacked to pieces by the cruel knives of the fanatical Boxers, and, knowing their hatred for us, we knew well that if the men were overcome, the women and children must suffer a horrible death or worse.
>
> Many of the men had resolved that at the last fight they would themselves kill their wives and daughters to prevent their suffering at the hands of the incarnate devils that surrounded us.

Robert Coltman, *Beleaguered in Peking,*
The Boxer's War against the Foreigner
(Philadelphia: F. A. Davis & Co., 1901), 182–4

The voice of the god Guandi, speaking through one of the Boxers, and posted on placards in Beijing:

> I am none other than the Great Yu Di come down in person. Knowing that you are of devout mind, I have now descended to make known to you that these are times of trouble in the world.... Disturbances are to be dreaded from the foreign devils; everywhere they are starting missions, erecting telegraphs and building railways; they do not believe in the sacred doctrine, and they speak evil of the gods. Their sins are numberless as the hairs of the head.... For this reason, I have given forth my decree that I shall descend to earth at the head of all the saints and spirits, and that wherever the Yihequan are gathered together, there shall the gods be in the midst of them.... The will of Heaven is that the telegraph wires be first cut, then the railways torn up, then shall the foreign devils be decapitated.

Roland Allen, *The Siege of the Peking Legations*
(London: Smith, Elder & Co., 1901), 18–19

---

pleased. At one extreme, Governor Yuxian of Shanxi promised refuge to foreign missionaries and then turned on them, killing dozens of men, women, and children, along with hundreds of Chinese Christians. At the other, Governor Yuan Shikai (1859–1916) of Shandong ignored the declaration completely and turned his elite New Army on the Boxers themselves. Muslim regiments in the regular army were notoriously antiforeign, but few entertained much sympathy for the Boxers, either. When these troops were sent in to suppress the Boxers, they did so with particular ferocity. The fact that the foreign legations in Beijing were

Figure 7.2 Foreign occupation of Beijing. Suppression of the Boxers left Beijing occupied by troops of the Eight Nation Army. Here American marines parade through the city. Property of the Wason Collection on East Asia, Cornell University Library.

able to survive shelling for more than three months suggests that at least some of the Qing forces sent to dislodge them were less than committed to the job.

By the close of the summer, the foreigners had prepared their response: an Eight Nation Army landed near Tianjin and began marching toward Beijing. At this moment, it became clear that reports of Boxer invulnerability to foreign weapons had been greatly exaggerated. Eighteen thousand foreign troops arrived, the largest number sent from Japan and Russia (one scholar suggests that these two countries were already sizing each other up for the war that would begin five years later).[5] German and Russian troops were particularly violent and, by many reports, slaughtered Boxers and civilians indiscriminately. Others looted cultural treasures and finished off the destruction of the Yuanming Palace, which had been designed by Jesuits three centuries earlier. The Eight Nation Army occupied Beijing, and paraded troops through the streets in a show of force (see Figure 7.2). In a final act of

[5] Urs Matthias Zachmann, *China and Japan in the Late Meiji Period: China Policy and the Japanese Discourse on National Identity, 1895–1904* (London: Routledge, 2009), 128–52.

degradation, the empress dowager and the imperial family disguised themselves as commoners and fled Beijing for the hills of Shanxi.

The Boxer Uprising marked the absolute nadir of China's century of decline and, thus, the beginning of a new era. The faction that had supported the Boxers was irremediably disgraced: even the powerful empress dowager could no longer hide her head in the sand and began making small steps toward political reform. The court offered an indemnity for the lives of the murdered missionaries and initiated a surprisingly thorough investigation into lives and property lost by Chinese Christians.[6] Everything connected to the Boxers was discredited: their violence, their bellicose xenophobia, their anti-Christianity, and their superstition. The Boxer debacle drew one era to a close, and a desire to escape the Boxer legacy would dominate much of the next.

II. Kill the Buddha! Shintō and the new traditionalism of Meiji Japan

Just as it had been in China, the nineteenth century was a period of quickly changing fortunes for Japan. In 1800, the Qing Empire was at its apex. It had extended its reach far into Central Asia and was just beginning to see, in the form of small religious rebellions, the first few cracks developing in its rule. By the middle of the century, these cracks had grown and were beginning to threaten the very foundations of the dynasty. Tokugawa Japan was not nearly as significant as a regional power, but it was no less troubled. Its social and political institutions had been finely tuned to fit the early 1600s but were poorly suited to change. But change there was, even in a secluded country. Just as in China, the crisis resulted from prosperity. Trade had flourished during the stable and peaceful Tokugawa reign, creating very clear winners and losers. Urban merchants became exceedingly wealthy, and a new world of entertainments and diversions opened up in commercial cities such as Edo and Osaka. The Tokugawa government fared far worse. As the economy expanded, it increasingly relied on debt to finance its expenses. Its fixed-income retainers, most notably the once-privileged class of samurai, suffered the most. As the internally peaceful Tokugawa had little need for an armed warrior class, many samurai had already turned their hands to administrative tasks. As their economic station declined, others were forced to take up jobs as bodyguards or even

---

[6] The total size of the indemnity, 450 million taels, was ruinously large. Esherick, *Origins of the Boxer Uprising*, 311. The United States used its share to fund scholarships for Chinese students to study in American universities.

artisans. Some were thrown into absolute penury. Because samurai loyalties had always been to their own domain lords, rather than to the shōgun, the decline in their fortunes quickly spelled trouble for the Tokugawa regime.[7]

The political deterioration of the Tokugawa regime augured trouble for Buddhism. For more than two centuries, the Tokugawa had presided over a vast expansion of the Buddhist institution. The *danka* system prompted a vast increase in the number of temples, making them far more prevalent in local society than they had ever been in China. The temples acted as eyes and ears for the state, registering subjects in the name of rooting out hidden Christians. At the same time, they grew wealthy off their government-secured funeral monopoly. Already, popular images of the Buddhists portrayed them as corrupt and lax, and it was plain to all that their success was tied to Tokugawa patronage. When the shōgun finally abdicated in 1868, Buddhism would face a violent backlash.

But in many ways, dissatisfaction with Buddhism was just a symptom of deeper intellectual trends. Even before the Tokugawa ascended to power, a slow tide of interest was already rising in what was called "national learning" (*kokugaku*). Put simply, national learning was an attempt to return to Japanese native traditions, or at least what people imagined these traditions to have been. The movement was extremely broad: its interests touched upon literature, poetry, and politics, among much else. In each case, it sought to separate out the essence of the Japanese nation (*kokutai*) hidden underneath centuries of foreign pollution.

Religion, particularly Confucianism and Buddhism, presented a special difficulty. Motoori Norinaga (1730–1801), one of the pillars of the national studies movement, had begun life as a devout Buddhist. Although Motoori never fully abandoned the faith, he did come to see its strict moralizing tone as something alien to the Japanese aesthetic, which preferred to see the beauty even in a flawed individual. Motoori searched through classical texts, such as the eighth-century *Kojiki*, to find clues to this unspoiled Japanese spirit, the "Ancient Way" (*kodō*), which he and many others identified with Shintō. Motoori spent much

---

[7] The classic text on the long-term economic transformation during the Tokugawa period remains Thomas C. Smith, *The Agrarian Origins of Modern Japan* (Stanford, CA: Stanford University Press, 1959). On the radicalization of samurai during the later years of the shogunate, see Albert M. Craig, *Chōshū in the Meiji Restoration* (Cambridge: Harvard University Press, 1961), and Roger F. Hackett, *Yamagata Aritomo in the Rise of Modern Japan, 1838–1922* (Cambridge: Harvard University Press, 1971).

of his later life poring through the eleventh-century novel *Tale of Genji*, as though he were restoring a damaged painting, trying to uncover the original beauty hidden beneath layers and layers of Buddhist misinterpretation.[8]

Those who followed Motoori shared his interest in uncovering this Ancient Way but disagreed on exactly how to define it, particularly with regard to these other religions. Not all things foreign were necessarily or equally bad: Motoori himself had been more critical of Confucianism than of Buddhism. Other scholars accepted both Confucianism and Buddhism as derivatives of the Ancient Way and only objected when these two teachings were elevated above Shintō. (Christianity, it hardly needs saying, was opposed by all nativists.) Still others raised the earlier theme that worship of the Buddha angered the *kami*, who expressed their displeasure by visiting disaster upon the nation.

The harshest and most absolute criticism of foreign religions was that of a self-proclaimed disciple of Motoori named Hirata Atsutane (1776–1843). Like Motoori, he felt that Japan was a divine land and that the Japanese were literal descendants of *kami*. But Hirata was more violently xenophobic. His depiction of the Dutch, for example, paints Japan's only Western residents in terms that were literally bestial:

> As everybody knows who has seen one, the Dutch are taller than other people, have fair complexions, big noses and white stars in their eyes.... Their eyes are really just like those of a dog. They are long from the waist downwards, and the slenderness of their legs also makes them resemble animals. When they urinate, they lift one leg, the way dogs do. Moreover, apparently because the backs of their feet do not reach to the ground, they fasten wooden heels to their shoes, which makes them look all the more like dogs. This may also explain why a Dutchman's penis appears to be cut short at the end, just like a dog's. This may sound like a joke, but it is quite true, not only of Dutchmen but of Russians too.... This may be the reason why the Dutch are as lascivious as dogs, and spend their entire nights in erotic practices.[9]

Not surprisingly, Hirata was rabidly opposed to Buddhism. In his 1811 *Jests on Emerging from Meditation* (*Shutsujō Shogō*, the name itself is a pun on an earlier anti-Buddhist work), a text that would inspire later generations of anti-Buddhist activists, Hirata subjected all aspects

---

[8] Shigeru Matsumoto, *Motoori Norinaga: 1730–1801* (Cambridge: Harvard University Press, 1970).

[9] Donald Keene, "Hirata Atsutane and Western Learning," *T'oung Pao* 42, no. 5 (1954), 353–80, at 374.

of Buddhism to ridicule. He began by painting a very unflattering picture of India, explaining how its residents spread cow dung on the floors of their homes in order to enjoy the smell. But even this "vulgar" and "inferior land" had been wise enough eventually to rid itself of Buddhism. All the worse for Japan, where people remain entranced by the lies of monks, self-indulgently believing that a life of evil deeds may be forgiven simply by calling out "Amida."[10] Hirata was certainly not the first person to express such ideas; nor would he be the last. But we may see in him the rising wave of anti-Buddhist nationalism that would continue to grow over the next decades.

For the most part, these early thinkers had little to say about the actual conduct of government, but new crises toward the middle of the 1800s pushed politics to center stage. Though technically Japan was a closed country, the flow of information into the country had never stopped completely. The Dutch on Dejima had continued to take in books of science and philosophy (for this reason, all things Western were simply termed "Dutch learning"), and news of major events sooner or later found its way into the country. And in Japan, there could be no more major event than China's stunning capitulation to Britain in the Opium Wars. Although some Japanese no doubt reveled in China's humiliation, nobody could escape the fear that the divine country might itself be next.

By the middle of the century, all of these elements began to merge: the economic dislocation of the warrior class, the nativist search for Japanese essence, increasingly urgent calls for political reform, and a somewhat preemptive tide of anti-Western sentiment. When the U.S. fleet under Commodore Matthew Perry actually arrived in Edo harbor in 1853, and the shōgun reluctantly ended two and a half centuries of seclusion by signing a treaty of friendship one year later, the call went up to "revere the emperor and repel the barbarians" (sonnō jōi). The latter part of this phrase is straightforward enough, but the first part deserves more explanation. The call to revere the emperor was more than just a call to patriotism – it was also a criticism of the shōgun who had signed away Japan's dignity. The struggling Tokugawa regime found itself embattled on all sides, as increasingly nationalistic groups of samurai (especially those from the southern domains of Satsuma and Chōshū, which were, not coincidentally, the closest to China) threatened to plunge the country into civil war. In 1868, the final shōgun ceded power to the young Meiji emperor (1852–1912).

[10] James Edward Ketelaar, *Of Heretics and Martyrs in Meiji Japan: Buddhism and Its Persecution* (Princeton, NJ: Princeton University Press, 1990), 30–7; Mark McNally, *Proving the Way: Conflict and Practice in the History of Japanese Nativism* (Cambridge: Harvard University Asia Center, 2005).

We know this event not as a coup or a revolution, but as the Meiji *Restoration* because, it was felt, reinstating the emperor to real power marked the return to a more pure form of Japanese governance. It was also to be the beginning of a vast spiritual reform of the Japanese people. Not surprisingly, Buddhism was the first on the chopping block. Even before 1868, samurai in domains such as Mito had spearheaded local campaigns against Buddhist temples. Now with a supportive government behind them, they set out not only to punish Buddhism, but also to reverse centuries of Tokugawa policy by elevating Shintō in its place. The rallying cry was to "revere the *kami* and destroy the Buddha" (*keishin haibutsu*).

To understand the new religious policy, it is important to appreciate the profound contradictions of the early Meiji period. On the one hand, the new government was deeply conservative, in that it sought to recreate a semimythical past and return to a pre-Chinese tradition. The emperor was to play a central role in this. Reflecting the aspiration of nativist thinkers like Hirata to elevate Shintō to a central political role, the emperor was to be not only the head of state, but also the center of a network of ritual observances. Early Meiji activists called this new arrangement the "unity of ritual and government" (*saisei itchi*).

At the same time, many of the reforms from the early Meiji period were distinctly progressive. One primary goal of the Meiji Restoration was, after all, to prevent the divine country from falling prey to the Western powers, and, to do that, Japan needed to emulate them. Not long after the political change opened the door for international travel, Japanese delegations began visiting Western countries, learning everything they could about science, technology, and even customs. For a political movement that had begun with the slogan of expelling the barbarians, Meiji Japan became very quickly infatuated with everything Western, at least for a time. More profoundly, the entire Tokugawa social structure was dismantled, piece by piece. The first to go were the samurai, who lost their marks of status and were replaced by a conscript army drawn primarily from commoners. Such steps may appear to be part of a liberalizing of society, but they were less in the tradition of Thomas Jefferson than of Napoleon. The new Japanese was not a citizen, in a democratic sense, but a *subject* of the emperor. It was the responsibility of the new circle of Meiji elites to mold and shape the new subject, giving him a patriotic mind-set and inculcating in him traditional Japanese values. This sort of government-directed program of social transformation is sometimes referred to as social engineering. In the case of Meiji Japan, perhaps it is more appropriate to think in terms of *spiritual* engineering.

Shintō was thus to be the center of the new government and of the new society. The newly created Department of Shintō Divinity (*jingi-kan*), which was higher than all other departments in the new government, would preside over its rituals and sacred sites. But even with unimpeded official backing, putting this plan into practice raised some rather fundamental problems. The first was deciding exactly what Shintō was. For well over a thousand years, since the Nara period, Shintō and Buddhism had been inextricably mixed together. Buddhist temples and Shintō shrines often shared the same physical space, and the question of *true* nature aside, few people had problems reconciling the idea that the same deity could share an identity as both bodhisattva and *kami*. Even those who had wanted Shintō to stand alone found it difficult to separate their ideals from standards set by Buddhism. This had long been a problem. In answer to the venerable Buddhist scriptural tradition, an unknown contemporary of Kitabatake Chikafusa had forged the so-called *Five Classics of Shintō*, a text that tried to trump Buddhism by claiming it to be even older.

But with the political transformation of the Meiji state, a solution now came directly from the top: in 1868, the government issued the first of a series of laws formally dividing Shintō and Buddhism. Not surprisingly, this "separation of Shintō and Buddhism" (*shinbutsu bunri*) greatly favored the former. Temples that combined shrines of the two religions (which is to say, nearly all of them) were to be purged of their Buddhist elements and made Shintō by default. Buddhist monks attached to such properties would become Shintō priests or return to lay society. In some places, the picture was more violent. In hotbeds of samurai radicalism such as Mito, bands of activists scoured the countryside beating priests, destroying temples, and plundering Buddhist treasures. One student of the nativist scholar Gonda Naosuke recalled the atmosphere of the times:

> The reason we established the unity of "rites and rule" as it was practiced in Emperor Jimmu's time was in order to eliminate Buddhism.... Nativist scholars were the most ardent anti-Buddhists, and the Hirata school, frequently citing the *Essay on the Two Enemies of the Kami* from Hirata's *Shutsujō shōgo*, was among the most active.... We students would go through town every day smashing every roadside Jizō or other Buddhist statues we could find. If even one were missed, it was a great disgrace to us. Fire, being a danger in the city, was not used to destroy pagodas and temple buildings, but we did our best in burning Buddhist artifacts.[11]

---

[11] Ketelaar, *Of Heretics and Martyrs*, 33.

Box 7.b. The imperial Rescript on Education

The rescript (*chokugo*) was a type of document used rarely, but with great effect, from the Meiji reign through the 1940s. Rescripts were issued directly from the emperor himself and were thus above ordinary pronouncements or laws. The Rescript on Education (*kyōiku chokugo*), promulgated in 1890, was sent to schools throughout the country, along with a picture of the Meiji emperor. Teachers and students were instructed to commit it to heart and demonstrate respect by bowing before the document. (The Christian educator Uchimura Kanzō created a major incident when he refused to do so.) Yet despite the sacred aura that surrounded the rescript, its content is a relatively bland expression of Confucian principles:

"Know ye, Our subjects,

Our imperial ancestors have founded Our Empire on a foundation broad and everlasting, and subjects ever united in loyalty and filial piety have illustrated the beauty of it from generation to generation. This is the glory of the fundamental character of Our Empire, and therein lies the source of Our education. Ye, Our subjects, be filial to your parents, affectionate to your brothers and sisters, be harmonious as husbands and wives and as friends be true. Conduct yourselves with modesty and moderation; extend your benevolence to all; pursue learning and culti-vate arts, and thereby develop intellectual facilities and perfect moral powers. Furthermore, advance the public good and promote common interests; respect the Constitution and observe the laws. Should emer-gency arise, offer yourselves courageously to the State, and thus guard and maintain the prosperity of Our Throne coeval with Heaven and Earth. So shall ye be not only Our good and faithful subjects, but also render illustrious the best traditions of your forefathers.

The Way here set forth is indeed the teaching bequeathed by Our Imperial Ancestors, to be observed by Their Descendants and subjects alike, infallible for all times and true in all places. It is Our wish to lay it to heart in all reverence, in common with you, Our Subjects, that we may all attain the same virtue."

Hardacre, *Shinto and the State*, 121–2

The combination of government fiat and local violence was devas-tating. Of the estimated 200,000 temples in Tokugawa-era Edo, only 74,000 survived. In Toyama province, 1,730 temples were reduced almost overnight to 7.

In some ways, Meiji support for Shintō closely mirrored Tokugawa policy toward Buddhism. Just as the Tokugawa had with Buddhist temples, the new government made a survey of shrines, ordering them into a national hierarchy, capped by the great shrine of Ise. Individual

Box 7.c. The Great Promulgation Campaign

In 1870, a coalition of Shintō and Buddhist priests initiated the "Great Promulgation Campaign" (*taikyō senpu undō*), a drive to construct a new state religion, and to spread this teaching amongst the Japanese people. The movement faced problems from the outset. By creating a single national creed, it had hoped to heal the rift between Shintō and Buddhist priests, but its rituals, liturgies and even vestments all strongly favored the former. Its ideology, formulated in the Great Teaching Institute (*Daikyōin*), consisted of little more than anemic admonitions to serve the emperor and respect the gods. Even its own corps of evangelists had trouble grasping the point of the ideology, much less presenting it to the Japanese people. Moreover, the political nature of the movement meant that its leadership quickly factionalized around individual schools and shrines. Buddhist monks, by far the more experienced and effective preachers, soon abandoned the campaign, and a dispute between the Ise and Izumo shrines divided the remaining proponents. As time went on, many more groups splintered off from the campaign: some became the schools of Sect Shintō, others took on an independent existence as the so-called "new religions" of the late Meiji era.

Ridiculed in the press, and abandoned by much of the clergy, the movement was officially called to an end in 1884.

Hardacre, *Shinto and the State*, 42–59

families were required to keep a shrine (*kamidana*, literally a "spirit shelf") within the home, and within the shrine to keep a talisman from Ise – technically making every home in the nation a branch of the Ise shrine. In 1871, responsibility for household registration was transferred from the Buddhist network to the new Shintō one.

Through a variety of methods, the new government sought both to promote ritual and to control the way it would be interpreted. It arranged well-publicized trips for the emperor to worship at Ise, something no reigning emperor had done for a thousand years. Not only was the emperor the most important ritual practitioner, but the rituals themselves increasingly emphasized his divine lineage. A shrine to Amaterasu, the progenitress of the imperial house, was installed on the grounds of the palace, and an unsuccessful attempt was made to build a popular cult of Jimmu, another imperial ancestor. Imperial rituals were now made into a model for *national* rituals: the entire population was expected to emulate the emperor – his and their activities were coordinated in a national calendar of Shintō observance. The new government created ambitious plans to foster Shintō values among the populace.

For fourteen years, it embarked on what could only be called religious mission among its own people. This "Promulgation Campaign" sent activists and newly appointed priests into the countryside to establish Shintō and displace Buddhism. The campaign itself was an utter disaster. Its failure to win converts revealed both the lack of substance in the mixture of invented rituals and political rhetoric and the limitations of even a very activist state to force religious belief on its people.[12]

This level of enthusiasm for national Shintō could not be sustained for very long. As we will see in a later chapter, the Buddhists quickly regrouped and began to portray their own religion in the same sort of nationalist terms as used by their onetime tormentors. At the same time, political will for Shintō began to waver. Many Meiji politicians had been ambivalent about making Shintō the foundation for their new, modern state and were concerned that overly generous state funding of Shintō would make the new clerical elite just as corrupt as the old elite had been. Others found Shintō to be a diplomatic liability. Meiji foreign policy was a complete reversal of Tokugawa seclusion: Japan was desperate to earn the respect of the Western powers and to engage them as diplomatic equals. To this end, they were willing to make numerous changes. Some were cosmetic, such as adopting Western hairstyles and dress. Other changes, such as the transformation of Japan's legal system to fit Western ideas of justice, were much more profound. Meiji politicians quickly learned that state support of Shintō and the persecution of Buddhists and Christians were harming Japan's image as a civilized power. In order to be accepted by the international community, Japan had to present at least the appearance of religious tolerance. It was at this point, incidentally, that Japanese diplomats engaged in treaty negotiations first coined the word that is still used for "religion" in Japanese (and Chinese) today.

By the 1880s, then, it was clear to most that Shintō would not, and should not, become a national religion. The failures of the previous decade had revealed the limitations of Shintō as a pastoral religion, as well as the high political and diplomatic cost of promoting a national religion too aggressively. Moreover, even among Shintō supporters, there were many who rejected the idea. Shintō priests sent into the countryside during the Promulgation Campaign had balked at the idea of performing Buddhist-style ritual services, especially polluting ones such as funerals. More generally, it was felt that the new category of "religion" was simply too lowly and restrictive a definition for what was

---

[12] Helen Hardacre, *Shinto and the State, 1868–1988* (Princeton, NJ: Princeton University Press, 1989), 42–59.

in reality the Japanese national soul. Ironically, both sides reached the same conclusion: what they wanted from Shintō was not its rituals or clergy, but its spiritual and moral essence.[13]

The solution was to separate out the religious and moral aspects of Shintō. In 1882, the government did just that, legally dividing it into Sect Shintō (shūha Shintō) and Shrine Shintō (jinja Shintō). The former consisted of the thirteen specific sects that had evolved to gain government recognition as "churches" (*kyōkai*) and would be administered by the Department of Religion. The latter consisted of everything else: all Shintō sites that were not identifiably part of these thirteen recognized sects. These unaffiliated shrines, which constituted the great majority of Shintō sites nationwide, would be administered by a *secular* chain of command: the Bureau of Shrines, which was under the Department of Home Affairs. A draft of the Japanese constitution from that same year outlined this new, and much more modest, role for Shintō:

> Worship at indigenous Shintō shrines is the symbolic expression of civic obligations and human virtues, and shall not be understood as a matter of religious belief. Shintō worship shall be based on the popular will and donations made at such occasions shall be decided by citizens in accordance with local customs and individual resources.

This new arrangement was very good news for the government. On the one hand, it allowed it to exert more aggressive control over the shrines, restricting financial support to only the most important shrines (such as Ise) and ordering villages to consolidate their existing Shintō sites into one single shrine each. On the other, it also gave them a free hand to use Shintō to unify the state. The final version of the constitution, promulgated in 1889, did not mention Shintō specifically, because it did not need to mention it. Instead, Article 28 promised the Japanese people freedom of religion, so long as the exercise of such freedom was "not prejudicial to peace and order, and not antagonistic to their duties as subjects." In other words, a religion (such as Sect Shintō, Buddhism, or even Christianity) was a matter of conscience and choice. But Shrine Shintō, or more specifically, what historians looking back on the period would call State Shintō (kokka Shintō), was more than religion: it was the spiritual core of the Japanese people. As such, it was anything but optional.

---

[13] An important inspiration for Japan was Germany, which was undergoing a similar process of national unification and used a national religion to create a spiritual bond with the state.

8   Into the abyss: Religion and the road to disaster during the early twentieth century

I. Toward Confucian fascism: China searches for direction

One frozen Beijing morning early in 1898, a Confucian scholar named Kang Youwei (1858–1927) sat somewhere in the maze of antechambers of the Forbidden City, waiting for an audience with the young Guangxu (1871–1908) emperor. For Kang, an improbably youthful forty years old, this was a once in a lifetime honor, albeit one that would eventually end with his fleeing the country and the emperor a prisoner within his own palace. It occurred at a particularly momentous time. China had just lost a disastrous war with Japan, defeated by a country that nearly all had considered a laughably insignificant foe and losing its traditional sovereignty over the Korean Peninsula in the bargain. It would not be long before Beijing itself was overrun, first by the Boxers, and soon afterward by foreign troops. But for a brief moment, the meeting of minds between Kang and the Chinese emperor offered a glimpse of a radically different future.

Kang himself had led something of charmed and sheltered life. Like many of the political reformers who would follow him, Kang was a Cantonese, originally from the distant South, thousands of miles from the political intrigues in Beijing. As a child, he had displayed all the signs of becoming a promising scholar and was groomed from an early age to take the Confucian civil service exams. Even for a prodigy such as Kang, preparing for the exams was an extremely demanding task, requiring hours of cloistered study and rote memorization of the Confucian classics. The stress of these examinations was enormous. Repeated failure in the examinations was probably enough to have driven the rebel Hong Xiuquan out of his mind. Kang himself took solace in Buddhist meditation. But even successful candidates were at best hothouse flowers. By the time they were ready actually to sit for the exams for the first time, many students had spent their entire lives within the rarified world of scholars, libraries, and elite literary circles.

Few had any direct experience with the real woes ordinary people faced, and fewer still with the foreign powers that were causing China such problems.

Initially, at least, Kang was a rather typical member of this naive and cloistered elite, prone to spouting dilettantish opinions on the world and what ailed it. On the basis of little more than the deeply entrenched biases of his class, he developed a vocal hatred for all things foreign. This lasted until he was able to take a trip to Shanghai, large sections of which were divided into the "concession areas" administered directly by foreign powers, principally the French and British. There he saw something he would never have expected: foreign-run areas that were well ordered, with clean streets, gas lamps, professional police, and efficient public services. Kang then did a complete about-face, becoming convinced that the path for China lay not in retreating to the past, but in facing the future, which meant, at least in part, the radical transformation of China's social and political structure. He aired these views to whoever would listen, sympathetic younger students mostly. He wrote official letters to the emperor, but these were never delivered.

When he finally did meet the emperor (through the influence of a well-connected tutor), Kang aired the views he had been gestating for years. Some of these were sweepingly radical. Turning his back on his own career path, Kang called for the government to be staffed not by generalist Confucian scholars, but by persons of technical competence: people with training in finance, engineering, foreign languages, and the like. Up until that point, the Chinese government had for nearly a thousand years recruited its officials under the assumption that the moral attitude that a good scholar gave to his task would more than make up for his lack of technical training. That is why lower-level officials such as county magistrates were tasked with all of the duties of government – keeping the tax rolls up to date, investigating crimes, maintaining intricate systems of dams and levees. These technical jobs, Kang insisted, were far too complex for what were essentially well-intentioned laymen to handle.

The most important transformation was to occur at the very top, the restoration of real power to the emperor himself. The Guangxu emperor, thirteen years Kang's junior, had been instated emperor in 1875, at age four. Since that time, the emperor, whose personal name was *Zaitian*, had lived and reigned in the shadow of his aunt and former regent, the empress dowager, Cixi. Even before then, Cixi had reigned as the power behind the throne, as regent to another child emperor, her own son, who had died at the age of nineteen. (The official story was that he had died of smallpox, but rumors at the time attributed his death to syphilis that he had contracted with local prostitutes. Since court records have an uncanny way of scrubbing such problems clean, we will likely never know for certain.) At any rate, Zaitian, the Guangxu emperor, was now in his twenties and had never been able to exercise any real power over his aunt, who held, among other cards, the loyalty of many top officials and the most important military commanders. Kang Youwei encouraged the frustrated emperor to seize power from the "evil influences of eunuchs and palace maids" and, in emulation of Russia's Peter the Great or the Meiji emperor in Japan, to use his personal prestige to launch a wave of modernizing reforms in China. Inspired by his newfound friend and adviser, the Guangxu emperor did indeed embark on such a program. It lasted, however, only until Cixi was able to organize a countercoup, which unfortunately was not very long at all. The ephemerality of this short-lived attempt to rule is evident in the name history gives the period: the Hundred Days of Reform.

Yet, however radical Kang's ideas were, they were nothing compared to the ones he did not talk about. Writing in China before the ill-fated Hundred Days of Reform and in Japan after having been forced to flee the country (Cixi had called for him to be executed by the infamous "death by slicing"),[1] Kang developed a radically utopian vision of the future, which he called the Great Unification (*da tong*) in a book of the same name. In this world, there would be no nations. Instead, people would be united under a single, democratically elected government. Likewise, families or clans would cease to exist; men and women would freely choose with whom to cohabitate and then switch to new partners at the end of each year. All citizens would live in public dormitories and eat in giant common halls. The dead would be cremated and made into fertilizer.

Although this titular Great Unification is a reference to an ideal espoused by Confucius, Kang's plan in fact represented the systematic dismantling of the entire Confucian worldview. Kang's vision undermined two of the fundamental pillars of Confucian society: loyalty to the nation and hierarchy within the family. Even his proposal to cremate rather than bury the dead was a response to the popular custom of holding funerals so lavish that they could bankrupt the living, which itself

---

[1] This method of execution represented the harshest punishment in the imperial penal system. Aside from having a name that sounds strikingly sadistic, this type of execution not only killed the victim, but also mutilated the corpse, thereby violating the Confucian requirement to keep one's body intact. By this same logic, decapitation was a lesser form of punishment, since the head could be recovered and buried with the body. The lightest form of execution was thus by smothering or strangulation.

derived from social pressure to conform visibly to Confucian norms of filial piety. In place of particular loyalties to one family or one nation, Kang wanted mankind to become one giant family, one great nation. This, he insisted, had been the true goal of Confucius's teaching.

As the years passed, Kang would lose his reputation as a radical and eventually become known as something of a reactionary irrelevance. He was a lifelong advocate of constitutional monarchy, rather than revolution, and remained devoted to the emperor, even after the imperial system was finally toppled in 1911. Once this happened, however, China quickly became a very different place. Within a few years, trolleys and motorcars traversed the streets of Beijing, and real power fell into the hands of a number of regional warlords. Vastly miscalculating the mood of the public, one of these militarists in 1917 proclaimed the rebirth of the empire and briefly attempted to reinstate the deposed boy emperor Pu Yi (1906–67).[2] In response, Kang donned his official mandarin robes and presented himself at the Forbidden City, ready to offer his services.

Yet, however anachronistic this erstwhile reformer would appear to later generations, his ideas were indeed prophetic, and an appropriate way to punctuate the end of the nineteenth century and the imperial system. Over the previous century, a succession of reformers had sought to accommodate China to an increasingly intrusive world order by posing concrete answers to a growing list of problems. To answer the country's military weakness, they purchased ships and built academies. When this effort proved insufficient, they built an industrial infrastructure of telegraphs, coal mines, munitions factories, and dockyards. But the complete inability of any of these measures to stem the advance either of foreign imperialism or of homegrown crises such as the Boxer debacle revealed that China's problems were more profound than simply the state of its military. In the new century, new generations of reformers, of whom Kang was among the first, would seek to find the roots of China's problems in something more fundamental, and more intangible. People like Sun Yat-sen (1866–1925, another Cantonese), a political organizer commonly accorded the distinction of being named the "father of the Chinese nation," set their sights on toppling the decayed monarchy and founding a republic. But when political change made the situation worse, not better, it led people to consider more fundamental reform, of the last and most venerable bastion of tradition – China's spiritual culture.

---

[2] This was his name. As emperor, his reign was titled *Xuantong*, meaning "to declare authority."

It is probably no surprise to learn that this new generation of reformers deeply despised popular religion, the type of beliefs and practices that had inspired the Boxers. Yet they were hardly the first to do so. When one speaks of "reformers" during this period, a certain image comes to mind: an inveterate modernizer, bilingual or multilingual, wearing a Savile Row suit and jaunty straw hat; educated in a missionary school and possibly the recipient of a scholarship to Yale or Cambridge; with an improbably Anglicized name such as *Aloysius Koh* or *Ethelbert Wang* – in other words, of an elitist cultural hybrid, someone who had at least partially turned his back on Chinese traditions and consciously embraced those of the West.

Certainly, more than a few self-styled reformers fit exactly this image, yet the desire to curb religious superstition was nothing new to China. Remember that for centuries, the imperial government was paternalistic in a literal sense. The Confucian gentry saw themselves as "father-mother officials" to the masses of ordinary people, whom many thought of and described as stupid, childlike, and in need of constant guidance. Like elites anywhere, generations of Confucian scholars competed to outdo each other in expressing their shock and dismay at the ignorance of the ordinary people, and in particular at their immoral religious practices. During the Ming dynasty, for example, it became the custom for the native sons of a particular area to compile a guidebook for their county or province. These tended to be exceedingly detailed, including such information as local cuisines, styles of dress, and handicrafts, as well as the names of virtuous widows and filial sons. They also presented an insider's view of local religion, introducing any historic temples or famous monks, but often omitting details that the writers found unpalatable. A few did choose to air their dirty laundry by appending a short, almost apologetic section on popular religion: practices such as folk healing, shamanism, possession, spirit writing séances, and the like. Often this section would begin with a long disclaimer about how the people of that area are traditionally stubborn, ignorant, and gullible – all but inviting the reader to join the author in an exasperated sigh.

Beginning with the energetic policies of Zhu Yuanzhang, the Ming and Qing states had sought to control certain aspects of religion: preventing illegal teachings from taking root and preventing legal ones, such as monastic Buddhism, from becoming too strong or political. As the Qing dynasty began its long, slow decline, even these modest efforts fell by the wayside. White Lotus groups freely organized in the very shadow of the capital. By the latter years of the eighteenth century, a time when the Qing to all outward appearances remained the greatest empire on earth, even the system of Buddhist registration had largely disintegrated. This system, designed to ensure that all monks were offi-cially ordained, had fallen into such disuse that, in the words of Philip Kuhn, the eminent historian of Qing statecraft, "virtually anyone with a robe and a shaved head" could call himself a monk "whatever his state of religious commitment or education."[3]

The religious reforms of the early twentieth century were a great deal more ambitious in scope. This generation of reforms was actually more in the tradition of Zhu Yuanzhang's other notable religious policy: his attempt to force Confucian rituals and ethics into the lives of the com-mon people. More than simply banning bad practices or dangerous sects, these reforms aimed to use religion to transform society. One can see glimpses of such big ideas in Kang Youwei's ideal of the Great Unification, which was nothing less than a complete overhaul of the most venerable institutions.

But for those who thought along such lines, China's vast rural popu-lation posed a particular difficulty. Many Chinese intellectuals of the early twentieth century inherited a deeply felt derision for the unlet-tered rural masses. Some may have felt a kind of guilty satisfaction at the ability of mass movements such as the Taiping or Boxer Rebellion to strike a blow against the Qing or the foreign powers, but the images of ignorant peasants praying to idols, speaking prophecies, or burning magic charms to protect themselves from bullets were hardly what any forward-looking intellectual would have wanted for his country. Like urban intellectuals elsewhere, Chinese elites saw it as their duty to pro-vide education and enlightenment for "their" peasants.

Such sentiments were based on a curious combination of contempt and patronizing affection. A few decades earlier, a generation of Russian intellectuals had faced a similar dilemma: they romanticized village life as the soul of Russia yet felt that the peasants needed urban intellectu-als to shape and train them.[4] But when they actually went to the coun-tryside to spread their gospel of progress, these intellectuals soon found that "their" peasants were suspicious of, and sometimes violently hos-tile to, outsiders. Those who managed to escape with their skins intact returned home deeply disabused of their romantic images and might have found much to agree with in the shock and revulsion expressed

---

[3] Philip A. Kuhn, *Soulstealers: The Chinese Sorcery Scare of 1768* (Cambridge: Harvard University Press, 1990), 112.

[4] This was the *narodnik*, or populist movement, which dates from roughly half a century before the Russian Revolution and presents a particularly striking image of a class of well-to-do intellectuals going "to the people," and "the people" sending them right back where they came from.

by one character in Anton Chekhov's *Peasants*, who had left Moscow to live out his old age in the village in which he had been born. "In his memories of childhood he had pictured his home as bright, snug, comfortable," but having seen them up close, it now seemed that "these people lived worse than beasts, and to live with them was terrible; they were coarse, dishonest, filthy, and drunken."

While few Chinese reformers of the time suffered this sort of nostalgia for rural life, neither did they go as far as Kang in wanting to destroy it entirely. Most still saw a kernel of potential in the countryside and tried to use natural structures, such as the village, as a foundation for their various modernization programs. This was the origin of a plan to wean peasants off religion by spreading universal education, in effect replacing one with the other. The remedy was simple: to take the temple that sits in the center of every village and turn it into a free school. The peasants could take care of the details and even pay for it themselves – they just needed guidance and a good kick to get the program moving. This call to "destroy the temple and build a school" (*hui miao xing xue*) was first voiced during the Hundred Days of Reform, and often thereafter. It was more than once written into law but, given the weak state of the central government, was impossible to enforce.

When such reforms were put into practice, it was usually on a small scale. In his famous surveys of rural Hebei province, the Chinese sociologist Li Jinghan noted that many village temples had indeed been turned into schools, but this was often entirely at the initiative of some unusually energetic county official. In some cases, the villagers themselves would immediately dismantle the school and reconvert the building back into a temple almost as soon as those officials left. In others the opposite was true. Images of blind superstition aside, these peasants were extremely practical people. Weighing the expense of maintaining a temple against the potential benefits of providing education to their children, many villages made the switch themselves, pooling resources to buy supplies and hire a teacher. Local authorities might then step in to take credit, or else wave the banner of reform in order to confiscate valuable religious landholdings or buildings.

These piecemeal efforts were a preview of the more sweeping changes that were to occur, much more quickly than anyone would have expected. The pace was such that by the late 1910s and early 1920s, many elements of Kang Youwei's radical proposals had become quite mainstream, at least among the new class of intellectuals clustered in the major cities, notably Beijing.

During these years, the universities, and especially Beijing University, became hotbeds of social reform. Western-style universities were still

something of a novelty in China. Large schools and imperial academies had existed for centuries, but these had been essentially centers
of Confucian learning, concerned with relatively little else. Kang and
many others recognized the need for technical training, a broad cur-
riculum in such traditionally shunned topics as science, mathemat-
ics, and foreign languages. The Imperial Capital University, the first
of its kind in China, was created during the 1898 reforms but, unlike
much else dating from the time, actually lasted for more than a hundred days. Eventually, it would become Beijing University, renamed
after the revolution of 1911 had made the imperial appellation obsolete.
Beijing University was followed by others, established by the state or
by missionaries, but remained unique, not merely because it was the
first of its kind, nor even by virtue of being in the capital, but because
it developed into a center of student activism the likes of which China
had rarely seen.

There was certainly reason for students, or anyone else for that matter, to be upset. For decades, most people had placed blame for China's
humiliation solely on the corrupt and incompetent government of the
Manchu Qing. The revolution of 1911 presented great cause for opti-
mism – the country would finally be run by a modern government and
was back in the hands of Han Chinese – and those of a reformist mind-
set expected that happiness and prosperity would naturally follow.
However, the result was very different. In the wake of the revolution,
China had in fact traded a weak central power for no central power at
all, and the country quickly devolved into a civil war among a handful
of militarists. To earn quick cash for troops and arms, local militarists
made some very shady deals. Some sold assets and rights to the areas
they controlled. Whoever held the city of Beijing at the moment had the
power to sign treaties and take out foreign loans in China's name, often
on disastrous terms, with little concern for the ability of the country to
make good on his promises later. With no army of its own, the national
government was quite literally a hostage of these warlords. When, for
example, the newly convened parliament in Beijing had the temerity to
object to one of these deals, the general Duan Qirui (1865–1936) surrounded the building with artillery and politely asked them to recon-
sider. More often, deals were simply made in secret, such as when Yuan
Shikai, who had himself named president of the Republic, signed away
many of China's rights to Japan. Those who had any knowledge of what
was happening could only watch in dismay as the country seemed to
spiral out of control.

The final straw was in 1919, at the close of the First World War.
China had not actually fought in the war but had supported the Allied

cause by sending 200,000 laborers to dig trenches in the battlefields of France. This was supposed to be the debut of a new, progressive China on the stage of world affairs, and those who had supported the war expected to see some recognition of their nation's contribution. Instead, it was revealed that these boons, including German assets seized in the Chinese city of Qingdao (formerly a German colony, hence the city's unique architectural legacy of Bavarian-style villas, as well as the original brewery of Tsingtao Beer), were to be ceded to Japan and, moreover, that the world's politicians had sealed the secret deal long in advance. The Chinese diplomats sent to Versailles to sign the treaty had known nothing of this arrangement, but it would not have mattered even if they had: once word of this treachery got out, enraged Chinese students studying in France surrounded the Paris hotel where the diplomats were lodged, preventing them from taking part in the signing ceremony.

When word of the treaty reached China, the public reaction was fierce, particularly among university students, who held numerous marches, including one famous demonstration on May 4, 1919, that gives the activism of this noisy decade the general name the *May Fourth Movement*. Beyond political demonstrations, the greater and more long-lasting influence was a broad social movement that took a hard look at Chinese culture and did not like what it saw. Young, reform-minded students increasingly began to believe that the reason for China's weakness lay not in its industry or politics, but in a culture of empty self-righteousness that served only to paper over a deeper rot of greed, dishonesty, and incompetence.

Perhaps unexpectedly, given the gravity of the situation, much of this criticism was delivered via the literary vehicle of fiction, deeply satirical short stories that the reading public simply devoured. One step removed from Kang Youwei, but still in his same iconoclastic spirit, these stories directed their attacks at the Confucian heart of Chinese culture. The 1931 novel *Family* by the anarchist author Ba Jin (1904–2005) is typical.[5] The story recounts the intrigues of a wealthy but declining rural family in the southwestern province of Sichuan (circumstances that closely matched Ba Jin's own background) and reads as a traditional morality tale presented as a serial soap opera. After numerous twists and turns, loves and betrayals, nearly every character is in the end done in by weakness or personal corruption, but all remain blinded to their faults and their fate by a veneer of Confucian hypocrisy. The only

[5] As did many authors in this period, Ba Jin wrote under a literary pseudonym. His real name was *Li Yaotang*, and his adopted moniker allegedly derives from a combination of the Chinese names of two Russian anarchists, Bakunin and Kropotkin.

sympathetic character, and the only one to escape the moral quicksand that eventually swallows the other family members, is the youngest son, who runs off to join the communists.

The most iconic figure of the period was the writer Zhou Shuren, better known by his pen name of *Lu Xun* (1881–1936). For years after his untimely death, Lu Xun would be hailed as the voice of the Chinese conscience by Mao Zedong, and for a period, he held iconic status that few Chinese authors have since enjoyed. During the 1960s, countless roads, parks, and universities would be named after him. Statues of Lu Xun (easily recognizable by his characteristic pushbroom mustache) often portray his figure emerging out of a chunk of rough-hewn rock, as if he were an elemental force of nature, rising up out of the very earth of China.

Zhou Shuren was born in the southern province of Zhejiang, into a wealthy and well-connected family that, like the one depicted in the story by Ba Jin, was facing declining fortunes. After his father's death, Zhou began to study medicine, eventually traveling to the Japanese city of Sendai to continue his studies. Although he had up to that point never expressed any interest in politics, Zhou had an experience in Sendai that would turn him from medicine to social activism. Famously, he went to view a lantern show of scenes from the Russo-Japanese War (much of which had been fought on Chinese soil), including a picture of a bound Chinese prisoner awaiting execution by Japanese soldiers. More than hatred of Japan, this experience inspired in him a profound concern for what had become of the Chinese character. Zhou was learning to heal people's bodies, but the problem with his compatriots lay deeper. "Physically," he would later write, "they were as strong and healthy as anyone could ask, but their expressions revealed all too clearly that spiritually they were calloused and numb. According to the caption, the Chinese whose hands were bound had been spying on the Japanese military for the Russians and was about to be decapitated as a 'public example.' The other Chinese gathered around him had come to enjoy the spectacle."

When he returned to China and began publishing his short stories, Lu Xun created a series of memorable characters who embodied his assessment of China's grim situation. Possibly the best known of these is Ah Q, a comic figure and a rather obvious allegory for China itself. Famously depicted by the illustrator Feng Zikai (Figure 8.1), Ah Q begins his tale as a lowly laborer. Through a series of misadventures, he ends up ostracized from his small village, reduced to begging, and finally being taken away to execution after having been falsely accused of a crime. At every stage, Ah Q is entirely the cause of his own undoing: his comically misplaced pride leads him to bully the weak and pick fights he cannot win. The story is purposefully written in a heroically

Figure 8.1 Ah Q. These illustrations by the cartoonist Feng Zikai accompanied a 1939 edition of the book. **A**. Ah Q (at center) is caught posing as a member of a prestigious family.

B

Figure 8.1 **B**. The classic image of Ah Q on his way to be hanged.

grandiose style, yet the stakes of the game are pitifully low – at one point, Ah Q becomes enraged at another beggar for being more skilled at picking lice than he, and the two fight in the street, each holding the other by the hair, neither able to best the other, nor willing to let go. Yet the only one unable to appreciate the depths of the protagonist's decline is Ah Q himself, because of his unique talent for turning every defeat into a moral victory. When he is publicly caned by a local scholar, Ah Q turns the event over in his mind until he comes upon the idea that since he was humiliated by a great man, he must be a great man himself, at which point he feels a flush of pride. Lu Xun saw this habit of creating a comforting deception to mask an uncomfortable truth as a flaw unique to the Chinese character. It is still known in China as "Ah Q-ism."

Like most of his generation, Lu Xun was deeply uncomfortable with Confucian rhetoric and what he saw as empty ritual. His short story "The New Year's Sacrifice" in some ways resembles Ba Jin's *Family* in its satirical unvarnishing of Confucian hypocrisy. Yet during this same period, others would attempt to use a newly reformed Confucianism toward what were essentially the same ends as leftist writers of the May Fourth generation: the revival of Chinese culture and resuscitation of the Chinese spirit.

Not everyone wanted to do away with religion entirely. Many of the reformers were themselves Christian, and even some of those who were not found much to admire in Christianity. A 1906 article in the Japanese-owned newspaper *Shengjing Times* attributed Western civic-mindedness to Christianity, which grounded people in the absolute moral concepts of good and evil, and in particular of heaven and hell (the opposite, in other words, of the sort of moral relativism exemplified by Lu Xun's Ah Q). The article ended with the hope that Christianity would spread more widely in China, not for its promise of salvation, but for its positive moral influence.

There was also much to be salvaged from Chinese religion. In 1927, the legislature passed a measure that would sift through the many gods and deities venerated in China to identify and promote those considered to have redeeming social value. These gods, who included Confucius, the Buddha, Muhammad, and Jesus Christ, represented the philosophical ideals of high religion, and their worship was to be encouraged. Many of the others, especially the small and esoteric popular deities – gods such as the Spotted Pox Matron, the Fire Avoiding Pig, the Fire Eating Monkey, or the Stupid Older Brother (all of which appeared in the Temple of the Empress of Heaven in Tianjin) – were to be eliminated. The instinct to weed out retrograde culture was, of course, not unique to China. However, since the Chinese Republic had now adopted the rhetoric of liberal democracy, which included the freedom of religion, it would have to work hard to justify an official movement to eradicate popular gods. Just as with the creation of State Shintō in Japan, the answer to this dilemma was to be found in political spin. According to the statute, the "poison of popular superstition" had retarded the sense of judgment among the common people, preventing them from exercising *true* free will. The fact that such ridiculous gods continued to exist at all was itself ample proof that the Chinese people were too infantile to be trusted with making their own decisions. The government must therefore take up the burden of thinking for them, all in the name of one day training them for true popular sovereignty.

Perhaps not surprisingly, the impetus to revive Confucianism would originate from a position of political strength. By the mid-1920s, the general Chiang Kai-shek (Jiang Jieshi, 1887–1975) had formed an alliance with the newly formed Chinese Communist Party. With significant help from the Soviet Union, he had managed to raise, train,

Box 8.a. Old and new deities in the Temple of the Empress of Heaven

Actual religious practice in China is very diverse. Beyond the integration of the "three religions," it includes dozens, or even hundreds, of local, highly specialized deities, most of which were highly unpalatable to the reformers of the May Fourth era. The chart shows the various deities that were housed in the Tianjin Temple of the Empress of Heaven (Tianhou gong) in 1869. By 1999, only a small number (those marked with an *X*) remained in the temple.

1. Empress of Heaven	天后	X
2. Kingly Efficacious Official	王靈官	X
3. Seer of One Thousand Li	千里眼	X
4. Hearer of Sounds Carried on the Wind	順風耳	X
5. Fierce Spirit	凶神	X
6. Evil Demon	惡煞	X
7. Bright Eyed Goddess	眼光娘娘	
8. Bringing Children Goddess	子孫娘娘	
9. Bright Ears Goddess	耳光娘娘	
10. Spotted Pox Goddess	斑疹娘娘	
11. Thousand Children Goddess	千子娘娘	
12. Birthing Mother Goddess	引母娘娘	
13. Nursing Mother Goddess	乳母娘娘	
14. Hundred Children Goddess	百子娘娘	
15. Guanyin Pusa	關音菩薩	X
16. Grandma Wangsan	王三奶奶	X
17. Goddess of Mount Tai	泰山娘娘	
18. Speedy Birth Goddess	催生娘娘	
19. Granting Birth Goddess	送生娘娘	
20. Palace Official in Charge of Nursing and Feeding	兼管乳食宮官	
21. Child who Disperses Pox	散行痘疹	
22. Immortal Woman Who Dispenses Heavenly Flower (Medicine)	散行天花仙女	
23. Immortal Official Who Dispenses Medicine to Those in Need	救急施藥仙官	
24. Great Scholar of the Southern Sea	南海大士	
25. Immortal Zhang	張仙	
26. Grand Mr. Scratcher	撓司大人	
27. Brother Who Delivers the [Medicinal] Paste	送漿哥哥	
28. White Old Matron	白老太太	X
29. Stupid Older Brother	傻哥哥	X
30. Stove God	灶王爺	
31. Three Officials	三官	

32. Medicine King	藥王	X
33. Grandmother Big Dipper	斗姥	
34. Guandi	關帝爺	
35. Fire Emperor	火帝	
36. Restraining Fire Snake	抑火蛇	
37. Avoiding Fire Pig	避火豬	
38. Eating Fire Monkey	食火猴	
39. Encircling Fire Tiger	圍火虎	
40. Caishen (God of Wealth)	財神爺	
41. Patriarch Lightning	雷祖	
42. Duke Lightning	雷公	
43. Flowing Rain and Flashing Lightning Goddess	行雨閃電娘娘	
44. Duke Cao and Duke Ma	曹公馬公	
45. Most Supreme Lord Lao	太上老君	

Source: Tianjin huanghui kaoji 天津皇會考記 [A record of the Empress of Heaven Festival in Tianjin] (late nineteenth century).

and equip an army that by 1927 had captured much of the country back from the local warlords. Chiang was never able to control the entire country. Large swaths of territory, including Beijing itself, remained outside his grasp. This is why he had the capital moved south to his own power base in Nanjing. (The name Beijing simply means "northern capital." When the seat of power was moved south, the name was changed to Beiping, or "northern peace.") It was a precarious situation, and for the next ten years, Chiang would remain preoccupied with threats not only from remaining militarists, but also from Japan, which was becoming increasingly aggressive on Chinese soil, invading Manchuria in 1931 and showing no signs of intending to stop there.

More than external threats, Chiang felt increasingly threatened by infiltration from his former Communist allies, whom he had betrayed in a rather spectacular manner after the capture of Shanghai in 1927, and who were demonstrating an uncanny talent for organizing peasants into large and heavily armed base areas, into which Chiang's army dared not tread. Of the many crises he faced, Chiang considered the Communists the most dire. Even as the Japanese massed troops on the northern border, Chiang famously dismissed the foreign threat as "a disease of the limbs." The Communists, on the other hand, were "a disease of the heart," which must be excised completely, and without delay. The cure for the Communist disease was to be found in a spiritual transformation.

This instinct for spiritual engineering was not restricted to China. We have already seen it at work in Meiji Japan. Throughout the world, in fact, the early twentieth century (particularly the period between the two world wars) was characterized by an overwhelming confidence in the ability of states or civic groups to transform the human spirit. A variety of new political doctrines – Soviet communism, anarchism, anti-imperialism – aimed at massive transformation of society by effecting fundamental change in the heart and soul of the individual.

Perhaps more than any other political doctrine of the time, this instinct to reweave the basic fabric of society is seen most clearly in fascism. Fascism is the very portrait of mass ideology, visually captured in images of crowds marching, drilling, or saluting in unison. But the other side of mass ideology is precisely the process of convincing or forcing the individual to surrender his will to the process of transforming the individual. Mussolini waxed poetic about *uomo nuovo*, the "new man" forged in the crucible of war. Hitler described the new fascist German as "slim and slender, quick like a greyhound, tough like leather, and hard like Krupp steel." Children were to be inculcated in military values and discipline from the youngest age (see Figure 8.2). Above all, the new fascist man would be one of action, cold, remorseless, and free of the cerebral sentimentality that sapped the strength of liberal democracies.

Such ideas proved extremely attractive in Asia. By the 1930s, fascism had more than a few admirers in China. Just as Kang Youwei had once encouraged the Guangxu emperor to become China's Peter the Great, some of the Confucian scholars who remained with the deposed child emperor Pu Yi harangued him to emulate Mussolini. Many within Chiang Kai-shek's own Nationalist Party (Guomindang) praised the speed with which fascism had stabilized the weakened economies and military machines of Italy and Germany. While Chiang himself was no doubt attracted to fascism's tendency to elevate the national leader to godlike status, he was especially drawn to its promise to stem the advancing spiritual rot of communism.

During the 1930s, Chiang copied many of the institutions that had proven so successful in establishing fascism elsewhere. Within his own government, Chiang's supporters established a group called the Society for Vigorous Action, a clandestine movement that coordinated the creation of propaganda campaigns, military-style scouting and training camps, and numerous affiliated political groups, most notoriously a youth movement called the Blue Shirts, which was modeled on the black and brown shirts in Italy and Germany, respectively. Although the Society for Vigorous Action may have had as many as half a million members, it led the shadowy life of a party within a party. Very few outsiders knew of its existence at the time – it was not until the publication

Figure 8.2 Martial values in fascist propaganda. Fascist regimes idealized the militarization of all segments of society. This 1935 image of the Italian youth organization Giovinezza in Marcia is from a child's school workbook. From the Fry Collection. By courtesy of the Department of Special Collections, Memorial Library, University of Wisconsin-Madison.

of posthumous memoirs that scholars learned anything more than its name. Supporters, many of whom had studied in Germany or Italy, referred to Chiang not as president, but as *lingxiu*, which in normal use simply means "leader," but here was obviously meant to echo something more along the lines of *Duce* or *Führer*. Chiang openly called for China to embrace the new ideology. "Fascism," he proclaimed, "is what China now most needs. At the present stage of China's critical situation, fascism is a wonderful medicine exactly suited to China, and the only tonic that can save it." For movements such as the Blue Shirts, fascism meant above all loyalty to Chiang himself. Newspapers associated with the movement made the point plain: "we must not disguise that we demand a China's Mussolini, China's Hitler."[6]

These two elements – the inability to stem Communist insurgency and his desire to lead his country into a spiritual renewal – motivated Chiang to initiate the New Life Movement (*xin shenghuo yundong*), his signature social initiative. This campaign, dubbed "Confucian fascism" by the historian Lloyd Eastman, was launched in 1934, just as Chiang was preparing a final push against the Communist stronghold in the mountains of Jiangxi. Chiang addressed the nation with a radio speech that sounded like a slightly updated version of the otherwise staid Confucian themes of social order based on attention to hierarchy:

> The general psychology of our people today can be described as spiritless. What manifests itself in behavior is this: lack of discrimination between good and evil, between what is public and what is private, and between what is primary and what is secondary.
>
> Because there is no discrimination between good and evil, right and wrong are confused; because there is no discrimination between public and private, there is graft and bribes; and because there is no distinction between primary and secondary, first and last are not placed in the proper order. As a result, officials tend to be dishonest and avaricious, the masses are undisciplined and calloused, the youth become degraded and intemperate, the adults are corrupt and ignorant, the rich become extravagant and luxurious, and the poor become mean and disorderly. Naturally it has resulted in disorganization of the social order and national life, and we are in no position either to prevent or to remedy natural calamities, disasters caused from within, or invasions from without. The individual, society and the whole country are now suffering. ("Essentials of the New Life Movement," 1934)

These claims themselves were nothing new – they could have been made by Zhu Yuanzhang himself. What was unusual was the prescription Chiang's New Life Movement had for China. In addition to a good dose of preaching – on radio, in public lectures, in schools – about the need to revive Confucian values, the New Life Movement created specific rules of good behavior, ninety-six of them to be exact, governing every aspect of dress, eating, speech, and deportment. Remember that at the opening of the campaign, Chiang was facing dire military threats on two fronts, from both the Japanese and the Communists. In answer

---

[6] Fan Hong, "Blue Shirts, Nationalists and Nationalism: Fascism in 1930s China," in J. A. Mangan, ed., *Shaping the Superman: Fascist Body as Political Icon* (Portland, OR: Frank Cass, 1999), 205–26.

to these very pressing problems, he gave his people the following words of inspiration: "Be quiet when you are watching a movie or at a meeting," "Don't make noise when you eat," "Button your clothes neatly," "Don't spit," "Don't throw garbage on the road." While hardly likely to inspire terror in the hearts of his enemies, Chiang's idea was that by changing the mental and behavioral minutiae of people's daily lives, it would transform their inner core, giving them a new sense of dignity, responsibility, and civic-mindedness. The transformation of the individual would translate into national strength.

In their political views, men like Kang Youwei, Lu Xun, and Chiang Kai-shek had little in common – indeed, one would be hard pressed to find three more different personalities. For all his talk of reform, Kang was a monarchist to the core, remaining loyal to the emperor even after all hope was lost. Lu Xun was equally patriotic, but an utter iconoclast. An immensely charismatic figure, Lu haunted the halls of Beijing's universities and salons, always surrounded by a gaggle of students and political hangers-on, eager to claim the influential scholar as one of their supporters. Chiang Kai-shek was anything but an idealist. Even Chiang's supporters conceded that his government was deeply corrupt and repressive. During the Pacific War, Allied propagandists portrayed Chiang as a great statesman, but in private, the U.S. president, Harry Truman, called Chiang's government a "bunch of grafters and crooks." Chiang's American attaché, General Joseph Stilwell, referred to the bald leader rather unaffectionately as "ol' Peanut Head."

Yet for all their differences, each of the three was a man of his times. Each perceived China to be on the precipice of national disaster and proposed programs of moral reform as the route to national salvation. Given the chaotic political situation, it was perhaps inevitable that none would make the type of permanent change that he had envisioned. That would only happen after 1949, when the remnants of Chiang's military had been chased to Taiwan, and the Communist insurgency that he had been fighting for two decades finally gained power.

II. Spirit of the rising sun: Japanese religious militarism

Japan had of course begun its political and social transformation much earlier and, over the last decades of the nineteenth century, had fundamentally reshaped its idea and practice of religion. After briefly flirting with the idea of establishing Shintō as a national religion, Meiji leaders had decided instead to be more selective in what they would promote. That which was defined as "religion" was effectively shunted off to the side.

Like Buddhism or Christianity (which after much bitter debate had been legalized in 1873), religious Shintō was formally divorced from the state. On one level, this meant that Japan would now adhere to Western norms of religious freedom, allowing its people the choice to worship as they wished. On another, the change had simply shifted the boundaries of what was optional and what was required. Even if it no longer cared, for example, whether people buried their dead with Buddhist rites, the Meiji government was no less concerned with religion than their Tokugawa predecessors. But while Tokugawa regulations had aimed primarily at policing behavior, the Meiji government increasingly relied on State Shintō to shape the ideology and spiritual core of ordinary people. Meanwhile, the new ideal of religious freedom meant that this program of spiritual engineering could be identified as Japanese culture, national spirit, or patriotic duty – anything but religion.

But this transformation was not solely the product of government initiative. Civic groups, individuals, and organized religions played their role, as well. By the final years of the nineteenth century, Japanese Buddhism had adapted to these new conditions and was poised to enter something of a renaissance. The actual persecution of Buddhism had been traumatic, but fairly short-lived. Even if the worst was over by the late 1870s, Buddhists still faced the question of what role their religion should play in the new Japan. At a basic level, Buddhists were keen to show that they were also productive members of the new society. Buddhist monks were active in the abortive Great Promulgation Campaign, and lay groups participated in various patriotic campaigns, such as the call to settle the northern island of Hokkaido.[7] But more deeply, Japanese Buddhists were also drawn into the same search for national essence that had animated Shintō.

Early nativist thinkers had once derided Buddhism as an alien religion, but a few decades into the Meiji reign, this same foreignness began to appear as a benefit. After two and a half centuries of isolation, many Japanese were eager to explore opportunities abroad. The West would provide Japan with the latest cultural and technological advances, while the Asian continent would provide a limitless market for Japanese goods. Perhaps most importantly, the world stage was a place to demonstrate Japan's own achievements. As China continued to decline as a regional power, and the earlier infatuation for any and all things Western began to cool, Japan's desire to display its unique culture and spirit to its Asian neighbors and to the world grew ever stronger.

---

[7] James Edward Ketelaar, *Of Heretics and Martyrs in Meiji Japan: Buddhism and Its Persecution* (Princeton, NJ: Princeton University Press, 1990), 73.

Japanese Buddhism was a perfect vehicle for engaging the outside world. Shintō may have been considered the crystallization of Japanese spirit, but it was never expected to take hold outside Japan. Buddhism, in contrast, linked Japan to a swath of cultures that stretched from China to Tibet and India. Not coincidentally, all of these countries, with the exception of Japan, were politically weak and, it was felt, culturally backward. The once-mighty Qing was in free fall. India and Indochina had already become colonies of the advanced West. In response, Buddhists such as Ogurusu Kōchō (1831–1905) put out the call for Japanese monks to revive the dharma in India and China. Even while they were being persecuted at home, monks from Japan began visiting the Asian mainland. Ogusuru visited Shanghai in 1873. The Eastern (Higashi) Honganji branch of True Pure Land established a temple there in 1876 and a mission in Korea one year later. Within a few years, delegations of monks were making their way to India, Sri Lanka, Burma, and Tibet.

But their desire was less to learn than to teach. Most Japanese monks expressed the view that the Buddhism practiced on the continent had lost its way, having become superstitious and formulaic. In India, the birthplace of Buddhism, the dharma had disappeared almost completely. In the worst cases, such as Indochina, the decline of Buddhism had even opened the door for Christian missionaries to enter and fill the gap. It seemed that within a few years China might be destined to share the same fate. By the end of the century, sects such as True Pure Land and Nichiren were sending their own missionaries to China to reinvigorate Buddhism and counter the Christian influence. By and large, Buddhist activists remained strong opponents of Christianity, both in Japan itself and abroad, and were willing to use the weapons of the Christians against them. Shaku Sōen (1859–1919) and Inoue Enryō (1858–1919), two of the most vocal proponents of the Buddhist revival, each urged monks to copy the Christian tactic of building missions around institutions, such as hospitals and charities. Over the next few decades, Buddhist missionaries in Korea and China established Sunday schools, created a sort of wedding ceremony, and in 1894 founded a civic organization modeled on the Young Men's Christian Association (YMCA): the Young Men's Buddhist Association.[8] They also imitated the Christians in lobbying their own government to push for special rights for Buddhist missionaries in China.[9]

[8] The YMBA movement was not solely Japanese. In some places, most notably in Burma, similar organizations became a focus of anticolonial activity.

[9] Nakano Kyōtoku, *Tennōsei kokka to shokuminchi dendō* [The imperial state and colonial missionization] (Tokyo: Kokusho Kankōkai, 1976), 18–24; Brian Daizen Victoria, *Zen at War* (Lanham, MD: Rowman & Littlefield, 2006), 17.

Japanese Buddhists wanted to present their religion beyond Asia. Having spent decades absorbing Western culture, Japan was eager to show that it was more than a good student and, in fact, had something tangible to offer to world civilization. In 1893, a delegation of monks led by Shaku Sōen attended the first World Parliament of Religions in Chicago. Despite the name, this parliament was primarily a gathering of American Christians. (Besides the Buddhists from Japan and a sprinkling of Hindu speakers, most of the Asians in attendance were there either to bear witness to Christian mission in their own countries or to participate in mock-up displays of life in exotic lands.) The Japanese delegation thus faced an audience that was interested but politely skeptical. For one thing, many people did not accept that the delegation truly represented Buddhism. In the Western idiom, religious authority derives from the words of the founder and thus from scriptures, the more ancient the better. Thus, the Mahāyāna scriptures used by Japanese Buddhists were considered inferior to the much older Pali texts that were traditionally the purview of academic specialists, such as the Oxford philologist Max Müller (1823–1900). As one such scholar described it, Asian practitioners were "merely nominal Buddhists who know little if anything about genuine Buddhism as elucidated in the texts." However well intentioned the World Parliament may have been, the event showed how far the Western conception of religion was from the one developing in Japan. The monks presented their tradition as an *evolution* of the Buddha's teaching, but the Christian delegates, who understood scripture to be the most fundamental truth, saw only degeneration.[10]

The problem, and the solution, was yet again one of definitions. Just as with Shintō, one response from Japanese Buddhists was to discard the label of religion. Inoue Enryō had trained as a monk in Eastern Honganji but left the *sangha* in order to preach the values of Buddhism in lay society. Inoue was well acquainted with Western thought, having studied it at Tokyo Imperial University, and argued that Buddhism in fact represented the culmination of Western philosophical truth, even more so than Christianity. To his own countrymen, Inoue argued that genuine Buddhism, as developed in Japan, would serve the nation by creating enlightened citizens. It would allow Japan to surge ahead of the West, by mastering and improving upon the spiritual basis of Western society, and to a spiritual revival of Asia by replacing the inferior forms of Buddhism found elsewhere.[11]

---

[10] Judith Snodgrass, *Presenting Japanese Buddhism to the West* (Chapel Hill and London: University of North Carolina Press, 2003), 85–114; quotation from p. 86.

[11] Snodgrass, *Presenting Japanese Buddhism*, 139–54.

More than any other school, it was Zen that took the lead in portraying itself as something *more* than religion. In his 1913 *Religion and the Samurai*, the Sōtō monk Kaiten Nukariya (1867–1934) described Zen as religion, yes, but also a philosophy and culture, one that had a broad impact on all areas of Japanese life. Perhaps the most famous example of this trend is Suzuki Daisetsu (1870–1966), better known to English readers as D. T. Suzuki. In order to have his views on Buddhism accepted in the West, Suzuki knew that he first had to gain the proper academic credentials, and to master the classical languages of Buddhism.[12] But once he had done so, this very prolific author would then spend the rest of his long career making one point very plain: Zen is the essence of Asian culture, but also something far more profound than any single religion:

> As I conceive it, Zen is the ultimate fact of all philosophy and religion. Every intellectual effort must culminate in it, if it is to bear any practical fruits. Every religious faith must spring from it, if it has to prove at all efficiently and livingly workable in our active life. Therefore Zen is not necessarily the fountain of Buddhist thought and life alone: it is very much alive also in Christianity, Mahommedanism, in Taoism, and even in positivistic Confucianism. What makes all of these religions and philosophies vital and inspiring, keeping up their usefulness and efficiency, is due to the presence in them of what I may designate as the Zen element.[13]

Of course, Japan's influence on the continent consisted of much more than Buddhist mission. The arrival of the West had fundamentally changed the rules of diplomacy in East Asia. Gone were the days of tribute states and informal dominions. The new international order demanded clear and absolute boundaries, opening a new race to take and control marginal territories. This was a hardship for the waning and hopelessly overstretched Qing Empire, but a boon for Japan. Throughout the Meiji period, Japan had strengthened its hold on the surrounding islands of Hokkaido and Okinawa, and as China continued to decline, Japan stepped in to fill the vacuum. In ten short years, Japanese forces defeated Qing China (1894–5) and tsarist Russia (1904–5), gaining dominion over Taiwan and unofficial hegemony over Korea and Manchuria. Even where troops were not present, Japanese commercial interests penetrated every corner of East Asia, and Japanese

---

[12] Judith Snodgrass, "Publishing Eastern Buddhism: D. T. Suzuki's Journey to the West," in Thomas David DuBois, ed., *Casting Faiths: Imperialism and the Transformation of Religion in East and Southeast Asia* (Basingstoke, England: Palgrave Macmillan, 2009), 46–72.

[13] D. T. Suzuki, *Essays in Zen Buddhism* (New York: Grove Press, 1925), 268.

settlers were soon to follow. Other Asians, to put it somewhat mildly, had mixed feelings toward Japan. There was certainly much about Japan to admire: its laws, its military, and its rapid industrialization. Nationalists throughout Asia, particularly those under Western colonial domination, were thrilled to see Japan emerge victorious over Russia – the first truly decisive defeat of a European power by an Asian military. But Japan quickly lost any goodwill through its own actions.

Within Japan, however, there was little question of the nation's manifest destiny on the continent. Support for wars with China and Russia was near-total, and often fanatical.[14] The wars themselves were widely viewed as the ultimate expression of Japanese patriotic duty, and religious groups, especially those whose own patriotism had been questioned in the past, competed to contribute their money and lives. Buddhists aided Japan's decade of war in a variety of ways. Many of the major temples released statements reminding the faithful of their duty as Buddhists to support Japan's military advance on the continent. These wars, they insisted, are morally just, and moreover, because the imperial state and dharma are one, they are fought in the name of the Buddha. On the eve of war with Russia, Inoue Enryō made this point in stark terms:

> In Russia, state and religion are one, and there is no religious freedom. Thus, religion is used as a chain to unify the [Russian] people. Therefore, when they see Orientals, they are told that the latter are bitter enemies of their religion. It is for this reason that on the one hand this is a war of politics and on the other hand it is a war of religion.... If theirs is the army of God, then ours is the army of the Buddha. It is in this way that Russia is not only the enemy of our country, but also of the Buddha, as well.[15]

Buddhist apologists continued to adapt their teaching to the needs of war. As discussed in an earlier chapter, there already existed a tradition of thought that allowed warriors to avoid the Buddhist prohibition against taking life. In an earlier era, Buddhist samurai were reminded that killing an enemy could actually be an act of compassion. Killing a wicked man prevented him from accumulating bad karma and demonstrated to others the folly of following a false path. Such arguments were again raised as Japan went to war.[16] Added to the Buddhist promise of

---

[14] For a very thorough analysis of how the decade between these two wars was treated in the Japanese press, see Urs Matthias Zachmann, *China and Japan in the Late Meiji Period: China Policy and the Japanese Discourse on National Identity, 1895–1904* (London: Routledge, 2009).

[15] Brian Zaizen Victoria, *Zen at War* (Totowa, NJ: Rowman and Littlefield, 2006), 30.

[16] Xue Yu, *Buddhism, War, and Nationalism: Chinese Monks in the Struggle against Japanese Aggressions, 1931–1945* (New York and London: Routledge, 2005).

postmortem salvation, they built a wall of faith around the Japanese soldier, steeling his resolve. As one contemporary described it:

> Reciting the name of Amida Buddha makes it possible to march onto the battlefield firm in the belief that death will bring rebirth in paradise. Being prepared for death, one can fight strenuously, knowing that it is a just fight, a fight employing the compassionate mind of the Buddha, the fight of a loyal subject. Truly, what could be more fortunate than knowing that, should you die, a welcome awaits in the Pure Land?

The two wars with China and Russia set the stage for much of what would follow: an ever-increasing militarism and the development of what would be called Imperial-way Buddhism (*kōdō Bukkyō*). Over the next few decades, the arguments that had been developed at the turn of the century would be, in the words of the Zen priest and historian Brian Victoria, "raised again and again in increasingly jingoistic language and shriller pitch."[17]

Nor were the Buddhists alone. Some of their enthusiasm, if not their ideas, was even reflected in the growing number of Japanese Christians. Since their religion had been legalized in 1873, Japanese Christians had been waiting for just this chance to demonstrate their loyalty to the nation. Even foreign missionaries, it seems, were not immune to war hysteria. French Catholic priests in cities such as Nagasaki blessed the troops on their way to the front and reported with obvious pride of the battlefield valor of Japanese Christians, such as the infantry captain who fell wounded on the fields of Manchuria with the final words "My heart with God and my body with the Emperor!"[18]

The two wars not only established a pattern for later militarism, but also drew a line in the sand from which it became impossible to retreat. Because Japan had paid such a high price in blood for its victories, its territorial gains took on a particular significance. When Japan was forced under Western pressure to return the Liaodong Peninsula, a territory that China had ceded after its defeat, an enraged Japanese public called it a betrayal of the Japanese soldiers who had died there. The wars also initiated the custom of venerating the war dead. The controversial Yasukuni Shrine in Tokyo was a forerunner of this trend. Now best known for housing the spirits of Pacific War dead, the Yasukuni Shrine was built in 1879, originally to enshrine those killed in the Meiji Restoration. During

---

[17] Victoria, *Zen at War*, 30–5.

[18] Recorded in the annual report of Monseigneur Pierre Osouf, bishop of Tokyo, October, 15, 1895. Osouf was of the order Missions Étrangères de Paris, the largest Catholic mission in Asia at the time. A wealth of documents from the mission is available at its Web site. Available online at http://www.mepasie.org.

the war with Russia, for which Japan had paid a staggering price, veneration of the war dead took on a special significance and increasingly came to be seen as the patriotic duty of all Japanese. The image of the war dead loomed large in the public imagination. Songs and poems commemorated the eighty thousand soldiers killed in the war. Shrines were erected to their memory overseas, as well as in Japan. The blood of the war dead had transformed Manchuria into a "sacred land," spawning a new patriotic tourist circuit to sites of famous battles.

Box 8.b. The Fengtian shrine

The shrine at Fengtian (Shenyang) was commissioned by order of the Japanese Kwantung governor in the forty-eighth year of the Meiji reign (1911). For two decades, the shrine primarily served the resident Japanese community, but after the capture of Manchuria and formation of a Japanese client state (called Manchukuo), it was increasingly used for indoctrination. Soon after the declaration of Manchukuo's independence from China, the following prayer was posted at the shrine in the name of the Japanese residents of Fengtian.

The precious blood of our predecessors spilled in war has consecrated Manchuria and Mongolia a sacred land. Over the past twenty years, the Chinese militarists have polluted this sacred land, and brought suffering upon the people with their misrule. Their policy has excluded foreigners, and been extremely cruel. They have obstructed the development of our divine people (*tengyō*), acting contrary to the will of Heaven and the heart of man. In September of last year, the Imperial Army took up the sword of destroying evil and bringing justice, and awakened the people of Manchuria and Mongolia, who spontaneously welcomed the Imperial Army and crushed the traitors. Thus purified, the grasses and trees of Manchuria and Mongolia bowed before the Imperial wind, giving honor to the Japanese flag. Thereupon, the races of Manchuria and Mongolia joined together to found the new country of the Kingly Way [a phrase used in Japanese propaganda to refer to Confucianism], together with the Imperial nation [Japan] to strive towards this pure ideal. We announce to near and far the birth of this new country of Manchukuo. The thirty million people of Manchuria and Mongolia pledged all their efforts to building this paradise. Before the great shrine, we make these grain offerings and pray.

We pray that the divine light will shine down to ensure the prosperity of the Imperial nation, the security of the new nation of Manchukuo, and the unbounded peace of the world. With fear and trembling we offer up our prayer.

March 11, in the seventh year of the Shōwa reign (1932)

Hōten jinja shi, 1939

The lands under Japanese control became the focus of numerous official and unofficial mission activities. The most ambitious of these was the planned cultural transformation of Korea, which was annexed by Japan in 1910. Asserting the historical and racial similarities between Japanese and Koreans, colonial authorities embarked on a policy to reshape the residents of Korea into dutiful subjects of the emperor (a policy called *kōminka*, sometimes translated as "Japanification"). This meant sharing with Korea the "spirit" of Japan: replacing Korean language, dress, surnames, and customs with Japanese ones, and thus making the Koreans culturally Japanese. Shintō ritual had a vital role in shaping these new imperial subjects: Koreans were encouraged to set up *kamidana* to house talismans from the great shrine at Ise. Schools, marketplaces, and public offices all established Shintō shrines, and

---

Box 8.c. Japanese shrines and temples in Manchuria

Japan only became extensively involved in the Asian continent after its 1905 victory over Russia. But once the door was opened, Japanese commercial, military, and religious influence immediately took root and would continue to grow for the next forty years. The chart shows the advance of Japanese religions into Manchuria. Although both Shintō and Buddhism grew gradually through the 1930s, the outbreak of war with China (1937) and the Allies (1941) prompted a vast expansion of construction. By the 1940s, most cities in Manchuria had at least one Shintō shrine, as well as a shrine to the sacred mission of national foundation and a monument to the war dead (see Figure 8.3).

	Shintō shrines	Pure Land (Ōtani) temples/missions	Sōtō Zen temples/ missions
1905	1	1	2
1910	6	4	9
1915	20	10	14
1920	31	17	27
1925	35	20	34
1930	36	22	35
1935	63	39	44
1940	171	76	54
1945	302	103	66

Source: Kiba Akeshi and Cheng Shuwei, eds., *Shokuminchiki Manshū no shūkyō: Nitchū ryōkoku no shiten kara kataru* [Religion in colonial Manchuria: Japanese and Chinese perspectives] (Tokyo: Kashiwa Shobō, 2007), 452–504.

Figure 8.3 Sacred sites in Japanese Manchuria. Shintō shrines were built throughout the empire. Initially for resident Japanese, such shrines were gradually adapted to a program of cultural indoctrination. **A**. Shintō shrine in the Manchurian city of Xinjing. **B**. Shintō shrine in the Manchurian city of Fushun.

Koreans were expected to pay their respect to the emperor and, increasingly, to the war dead, as well.[19]

---

[19] Cultural transformation in other Japanese possessions, such as Taiwan, was not a priority until the 1940s, a time when the Japanese military was becoming desperate for soldiers.

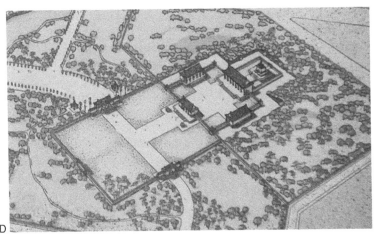

Figure 8.3 **C**. Artist's conception of the Manchukuo National
Foundation Shrine (*jianguo shenshe*) that was planned for the
southern edge of Xinjing. **D**. The complex was sited at an angle
so as to face the palace of the Manchukuo emperor. Neither the
shrine nor the palace was ever completed.

At the same time, Japanese Buddhist missionaries fanned out across
Asia. Although some had already established a foothold on the continent during the early Meiji period, it was the decade of war at the
turn of the century that initiated the greatest expansion of Japanese
Buddhism. Monks who had first traveled to Korea or Manchuria as
soldiers or army chaplains stayed on or returned to found temples.

Having established their first Korean presence in 1877, True Pure Land Buddhists had by 1918 founded ninety-two missions on the peninsula. Sōtō Zen established its first Korean mission in 1907, and by the end of the Japanese occupation, this number had grown to more than one hundred. Nichiren and Pure Land conducted mission throughout Korea, Taiwan, and Manchuria.[20]

Just as the Buddhists and Christians had sought to prove their loyalty during the Sino- and Russo-Japanese wars, a new wave of semilegal religions answered the needs and opportunities of the expanding empire. During the early 1900s, a number of "new religions," combining elements of Shintō, traditional folk belief, and often a heavy dose of political rhetoric, took root in Japan. Most of these new religions were viewed with suspicion by the authorities, and some were actively persecuted. Despite, or perhaps because of, their questionable legality at home, some of these teachings focused on expanding overseas. One, called the Teaching of the Great Source (Ōmotokyō), formed an alliance with religious groups in China, recruited heavily within Manchuria, and embarked on a conspicuously unsuccessful mission to Mongolia. When in 1936 the government announced a program to resettle five million Japanese in Manchuria, a group called the Teaching of the Divine Principle (Tenrikyō) responded. From the 1930s to the Japanese surrender in 1945, Manchuria was dotted with a sad string of what were called "Tenri villages."[21]

As Japanese imperialism became increasingly ambitious and violent during the late 1930s, the role of religion in justifying, governing, and resisting it kept pace. At home and abroad, State Shintō remained the most visible element. Shintō was at the core of the imperial cult, as well as of many of the rituals associated with the war, such as the preparation of airmen for suicide missions. Japanese society was increasingly structured around these ceremonies. Ordinary people had no way to opt out: all religions were forced to find a way to accommodate Shintō and imperial divinity in their own beliefs. For many of the Buddhists, especially the most shrill advocates of war, this was not a problem. High-ranking priests such as Yasutani Haku'un (1885–1973) and the Rinzai Zen master Yamamoto Gempō (1866–1961) fully accepted the divinity of the imperial system and sought to use Buddhism as a vehicle to spread "Japanese spirit" through the empire. At the urging of friends

[20] Victoria, *Zen at War*, 63.
[21] Li Narangoa, "Universal Values and Pan-Asianism: The Vision of Ōmotokyō," in Sven Saaler and J. Victor Koschmann, eds., *Pan-Asianism in Modern Japanese History: Colonialism, Regionalism and Borders* (London: Routledge, 2007), 52–66.

in the military, Gempō founded a temple (officially named a "spiritual training center," *shūyō dōjo*) in Xinjing, capital of the "puppet state" that the Japanese army had established in Manchuria.[22] Hoping to unite the hearts of conquered Asians under Japanese Buddhism, some even went so far as to claim that the emperor was a "Golden Wheel-turning Sacred King," the highest manifestation of a *cakravartin*.[23] This same tactic, you may remember, had been employed under very different circumstances by the rulers of Qing China and, before that, of the Mongols, a fact that Japanese diplomats may have had in mind when they suggested the formation of a new cult to Chinggis Khan in occupied Mongolia.[24]

But for those who chose to resist Japan, religion also proved a powerful weapon. Probably the most common forms of resistance were the small but still significant gestures of disrespect toward the symbols of Japanese rule, of which Shintō shrines and rituals were among the most obvious. The occupying forces certainly took such matters seriously, particularly when they involved Christians. In Korea, Christians were among the most stubbornly resistant to Japanese rule. Korean Protestants had been at the center of a massive uprising in 1919, and, for the next two decades, Japanese security forces kept a close watch on the diaspora of Korean Christians who had fled into Manchuria and China.

Conflict with the Christians came to a head after 1937, when Japan's invasion of China intensified both the implementation of its cultural policies and its security paranoia. Throughout the 1930s, Anglo-American Protestant missionaries in Korea had become increasingly vocal in their condemnation of Japanese colonial policy but had left actual conduct of church policy to Korean Christians. One of the fundamental questions these Christians had to face was how to respond to the Japanese demand that each church install a shrine to the *kami* Amaterasu, ancestress of the imperial house. Some Christians accepted the explanation that such ceremonies were merely expressions of civic duty, but most resisted the idea. Japanese authorities tried pleas and intimidation, but when it finally became clear that the remaining Korean Christians were not going to acquiesce, they simply organized a coup of church leadership.[25]

[22] Brian Daizen Victoria, *Zen War Stories* (Richmond: Curzon, 2002), 92–105.
[23] Victoria, *Zen at War*, 88–9.
[24] Nakano, *Tennōsei kokka*, 78–81.
[25] Wi Jo Kang, *Christ and Caesar in Modern Korea: A History of Christianity and Politics* (Albany: SUNY Press, 1997), 39. In a 1980 interview, the American Presbyterian missionary Bruce F. Hunt spoke about life in Korea under Japanese rule. Available online at http://www.wheaton.edu/bgc/archives/GUIDES/104.htm.

Box 8.d. *Plane compertum*

In the early twentieth century, the Paris Foreign Mission Society (Missions Étrangères de Paris) operated Catholic missions throughout Asia. In places like Indochina, they relied heavily on French colonial authorities, but in China and Japan, they were on their own. This was not always a problem. Many French priests greatly admired Japan and tended to see the Japanese occupation of places such as Korea as a legitimate and even positive act. And as Shintō ceremonies and veneration of the war dead became more common in Japan, priests were generally willing to accept the official reasoning that such ceremonies were acceptable for Catholics because they were civic in nature. (This was the same explanation rejected by the Vatican in the encyclicals *Ex illa die* and *Ex quo singulari*.) Moreover, as Japan swallowed Manchuria and, after 1941, Catholic strongholds such as Indochina and the Philippines, the Vatican was forced to contemplate the fate of millions of Catholics living under Japanese rule. The urgency of the situation prompted a sea change in Vatican diplomacy. It exchanged ambassadors with Japan and China, the first time it opened direct relations with non-Christian countries, at the same time professing neutrality in the Asian conflict. With *Plane compertum*, it also reversed the two-hundred-year-old ban on Confucian ceremonies.

Plane compertum (1939)

- Catholics are permitted to be present at ceremonies in honor of Confucius in Confucian temples or in schools;
- Erection of an image of Confucius or tablet with his name on it is permitted in Catholic schools.
- Catholic magistrates and students are permitted to passively attend public ceremonies which have the appearance of superstition.
- It is licit and unobjectionable for head inclinations and other manifestations of civil observance before the deceased or their images.
- The oath on the Chinese rites, which was prescribed by Benedict XIV, is not fully in accord with recent regulations and is superfluous.

George Minamiki, *The Chinese Rites Controversy:*
From Its Beginning to Modern Times (Chicago: Loyola
University Press, 1985)

By the time Japan declared war on the Allies in 1941, there was no possibility of changing direction, either at home or in the empire. Japanese policy, and the role of religion in promoting it, would continue to accelerate, particularly after the war effort began to turn against them. It would come crashing down in 1945, with the Japanese surrender and the complete collapse of the imperial system. With so much destroyed, Japanese society would need to be rebuilt from the ground up. But who would be there to speak for – or against – religion?

9 Brave new world: Religion in the reinvention of postwar Asia

I. Opiate of the masses: Why Marxism opposes religion

To abolish religion as the *illusory* happiness of the people is to demand their *real* happiness.

Karl Marx, *Contribution to the Critique of Hegel's Philosophy of Law*, 1844

October 1 is a national holiday in China, one that is increasingly marked by a massive flood of travelers taking to the skies and rails. The reason is that October 1 marks the anniversary of the founding of the People's Republic. On this day in 1949, Mao Zedong stood atop the red walls of what had once been the Forbidden City and, in his thick Hunan accent and unexpectedly squeaky voice, proclaimed to an ecstatic crowd that "the Chinese people have finally stood up!" For decades, pictures of that moment would adorn countless Chinese homes, schools, and workplaces.

There was no mistaking that this was a day of momentous significance. In 1911, the Qing dynasty had fallen not with a bang, but with a whimper. The Qing was not so much overthrown as much as the decaying structure collapsed under its own weight; the decades of chaos that followed occurred precisely because there was no power strong enough to take its place. In contrast, the 1949 Communist Revolution was led by a party that was highly organized, with an unmistakable ideology, decades of experience recruiting peasants and fighting guerrilla wars, and as many as five million tough and highly disciplined members. Some people loved Mao, others loathed him, but none would dispute that he and the new People's Republic would usher in a radically new era in Chinese history.

One thing that nearly everyone expected of the Communists was finally to make good on decades-old promises for social reform, to finish the elusive project that so many others had started. This would include religion. Over the past century, wave after wave of political elites and intellectuals had attempted to reform China's religion or to use religion to rebuild China's spiritual culture. The Chinese Communists were naturally part of this much broader trend, but they also brought to the table the ideas of Karl Marx. During the ideological battles of the Cold War, some did question whether the Chinese were truly faithful to Marxist thought. Stalin famously referred to Mao Zedong as a "radish communist," meaning that he was red (Communist) on the outside, but white (reactionary) on the inside. Yet there can be no doubt that China's Communists were indeed devoted to their ideology. During the years they had spent holed up in the remote Northwest, living in caves carved out of the sandy stone hills, they had never flagged in their devotion to Marxism. Even as the bombs fell around their heads, they engaged in constant political study and education and made indoctrination of Marxist ideology a focal point of their recruitment and training.

Yet even before Mao and his Party ever attained power, important cracks were already forming in the ideological façade of world communism. By the time the People's Republic of China was founded, the entire intellectual tradition of communism had already been evolving for the greater part of a century. The core of the ideology derived from classical Marxist theory: the mid-nineteenth-century writings of Karl Marx (1818–83) and Friedrich Engels (1820–95). For Marxist movements worldwide, this corpus approached something like a scriptural level of truth. It was simply inconceivable that these founding thinkers could ever be wrong – although there did exist a danger that they could be misinterpreted or misapplied. The next phase had occurred with the theories of Vladimir Lenin (1870–1924) and the historical experience of the Soviet Union. To classical Marxism, Lenin had added a theory of imperialism, the idea that powerful countries oppressed weaker ones overseas in order to buy off their own working classes and prevent revolution at home. This idea was deeply comforting to countries such as China that were themselves suffering under imperialism and is one reason why Marxism (or, more specifically, Marxist-Leninism) so often lay at the core of anticolonial movements in Asia, Africa, and Latin America.

The other reason is that these movements now had an ideological and material patron in the Soviet Union. The 1917 Russian Revolution had for the first time made Marx's ideas a reality, and since then, the Soviet Union had been the pioneer and model for Communist movements worldwide. Not only did the Soviet Union (through the Communist International, often shortened to Comintern) fund and support Communist Movements throughout the globe – the Chinese Communist Party was founded in 1921 under the tutelage of Soviet agents, and hundreds of its military and political officers had since trained in Moscow – they also provided a model for rapid socialist industrialization. Under Stalin, the Soviet Union had transformed one of the weakest powers in Europe into one of the most formidable (atrocities such as the Ukrainian famine clearly did not enter the official record of Stalin's glorious achievements), and this was to be the road that all socialist countries would eventually travel. This assumption of Soviet paramountcy would not play well with nationalist-minded Chinese such as Mao Zedong, who saw it essentially as imperialism with a different name. Mao had in the past chafed under the heavy-handed leadership of his Soviet advisers. Slavish adherence to Soviet military strategy had nearly cost the Communists their skins in one disastrous battle with Chiang Kai-shek. Further conflict was ahead. Yet even for Mao, Marxism was still a single, irrefutable truth, perhaps one that should be implemented differently in China, but nevertheless a complete and coherent intellectual worldview.

Marxism is at its core a theory of economics, or, more precisely, a theory of society wrapped in a theory of economics. Marx wrote in the mid-nineteenth century, a time of giddying economic growth, when industrialism had suddenly become a centerpiece of urban life, prompting millions across Europe to leave their farms to work in factories. Not surprisingly, Marx was interested in production, how things are made. Clearly there were winners and losers in these sooty Dickensian cities, and to be counted among the former, one needed above all money, specifically investment capital. Those with the means to invest in new industrial enterprises stood ready to increase their fortunes vastly; those without it had only their labor to sell, leaving them at the mercy of the market with no real chance of ever improving their lot.

It was unfair and unpleasant, but according to Marx, conditions had not always been this way – they used to be worse. Before the advent of modern industry sent productivity and investment returns into the stratosphere, the power of the investor (the capitalist, to use Marxist idiom) was not nearly as great. Instead, production was controlled by political power. Think, for example, of a landed nobleman directing the activities of his serfs, to produce millet, flax, wine, or other market commodities, and then reaping the profits. Marx certainly felt no nostalgia for this bygone age. Industrial production was more efficient and more lucrative, and, he insisted, it had only been a matter of time before the power of the dollar overthrew the power of the crown. We know this transformation as the American and French revolutions.

This logic may be a bit counterintuitive to many students of history. It is more common to see the big questions of history being settled by wars and political succession, with economic change left as something of a footnote. But for Marx, it was the other way around. Economic production was not only a basic reality – it was *the* basic reality – and the fundamental relationship between the people in charge and those who did the actual work – what Marx called the "relations of production" – was the key axis around which everything else revolved. It was the shift of real power from the crown to the dollar that had prompted the overthrow of monarchies in America and France. Talk of liberty or democracy in these revolutions may have been sincere, but it was incidental. The fundamental problem, what made the system unsustainable, was simply that there was more money to be made in a world without kings than in a world with them. Economics is thus the prime mover of history. Everything else – politics, culture, ideas – is only window dressing, a reflection and symptom of this deeper reality.

This applies equally well to religion. Generally speaking, Marxists are hostile to religion – most readers will undoubtedly know the famous quotation about religion being the "opiate of the masses" (a phrase that, incidentally, was actually penned by Engels, his longtime collaborator). This attitude deserves a bit of explaining, especially given that Marx was himself an advocate for social justice, a goal that seems laudable enough from the perspective of most religions, as well. Many movements later taken up in his name were themselves inspired or organized by religion or, in some cases, even led by clergy – the liberation theology of the Catholic Church in 1970s Latin America or the Philippines, for example. Why, then, the hostility?

For Marx, religion was a symptom of a deeper reality, admittedly a sad and unjust one. Writing in 1844, Marx outlined the basis of his criticism. "Man makes religion, religion does not make man. Religion is the self-consciousness and self-esteem of man who has either not yet found himself or has already lost himself again." Moreover, religion does not just reflect a problem; it contributes to it, both because it tends to ally with the forces of repression and because it provides just enough comfort to prevent people from doing anything to improve their lot. Simply put, religion is a problem because people pray for justice, instead of going out to seek it. For Marx, religion was at once "a universal source of consolation and justification." It told people that their misery was part of a divine plan and made them passive by keeping them drugged with false hope.

Even then, Marx did not demand the violent destruction of religion, as much as he hoped that people would gradually wean themselves off its sedating influence. He predicted that a more enlightened age would voluntarily abandon religion; that it, like our own imperfect political systems, repressive social mores, and much else of the world we live in today, would "wither away" from disuse. He did not advocate the use of violence against religion. Tactics such as the destruction of property, harassment of believers, and humiliation, beating, and murder of priests would be the unique innovation and inglorious legacy of the Soviet Union during the 1920s.

Marx's own beliefs toward religion aside, it was perhaps inevitable that in practice, a Communist revolution would face a showdown with religion. This was especially true for the young Soviet Union, owing both to the strength and popularity of the Russian Orthodox Church, to which an overwhelming majority of Russians belonged, and to Stalin's larger goal of pulverizing any social networks left over from the tsarist period. Soviet hostility to the church was especially evident in the countryside, where the purges ruthlessly targeted traditional elites, such as small landholders, and where the hold of the Russian Orthodox Church was strongest. That the church was also fabulously wealthy, not to mention deeply invested in the tsarist system, did not commend it to the Party. (In a way, it still is. After the fall of the Soviet Union, the newly revived church canonized members of the murdered Romanov family as saints.)

Put all of these forces together and you can appreciate the range of reasons, some ideological, some very pragmatic, behind the brutal repression of the Russian Orthodox Church across the young Soviet Union. During the 1920s and 1930s, nearly all of the church's clergy and many of its believers were shot or sent to labor camps. Theological schools were closed, and church publications were banned. In 1941, Stalin offered the churches a reprieve in order to use them to build patriotic fervor for the war against Nazi Germany, but by this point, there was relatively little to work with. Of the estimated fifty thousand Russian Orthodox churches that existed before the revolution, only about five hundred remained.[1]

Although the Russian Orthodox Church was their greatest bugbear, the Soviet government also targeted other religious groups within its borders, again, for a combination of ideological and practical reasons. The religions of ethnic minorities presented an especially sensitive problem. Jews had always been seen by some as a fifth column, and although many of the original revolutionaries had themselves been Jews, the long and shameful history of anti-Jewish pogroms in tsarist Russia

---

[1] Despite these years of repression, the Russian Orthodox Church has proven remarkably resilient. It expanded quickly under Stalin's brief reprieve, so much so that his successor, Nikita Khrushchev, instituted a new campaign against it in 1959. The story of the church's revival in the post-Soviet period is well known.

continued enthusiastically under the Soviet Union. For the most part, however, Jews were mixed into the Russian population, which again was overwhelmingly Orthodox. The real problem lay with the ethnic minorities who lived in border regions, many of which are now independent countries. Many of these areas were occupied territory, pure and simple. The people who lived there often had only weak emotional or cultural ties to Russia but did have very strong ties to their more immediate neighbors either in Europe or in Central Asia. This state of affairs raised the specter of religion serving as a conduit for divided loyalties or as a rallying cry for independence movements. (If you support such movements, you say that they are fighting for independence; if not, you must call them "ethnic separatists," or, if you wish to have a job in the propaganda department, "splittists.")

Figure 9.1 "Pope with cross and pistol in his hands." This 1929 cartoon appeared in the Soviet propaganda magazine *Atheist at His Workbench* (*Bezbozhnik u stanka*), which specialized in ridiculing Christian and Muslim clerics, as well as the capitalists who supported them. From: A. A. Kupetsian, ed., *Bezbozhniki: Listaya stranitsi zhurnalov "Bezbozhnik," "Bezbozhnik u stanka," "Krokodil," "Kapkan," "Bezbozhnii krokodil," "Perets," i drugie* [Atheists: Through the pages of "Bezbozhnik," "Bezbozhnik u stanka," "Krokodil," "Kapkan," "Bezbozhnii krokodil," "Perets," and others] (Moskva: Sov. khudozhnik, 1985).

On the European side, the Roman Catholic Church was powerful in the Baltic states (especially Lithuania) and in Ukraine, both of which could be seen as more tied to Central Europe than to Russia. And from Moscow's perspective, the fact that most Catholics recognized the authority of a foreign pontiff (depicted in Figure 9.1 as a scowling gangster) certainly did nothing to aid their cause. As it was for the Russian Orthodox Church, the tight clerical organization of the Catholics was their undoing. It was easy enough for authorities to walk in, eliminate the priests, and expropriate church property. And that was that. By 1926 there were no Catholic bishops in the Soviet Union. By 1941, only two of twelve hundred Catholic churches remained active.

Strategically speaking, the more sensitive border was not that with Europe, but the one with Central Asia, an area that was then as inextricably Muslim as it is today. The tsarist regime had been aware of the power of Islam to pull these regions out of the Russian orbit, and with the growing strength of pan-Islamic movements in the twentieth century, this threat became more urgent. As a result, Soviet policy toward Islam was frequently inconsistent, even contradictory, but always pragmatic. When times were good, and nobody was looking, Soviet policy turned vigorously repressive toward Islam within its own borders. When unity was the watchword of the day, especially when the nation went to war, repression eased.

This background is important because the Soviet experience was so deeply influential to world communism. To young Communist movements like the one developing in China, the Soviet Union was like an older brother – alternately protective and overbearing, a model to emulate, but also an example of mistakes to avoid. And although many Chinese Communists were truly grateful for Soviet guidance, others such as the headstrong and intensely nationalistic Mao Zedong were determined not to let big brother push them around.

Moreover, long before he gained power, Mao had developed his own views toward religion, and these, perhaps coincidentally, more closely matched the original spirit of Marxism. When we think of Mao, we often recall his later years – the enigmatic, jowly, and probably senile figure being adored by a sea of screaming students, each waving the famous "Little Red Book" of his collected quotations. Yet long before he became a household name, even among Communists, Mao Zedong was a fiery rebel against Party orthodoxy. During the 1920s, Mao had been an assistant librarian at Beijing University and there first encountered the small band of intellectuals who formed the core of the Communist Party. Mao had little patience for the endless discussion and empty theorizing of Marxist intellectuals and instead returned to his native

Hunan to take action. Mao toured the hills and valleys of the province, trying to organize a plan to generate a Communist revolution, not in the industrial cities, as Marx had envisioned, but in the countryside, where the vast majority of China's population actually lived.

In 1928, he published his "Report on an Investigation of the Peasant Movement in Hunan," a short and straightforward analysis of exactly how China's peasants were being exploited and why they seemed content to suffer under this yoke. As did Lu Xun and many of his contemporaries, Mao blamed a culture that caused peasants to be passive and fatalistic. Centuries of oppression had made peasants too weak, frightened, and dispirited to question the very forces that were bleeding them. These forces took many forms, but the three most important were the government, the oppressive family structure, and, of course, religion.

Mao was himself from the countryside and knew that peasants were not stupid, just badly misled. And religion was part of the problem because it taught people to accept their fate or else to pray in vain to the skies for help. In a speech that he no doubt repeated in dozens of villages in Hunan, and that would be echoed thousands of times more by his followers across China, Mao put the question directly to the peasants: What do you need, more prayer or more action? When asked about the gods, Mao replied, "Do by all means worship them," followed by the all-important question, "but if you had only Lord Guan and the Guanyin and no peasant association, could you have overthrown the local tyrants and evil gentry?" Of course, Mao was prepared to provide the correct response. "The gods and goddesses," he continued, "are indeed miserable things. You have worshipped them for centuries, and they have not overthrown a single one of your local tyrants or evil gentry! Now you want to have your rent reduced. Let me ask, how will you go about it? Will you believe in the gods or in the peasant association?"

This may seem to be typical political rhetoric, and at some level it certainly was, but it also shows Mao's resolve that the peasants *themselves* decide to abandon religion. When the Soviets sent in their activists from the cities to destroy churches, burn statues, and beat priests, they made no friends among the peasants and certainly did not win any converts to their cause. For Mao, the real revolution only occurred with a revolution of the mind. When asked about destroying statues, Mao replied, "The peasants are the ones who made the idols, and when the time comes the peasants will cast them aside with their own hands; there is no need for anyone else to do it for them."

Even after the Communists took power in 1949, Mao did not have complete control over policy. Other voices within his own Party had very different ideas about the direction China should follow, and Mao would need to spend the next few decades solidifying his place as the single paramount voice of the revolution. This would be an extremely violent process, one in which Mao not only purged his own enemies, but also enacted social and economic policies that directly resulted in the deaths of tens of millions of friends and foes alike. Yet his emphasis on creating a voluntary revolution of the mind, a transformation of thought, spirit, and culture, as the foundation for political revolution would remain a central feature of Maoist thought. Despite the immense chaos and suffering that his policies caused, Mao would insist to his dying day that that he was a champion of popular will. Mao never bullied or harmed the people; he embodied them. In his own mind, everything Mao did was demanded by the newly awakened consciousness of the "masses." Such magnificently self-referential logic of course leaves the door wide open for any manner of policy that a self-absorbed dictator would wish to enact. But the emphasis on popular will and awakened revolutionary consciousness meant that policies imposed from above would have to take on the appearance of voluntary and spontaneous actions by the masses. Just as before, Mao would insist that the people themselves should overthrow religion. But once he was in power, this ideal would take the form of an increasingly stylized and formulaic political theater, in which everyone would have a part to play, whether he wanted to or not.

II. The people's faith: How religion survived China's socialist paradise

Despite its Marxist heritage, the People's Republic of China has always professed religious tolerance. Article 88 of the 1954 Constitution (there have been others since then) states this unequivocally: "Every citizen shall have the right to religious belief."

On the surface, this sounds quite straightforward and would fit with the policy of allowing the Chinese people to abandon religion themselves, rather than forcibly taking it away from them. Look at the fine print, however, and the picture becomes a bit murkier. The key issue is terminology: although the people do have a right to religion, one must first define what one means by "people" and "religion."

By now, you are already well acquainted with the idea that governments separate legitimate from illegitimate religion by the judicious use of terms. Imperial China created legal categories of orthodoxy and heresy. Later era reformers separated religion and superstition. Japan, as we have seen, did something very similar in its treatment of Shintō during the nineteenth century. Regardless of the names, the idea was the same: "religion" was permitted and even encouraged, but by design, this was only the religion that was deemed acceptable by those who were doling out names.

To this, the Communists added a new concept of "the people." Put simply, the Chinese revolution was a class revolution, one with natural friends and enemies. In a variety of policies and campaigns, the Party drew these lines with a high degree of precision, at least theoretically. Nationwide campaigns to redistribute land, for example, divided farmers into four groups: poor, middle, and rich peasants, plus landlords. Poor and middle peasants were natural friends of the revolution; rich peasants were suspect, and landlords were by definition enemies. During successive land reform campaigns, Party operatives (cadres) were tasked not only with shifting land from the rich to the poor; they were also to identify landlords, rich peasants, and other "class enemies." This was an enormously impractical task and one that had very little relation to reality. In theory, class enemies such as landlords were expected to constitute 5 percent of any population, meaning that in a village with one hundred persons, cadres were to identify five as bad elements. They were then to gather the other peasants together to form a small-scale revolution, goading them to rise up against their enemies and accuse them of their crimes; to humiliate, beat, and sometimes kill them. Never mind the fact that in poor areas like the arid Northwest, even relatively well-off peasants still lived in abject poverty or that some villages were nothing more than large extended families where nobody felt particularly exploited by anyone else. What was important was the *process* of awakening, of helping the majority begin to realize class-consciousness and actively participate in revolutionary action. This required enemies, who it now seemed were to be found lurking in every village, factory, work unit, et cetera. Class enemies could not be reformed. They would have no place in the new society and were not counted among the eponymic "people" in the People's Republic of China. In other words, although "the people" had rights of free speech, religion, and the like, anyone who sought to exercise these rights, for example by questioning the Party, was definitionally an *enemy* of the people, for whom no such privileges applied.

In practice, China pursued numerous policies toward religion, often simultaneously. Although very different from the Soviet Union, in its policy toward religion China shared its combination of ideology and pragmatism.

The new government did initiate a number of violent campaigns against religion. These started very early; such campaigns were among the very first large-scale actions taken by the new government. These were not, however, Soviet-style purges of *all* religion, but rather surgical strikes against specific groups that the Party found threatening. One of the first targets was a teaching called the Way of Penetrating Unity (Yiguandao), which by 1950 was quite probably the largest organized religion in China. Today, the Way of Penetrating Unity remains especially popular in Taiwan and Southeast Asia.[2] But its real heyday was in the 1940s, when the teaching spread like a wildfire across China. By its own (no doubt highly inflated) count, the Way of Penetrating Unity at its peak had a hundred million members.

The Way of Penetrating Unity emerged from China's long tradition of popular religious teachings. It was founded some time in the late 1800s and led a secretive existence until 1932, when it was taken over by a former soldier named Zhang Guangbi (1889–1947). Zhang's innovation was essentially to franchise the teaching, allowing it to spread from city to city. As he sought to spread the teaching, Zhang and his disciples founded temples, where the faithful could communicate directly with the gods through spirit writing séances. In this way, the movement grew to resemble the Boxers – their ability to speak to the gods directly meant that individual temples could operate independently. The teaching spread quickly, and within a few years, there were temples in nearly every city in China. Cities such as Beijing had well over a hundred thousand members, but the real growth was in the countryside. A "seed temple" established in the county seat could quickly produce dozens of new temples and tens of thousands of members. Multiply this times dozens of counties and the numbers became either impressive or frightening, depending on where you stood.

The reason for this spectacular growth lay in the teaching itself. Like other teachings in the White Lotus tradition, the Way of Penetrating Unity combined Confucian, Daoist, and Buddhist elements in a master narrative that ended with the apocalypse. Upon assuming leadership of the teaching, Zhang had proclaimed himself the Maitreya Buddha. As mentioned earlier, the arrival of this figure announces the immanence of the apocalypse, a message that has more resonance at some times than others. Few had taken notice when Zhang's own predecessor made the same announcement ten years earlier. But Zhang rose to prominence in a very different world – a time that was so brutal, so catastrophic, that a discerning observer might well believe that the end of the world was indeed nigh. It is no coincidence that the teaching spread

[2] In Taiwan, the teaching has thousands of temples, vegetarian restaurants, and a university. Its adherents include some very powerful politicians and businessmen, including the founder and president of Eva Airlines and Evergreen Shipping.

most quickly in northern provinces, precisely those areas most traumatized by the Japanese occupation. The voice of the gods, channeled through the séances of local leaders, cleared up any doubt: the invasion was a divine punishment for the wickedness of the world. Even after the Japanese surrender, China would still face four more years of civil war that in some areas was even more catastrophic than the occupation. During this tribulation, as well, leaders spoke of the Communists as a divine cleansing of the world – like a plague of locusts. After the bombing of Hiroshima and Nagasaki, they predicted yet another punishment for China's wickedness: nuclear war.

Once the new Communist government had firmed up its borders and felt reasonably secure in its power at home, it began to move against its domestic enemies. For many reasons, the Way of Penetrating Unity was high on the list. Certainly, nobody likes to be compared to a plague of locusts, but, more importantly, the fact that the teaching had spread during the Japanese invasion caused many to suspect that they had in fact collaborated with the enemy. Perhaps even more damning from the new government's point of view was the security threat the teaching represented. This was an apocalyptic religion that its adherents directly to the gods, commanded the loyalty of countless millions, and propagated itself through underground networks. Such a group would rattle the nerves of any government, not least of all a Marxist one that still had only a fragile hold on power.

And once the government decided to act, it acted fast. Early in 1951, central authorities issued directives to local cadres to conduct covert surveillance on religious leaders and soon after announced a campaign to "suppress counterrevolutionaries." Posters, slogans, and movies spread the message that the teaching was traitorous and corrupt and that ordinary members had been duped by the machinations of its leaders. One serial cartoon (Figure 9.2) appeared in a Tianjin newspaper showing the sad descent of a gullible young man who was made to join by means of staged miracles and eventually became so thoroughly brainwashed that he sacrificed all of his money and even the virtue of his wife to the whims of the violent thugs who ran the teaching. In real life, leaders were rounded up and "reeducated" or, in some cases, simply executed. Ordinary members were encouraged to register voluntarily with the government and publicly renounce the teaching, as they did in numbers that surprised even the government. Overall, the campaign was a stunning triumph. Perhaps the best testament to its success was that when the government wanted to eradicate Falungong nearly fifty years later, it copied the methods and even the slogans of the 1951 campaign. The results, as we will see, turned out very different.

○心壞起見一師傅明·上壽求門婆婆給上壇到妻張（四十二）

斃死餓要，來悲關婆老的長道被叉，污姦師傅點被媳（七十二）

Figure 9.2 Propaganda cartoon from campaign against Yiguandao.
This month-long serial cartoon appeared in a Tianjin newspaper
during the 1951 campaign against the Way of Penetrating Unity.
In these scenes, a young woman who joins the teaching is subsequently kidnapped and murdered.

○ 妻張打泰師傳點令道，怒大婆老的首道（二十三）

○ 到看偷偷大趙，跡滅首屍了燒（四十三）

Figure 9.2 (*continued*)

Such was not the fate of all religion. The Way of Penetrating Unity, and a few other teachings like it, had spread quickly but had shallow roots. These were the religions targeted for eradication, and most evaporated with barely a trace. In contrast, the more established teachings

---

Box 9.a. Materialism and religion in the People's Republic

For the first few decades of the People's Republic, Marxist theory was used to explain every social and political phenomenon. The excerpts from the book *Religious Questions under Socialism in China* (published in 1987 by the Shanghai Academy of Social Sciences) show how the materialist view of society shaped official perspectives toward religion.

On Islam:

> The Marxist worldview is opposed to any kind of theism; but in political action, it is fully possible, in fact it is absolutely necessary, for Marxists to form a united front with religious believers in the common struggle for building Socialist modernization....

> From a political viewpoint, Socialism represents the basic interests of all of China's people, including the Muslim minority nationalities. The intrinsic difference in comparing Socialist society with slave-holding, feudalist and capitalist societies, is that the social phenomenon whereby some people oppress and exploit other people is wiped out. In the process of carrying out land reform and cutting rents and opposing local tyrants after Liberation, we seized the land which had been taken over by people in the feudal upper ranks of religious circles and redistributed it to the peasants who had little or no land....

On the continued attraction of Buddhism:

> Socialism has eliminated exploitation and oppression and the social sources for religion. But the many contradictions that remain in actual life often bring problems and disasters to the people. One often meets individuals who encounter these problems in the course of their daily lives. Different people approach these contradictions in different ways. Some press onward in the face of difficulties and become stronger. Others, not daring to face real life, lose faith in life or lose courage because of setbacks and turn to religion in the hope of gaining spiritual comfort.

> Cited in Donald E. MacInnis, *Religion in China Today* (Maryknoll, NY: Orbis Books, 1989), 159–60, 252

---

would present a much more challenging target, and with these, authorities took a very different approach, desiring not to destroy these religions, but to take over their leadership.

This was the tactic used for the more sensitive religions that, as in the Soviet Union, were associated with ethnic minorities living on strategic real estate. Of the millions of Chinese who embrace Islam, many are largely located in the western third of the country, along some of China's least secure borders. There was never any question of trying to wipe out Islam, but during the 1950s, local authorities gradually replaced local Muslim clerics with others who were more sympathetic to the government. When local religious leaders in any way resisted, matters could quickly become violent. Those who proved less than pliant were arrested and removed from their posts, often accompanied by a concerted propaganda campaign outlining a long list of crimes – rape, murder, theft, and, of course, treason – that the accused had been secretly perpetrating all along. Often the removal of troublesome clerics was made to resemble the little revolutions engineered in campaigns such as land reform. The story as it inevitably appeared in state newspapers was that the "people," here meaning the Muslim faithful, newly emboldened by the revolution, stood up and took action against a corrupt and tyrannical religious leader who had for years cowed them into submission. The Party, if it had been involved at all, was only serving the will of the masses in replacing him.

This same logic drove the subjugation of Buddhism in Tibet, but the role of lamas in resisting Chinese rule made their suppression all the more urgent. The question of Tibetan independence is a complicated one. Tibet was for most of its history an independent kingdom that was sometimes allied with China, and sometimes hostile to it. Much of what is now western China was at times under the control of Tibetan rulers. As discussed earlier, Tibet was part of the Qing Empire, somewhere between subject and ally. After the fall of the Qing in 1911, the leaders of the new Republic were keen to renounce the idea of "China for the Chinese," for the simple reason that this sort of Han chauvinism had been a fine rallying cry against the Manchu rulers but now stood to lose them the non-Chinese regions of Manchuria, Mongolia, Xinjiang, and Tibet – about half the country. Tibet was thus to remain part of China but was promised autonomy on most matters. (The official name of the province is the *Tibetan Autonomous Region*.) Under the Republic, Tibetan nationalists had been able to keep Chinese power at arm's length, but they were compelled to face the fact of Chinese suzerainty after 1949. During the mid-1950s, demonstrations against Chinese rule grew more frequent and violent. In 1959 the Chinese People's Liberation Army moved in troops to put an end to the movement once and for all. More than 120,000 monks and ordinary Tibetans followed the fourteenth Dalai Lama, Tenzin Gyatso (1935–), in flight across the border into India.

After 1959, the lamaseries were silenced. They were stripped of their economic power, a move that was perhaps inevitable, given that much of this power was based on landholdings. More importantly, the monastic institution was brutally suppressed. Thousands of monks were arrested and jailed. Many more simply disappeared. Officially, this was an action

taken by the Tibetan monks and people themselves against a feudal theocracy. Lower-level monks were forced to give statements thanking the
Chinese authorities for liberating them from the "corrupt Dalai Lama
clique." State propaganda portrayed this action as a boon for Buddhism
in Tibet. Newspapers reported that the monasteries were now models
of democracy and socialist reform. They even sponsored classes on how
true Buddhism could best flourish under socialist guidance.

Half a century later, the Dalai Lama himself remains a major irritant
to Chinese authorities. He has received the humanitarian Nobel Peace
Prize, among many other awards; has been feted by dozens of heads of
state; and is the darling of Hollywood. More importantly, he is deeply
revered by ordinary Tibetans. Even now, an unknown number of Tibetans
risk their lives to join him by fleeing their country on foot. Many more
engage in a more quiet protest of continued devotion. When the Dalai
Lama received the American Medal of Freedom in 2007, paintings of the
medal appeared on walls of monasteries across Tibet but were quickly
covered over by authorities. Much of this painting war was carried out in
secret, so that one could wake up one morning to see the face of the Dalai
Lama on a wall one day, only to see it disappear the next, and all without
ever having witnessed anyone actually picking up a brush.

With so much attention on the Dalai Lama, Chinese authorities are
most likely simply playing a waiting game, hoping to engineer a more
loyal replacement. This was the tactic taken with the second highest lama,
the Panchen Lama, who died in 1989 and was replaced with a boy who
was handpicked by Beijing but was not recognized by the Dalai Lama or
most Tibetans, who chose their own Panchen Lama. There are now two
Panchen Lamas, each of whom lives under a blanket of secrecy. In 2007,
the seventy-two-year-old Dalai Lama announced that he was considering taking the extremely unusual step of choosing his own successor.[3]

Christianity presented yet another unique challenge to Chinese authorities. Although only a small minority actually embraced Christianity,
the absolute numbers were still impressive. At the turn of the century,
when the Boxers went on their rampage, China had 178,000 Protestant
converts and nearly a million Catholics. These numbers continued to

---

[3] Similar to the way Qing emperors were seen as a continuation of the consciousness of
Chinggis Khan, high-ranking lamas are not officeholders but avatars of a single divine
presence. The Dalai Lama is thus an earthly manifestation of the deity Avalokiteśvara,
the same deity which in China is worshipped as Guanyin. The current Dalai Lama
is thus the thirteenth reincarnation of the first Dalai Lama, who died in 1474. The
successor is not trained but located as an infant by means of numerous portents. As
a reincarnation, the successor can logically only appear after the death of the current
Dalai Lama.

grow during the Republic. By 1949, the number of baptized Protestants had reached 936,000.[4] But like Jews in the Soviet Union, Chinese Christians (Catholics, in particular) were always suspected of harboring divided loyalties. Since the first Jesuit missionaries arrived back in the fifteen hundreds, Christianity had been associated with foreign cultures, interests, and empires. The link between Christianity and imperialism had prompted numerous explosions of xenophobic energy, most notably the uprising led by the Boxers. During the years that followed, many people were drawn to Christianity because they associated it with the West, with modernization, with everything China wanted to become. Many of the most prominent reformers, political figures, and business elites of the Republican period had been Christian. Little of this legacy was very attractive to the new government of the People's Republic.

The presence of foreign missionaries presented an immediate problem. Most of them were from Britain and the United States, powers that (particularly after the outbreak of war in Korea) were seen as irrevocably hostile to China. Since the time of the Boxers, many had considered the missionaries to be the cutting edge of Western imperialism. Now they were accused of everything from espionage (one movie from 1951 depicted Catholic nuns carrying radio transmitters under their habits) to the "mental enslavement" of the Chinese people. A few were jailed, but by 1952, most had simply been repatriated.

Frustration with the missionaries struck a chord even with the faithful themselves. By the time the foreigners were expelled, many missions had been active in China for close to a hundred years, meaning that the oldest Chinese parishioners would have been Christian for three or four generations. They had lived through the Boxer tribulation and no doubt proven the depth of their faith. But even with the likes of Rufus Anderson and James Hudson Taylor pushing for an indigenous church, many Chinese Christians felt that they were still being treated as a sort of second-class citizens within their own faith.

One of these was Wu Yaozong (1893–1979), who would become a vocal advocate not merely for an independent Chinese church, but for a distinctly Chinese form of Christianity.[5] Wu had converted to Christianity as an adult and attended seminary in the large foreign enclave in Shanghai. Although a devotee of a foreign religion, Wu also

---

[4] Donald E. MacInnis, *Religion in China Today: Policy and Practice* (Maryknoll, NY: Orbis Books, 1989), 313.

[5] Better known as Y. T. Wu, as abbreviated from the old spelling of his name: *Wu Yaotsung*.

developed deeply conflicting views about the Western presence in his own country, which gradually affected his view of Christianity. He began to lean toward what is known as the "social gospel," a view that sees the essence of Christianity not in theology but in the ethics of social equality and justice. During the 1940s, Wu became drawn to the ideal of Communist revolution and even began incorporating Marxist rhetoric into his own theological writings. He accused his own church, for example, of being a "reactionary organization molded by an anachronistic capitalist society."

Wu attracted the sympathy of the Communist Party and became the face of what was to be a new Chinese Christianity – free of the missionaries and wholly committed to the revolution. In 1950 he wrote in his "Three-Self Declaration" (*san zi xuangao*, often rendered in English as the "Christian Manifesto") of the need to "purge imperialistic influences from within Christianity itself." To the charge that the West was the true bearer of Christianity, Wu enunciated a litany of crimes – some real, some imaginary – that the missionaries had committed against China and stated baldly that a true Christian would put his own country first. This sort of rhetoric became the foundation for a new form of political Christianity, one that was dominated by the state-sponsored "Three-Self Patriotic Christian Churches." The idea of a "three-self" (self-governing, -supporting, and -propagating) church was of course much older, having derived from the American missionary Rufus Anderson, and very different from the version established in China, where "self-government" meant voluntary subjugation to political authority. Beginning in the early 1950s, all Christian congregations in China were gradually placed under political control and, in 1958, consolidated into two state-run bodies, the "Chinese Protestant Patriotic Association" (*Zhongguo jidujiao aiguo hui*) and the "Chinese Catholic Patriotic Association" (*Zhongguo tianzhujiao aiguo hui*). Only in this formulation was Christianity deemed to have been sufficiently purged of its dangerous tendencies and to be compatible with both socialism and Chinese nationalism.

Today the Patriotic Christian Churches (in total there are five of these: the same form is used to denote the other three legal religions of Buddhism, Daoism, and Islam) continue to thrive under state patronage, even as they face occasional accusations of being Party dupes. The conflict between state-sponsored and global Christianity is the more obvious in the case of the Catholics. The Vatican has a long history of conflict with communism, and the Chinese Catholic Church does not recognize the authority of the Roman pontiff. As in the conflict over the Panchen Lama, the result has been a standoff of dual systems of authority – Rome and Beijing each appointing bishops who are not recognized by the other. Foreign Protestants, who even during the mission days were less interested than the Catholics in maintaining a global organization, have generally been less critical of the developments within China and in some cases maintain very good relations with the official churches.

Rather, the conflict arises from within China itself, in the form of splinter organizations and illegal churches. In some cases, the indigenous Chinese churches look far more like White Lotus organizations than Christianity: the Eastern Lightning Teaching (*dongfang shandian*) claims to be Christian but also teaches that Jesus has been reborn as a woman in China. Given the shadow of the Taiping Heavenly Kingdom, it is perhaps not surprising that the state would vigorously pursue this particular sect. But other, more orthodox Christian groups have also been persecuted for organizing outside the official state church. In terms of its belief, the House Church movement, which has been growing in China since the 1980s, is largely the same evangelical Protestant Christianity seen in much of the world. However, because of their tight and secret organizational network, the state regards these churches as a threat to its own security and has on occasion thrown the full weight of its police apparatus against them.

But the best known, and perhaps least understood, conflict in recent years has been that against a teaching called the Dharma Wheel Method, better known as Falungong. Falungong was founded in the early 1990s by the former engineer Li Hongzhi (1951–) as a school of meditation and exercise. It operated quite openly in China until the summer of 1999, when approximately ten thousand members converged on Zhongnanhai, the headquarters of the central government in Beijing, to request that the group be recognized as one of China's official religions. President Jiang Zemin (1926–) reacted violently against the group, banning its practice, persecuting its followers, and initiating an intense propaganda campaign that fronted the news for weeks on end. In the face of such pressure, most followers abandoned Falungong, but a significant number, concentrated particularly among Chinese students overseas, remained with it and responded with a propaganda campaign of their own, demonstrating the violence of the repression. Today both sides remain deeply entrenched: the Chinese security apparatus closely follows Falungong movements abroad and pressures governments to drop any hint of support or sympathy for them, while Falungong itself has developed a variety of media outlets, including newspapers, cultural extravaganzas, and a television station, to propagate its message.

Why would the Chinese government see fit to unleash such an intense and costly (especially in terms of public relations) attack against this particular group? The charges levied against it– of spreading superstition, of theft, rape, and treason – are standard political scapegoating in China and tell us little about the real motivations behind the campaign. On the basis of a very unflattering depiction of Falungong itself, Maria Hsia Chang suggests simply that the Chinese Communist Party knows that socialism is an ideologically spent force and reacts violently against *any* competing ideas, regardless of how ridiculous.[6] In other words, the campaign indicates less about the danger of Falungong than the fragility of Communist Party rule. However, certain elements of Falungong's rise would attract legitimate official scrutiny: Li Hongzhi's own writings waver between pseudoscience and apocalyptic predictions, neither of which is welcome to the Party. Among the attractions of Falungong exercises are their supposed health benefits, which could be taken as an implicit criticism of the rising cost of health care in China. It is possible that the campaign was a panicked overreaction to the role that new communication technologies – cellular telephones and the Internet in particular – had played in organizing the ill-fated 1999 demonstration. Beijing was certainly aware that such technologies had toppled presidents in Indonesia and the Philippines and had added fuel to the "color revolutions" in Eastern Europe. The mere fact that such a large number of protesters was able suddenly to converge on the doorstep of the Chinese central government shows quite clearly that the security apparatus was caught by surprise. Most fundamentally, even if the group posed no threat in 1999, anyone with a knowledge of history would have known how quickly such a movement could spin out of control, even of its own leaders.

It would be a mistake to view the recent history of religion in China only as one of repression or manipulation. Even the formally atheist People's Republic recognizes the need for spiritual culture, even if it chooses to define this in purely ethical terms. As China seeks a new path for its future, it has again embraced Confucius. This is a significant reversal of earlier trends, the decades when leftist intellectuals lambasted Confucianism as the embodiment of everything that was wrong with China. Anti-Confucianism reached its peak during the 1960s and 1970s. The "Smash the Four Olds" (*po si jiu*) campaign of 1966 encouraged students to destroy all physical vestiges of China's prerevolutionary past, including Confucian temples, texts,

---

[6] Maria Hsia Chang, *Falun Gong: The End of Days* (New Haven, CT: Yale University Press, 2004).

and cultural treasures. Another campaign from 1972 singled out the Duke of Zhou for criticism. (In this case, criticism of the historical Confucian paragon was actually a thinly veiled allusion to the popular Premier Zhou Enlai, but Confucian temples and relics still came off no better for it.)

Nevertheless, Chinese scholars began to talk about Confucianism almost immediately after the death of Mao Zedong in 1976. Within a few years, the central government was offering special grants to any scholars working on the topic of how Confucius could be restored in Chinese culture. For a time, much of the inspiration was from out-side: Chinese in Taiwan, Southeast Asia, and the United States had never suffered under the political chaos of the Chinese mainland and had remained devoted to preserving their cultural roots. Scholars such as Tu Wei-ming of Harvard have advanced a theory of "New Confucianism" for modern societies and have been received with celebrity status in Chinese academic and political circles. The attraction for China was not merely the rediscovery of a lost cultural heritage. Just as Japan had once thought of Buddhism as its unique contribution to world culture, China now began to promote Confucianism in order to stake a claim to a world that, especially after the 1991 dissolution of the Soviet Union, seemed destined for domination by the might and culture of the United States. And when American or European observers condemned China's record of human rights, as they did with growing vehemence after the Tian'anmen massacre of 1989, China responded by saying that values such as freedom of speech and political association are not universal, as the West would claim. Asia has its *own* values of loyalty, respect, and benevolent patriarchy. As we shall see, such ideas found many friends elsewhere in Asia.

III. The peace paradigm and search for meaning in Japan

History has not been kind to the Japanese soldier. Popular images of the Japanese military during the Pacific War often focus on the sheer sadism of the Nanjing Massacre or Bataan Death March. But perhaps the most enduring image is of the Japanese soldier as a blind fanatic, an image best captured in the suicide missions that Japanese airmen carried out against American ships in the Pacific. Civilians were no less extreme. Even the hardened American troops who took the island of Okinawa were not prepared for the sight of Japanese women and chil-dren plunging off cliffs or blowing themselves up with hand grenades, rather than allowing themselves to be captured. Scholars continue to debate the degree to which these images were exaggerated by racism or propaganda, but the fact remains that when the war was brought to an unexpectedly abrupt end in August 1945, the Allied powers suddenly found themselves in possession of a land and people they only vaguely understood.[7]

But the Allies, and the United States in particular, had big plans for postwar Japan. The peace terms of the First World War had been impossibly harsh toward the defeated Central Powers: they had bankrupted and humiliated Germany and led directly to the rise of Adolf Hitler. This time, the Allies were less interested in punishing the defeated nations (top leaders and war criminals were another matter) than in rehabilitating them and restoring peace and stability as soon as possible. Nor was this simply a matter of being enlightened conquerers. Even before the Axis Powers had been defeated, the United States and Soviet Union had already begun jockeying for position in the postwar world. With Europe divided neatly down the middle, the Cold War had begun.

In the East, the United States had initially envisioned Chiang Kai-shek's China acting as a buffer against the Soviet Union, but with the "fall" of China to the Communists, all hopes were now pinned on Japan. The American secretary of state Dean Acheson (1883–1971) famously envisioned a "great crescent" of friendly states in the Pacific forming a cordon around Communist China, and of these, Japan was the key player. The goal for American policy was thus not merely to stabilize Japan, but to make it a firm U.S. ally. Work to this end was to commence without delay. In addition to the Communist threat emanating from the Soviet Union and China, it was feared that a demoralized and weakened Japan might even be ripe for a Communist revolution of its own.

From 1945 through 1952, Japan was effectively a military dictatorship, administered by the Supreme Command of Allies in the Pacific (better known as SCAP) and under the command of General Douglas MacArthur (1880–1964). Under the watchful eye of the SCAP administration, everything about Japan, its politics, economy, and society, was to be recreated from the ground up. It was not a delicate process. When Japanese jurists were unable or unwilling to rewrite the Meiji Constitution, MacArthur gave the job to two American army lawyers, who quickly produced a workable document. With a few minor revisions, this is still the constitution used in Japan today.

SCAP set about systematically replacing Japanese social values with what it considered to be American ones. The first target was the emperor

---

[7] On the issue of wartime racism, see John W. Dower, *War without Mercy: Race and Power in the Pacific War* (New York: Pantheon Books, 1993).

Figure 9.3 The Japanese Shōwa emperor and General Douglas MacArthur. Taken at the SCAP General Command, 1946. Photo courtesy of Harry S Truman Library.

himself. The Allies fully understood the importance of the imperial institution. They had assiduously avoided bombing the Imperial Palace during the war and, fearing instability during the occupation, decided against including him in the Tokyo war trials. But they were determined to destroy once and for all the idea of imperial divinity. The first article of the new constitution made the role of the emperor absolutely clear. He was to be a figurehead: "the symbol of the State and of the unity of the people, deriving his position from the will of the people with whom resides sovereign power." The emperor himself stated as much in his New Year radio address of 1946. As if to underscore the point, photos such as Figure 9.3, showing an impatient-looking MacArthur towering over the formally dressed emperor, left little question of who was in charge.

Along with the imperial myth, state support for religion was addressed. As a first order of business, government support for State Shintō was immediately cut off. On December 15, 1945, the Central Liaison Office made the point with characteristic directness: "The sponsorship, support, perpetuation, control, and dissemination of Shintō by the Japanese national, prefectural, and local governments, or by public officials, subordinates, and employees acting in their official capacity are prohibited and will cease immediately." At the same time, SCAP and Japanese jurists began preparing the ground for the legal separation of church and state. Article 20 of the new constitution made this point very clear:

> Freedom of religion is guaranteed to all. No religious organization shall receive any privileges from the State, nor exercise any political authority. 2) No person shall be compelled to take part in any religious acts, celebration, rite or practice. 3) The State and its organs shall refrain from religious education or any other religious activity.

Equally important was the 1954 passage of the Religious Persons Law (*shūkyō hōjin hō*), which defined certain legal rights to be enjoyed by all religions. This may not seem to be a particularly dramatic development. Japanese jurists had proposed such a law as early as the mid-Meiji and finally enacted the similarly named Religious Organizations Law (*shūkyō dantai hō*) in 1939, at the height of the war. But while the earlier law had delineated the legal subjugation of religion to the state, the postwar version did the opposite: marking the first time in the history of Japan (and one of the first times in Asia) that religion was guaranteed the right to exist as a matter of independent legal principle.[8]

The deeper problem was how to purge the values that years of indoctrination had produced. SCAP censors reviewed books and movies, excising anything that glorified militarism or ideas of Japanese racial superiority. Their brief extended even to religious activity, such as funerals and shrine visits. While they tried to purge Japan of its old values, they also introduced policies that favored American values. At a basic level, SCAP censors wanted Japanese to be optimistic. They flooded the Japanese entertainment market with American music and Hollywood comedies. To stimulate the economy and give people a new outlet for their energies, occupation authorities emphasized material

---

[8] Shūkyō Hōjin Hōrei Kenkyūkai (Bunkachō nai), *Shūkyō hōjinhō no kaisetsu to un'yō* [Explanation and implementation of the Religious Persons Law] (Tokyo: Daiichi Hōki Shuppan, 1974). On the previous law, see Helen Hardacre, *Shinto and the State, 1868–1988* (Princeton, NJ: Princeton University Press, 1989), 124–6.

progress and encouraged consumerism. The slogan of this economic plan, "prosperity through freedom," became a pillar of American foreign policy worldwide, and captures well the expectation that democracy and national affluence went hand in hand, and that both would naturally draw nations into the American orbit.

Aside from prosperity, the best cure for communism was Christianity. Both MacArthur and the American president, Harry Truman (1884–1972), were devout Christians and were at least sympathetic to, if not supportive of, a resurgence of Christian mission in Japan. SCAP supported the founding of the International Christian University in Tokyo and relaxed entry requirements for missionaries (including a portion of the flood of missionaries who were leaving China). Episcopalian missionaries alone soon numbered more than a thousand.

The SCAP administration was gradually phased out during the early 1950s, and by the time of the Tokyo Olympics in 1960, Japan was again on the road to prosperity. But more than policies of the SCAP years, the war itself had fundamentally changed Japanese society. Granted, a few diehards remained unrepentant, but the overwhelming opinion was that the war had been a disaster for Japan. Japanese society began to reject not just the Pacific War, but war in general. The nuclear destruction of Hiroshima and Nagasaki became a point of universal reference. Nuclear war, a constant threat during the heyday of the Cold War, was a particularly horrific image. Even Gojira (a.k.a. Godzilla), perhaps the most iconic symbol of 1950s Japan, was said to have been created by man's careless use of atomic weapons.

In this atmosphere, religion could not but adopt the cause of peace as a universal good. Although some monks such as Yasutani Haku'un remained openly supportive of Japan's legacy on the continent, most postwar Buddhism adopted a bland statement of peace and love.[9] Religious movements that had suffered during the war now wore their persecution as a badge of honor. One such movement was Sōka Gakkai (Society for the Creation of Values), founded in 1930 by Makiguchi Tsunesaburō (1871–1944) and his disciple Toda Jōsei (1900–1958). Makiguchi and Toda were both educators. In 1928, they converted to a particularly aggressive branch of Nichiren Buddhism that, among other things, taught that worship should be reserved for Nichiren alone. For this reason, they refused to participate in Shintō shrine worship, and both were jailed. Makiguchi would die in prison, but Toda survived and, after the Japanese surrender to the Allies, set to work rebuilding the movement.

[9] Brian Daizen Victoria, *Zen War Stories* (Richmond, UK: Curzon, 2002), 171–203.

Sōka Gakkai thrived in the postwar decades. Compared to the more ascetic schools of Buddhism, Nichiren is world-affirming, and Sōka Gakkai even more so. It welcomes worldly happiness, beauty, and even material gain and fits perfectly with the more optimistic society of postwar Japan. As much as a religion, Sōka Gakkai spread as a social movement. It quickly affirmed a stance of absolute pacifism, both as a retroactive criticism of Japan's militarist history and as the path for its future. Other concerns were closer to home. Sōka was particularly popular among women because volunteer members were organized to fulfill mothers' and housewives' needs, such as day care for children and material aid for struggling families. Education remained a centerpiece. Over the years, the movement sponsored numerous elementary and secondary schools, and the first campus of Sōka University opened its doors in 1971. Membership grew exponentially. From 200,000 in 1953, Sōka membership grew to 4,000,000 in 1959. Today, the movement known as Sōka Gakkai International (SGI) claims a worldwide membership of twelve million in dozens of countries.[10] Within Japan, Sōka Gakkai is not without its critics, particularly of the movement's success and broad influence. In the style of Nichiren Buddhism, SGI is very aggressive in spreading its message. Through a combination of publishing, donations, and investment, the movement has amassed significant wealth. Perhaps most worrying for those who would like to see religion make a permanent exit from politics, SGI founded and sponsors the Clean Government Party (Kōmeitō), which has been especially active in labor issues and manages to win a number of seats in Parliament each election.

Far more worrying developments started to unfold during the 1980s, at the height of Japan's "bubble economy." They began with Matsumoto Chizuo (1955–), a nearly blind practitioner of yoga and Chinese medicine who had spent much of the decade gathering a small following in Tokyo. During a 1986 trip to India, Matsumoto claimed to have achieved enlightenment, and, upon returning to Japan, he changed his name to *Asahara Shoko* and styled his teaching Aum Shinrikyō. The first part of the now-infamous name refers to the creative and destructive powers of the universe, hinting at the apocalyptic nature of the teaching. (*Shinrikyō* means the "teaching of the true principle.") Asahara's teaching was a mishmash of Buddhism, yogic practice, and a variety of apocalyptic traditions. He

---

[10] Joseph Mitsuo Kitagawa. *Religion in Japanese History* (New York: Columbia University Press, 1966), 329. Soka Gakkai International Web site. Available online at http://www.sgi.org/.

had predicted that the apocalypse would take the form of a major catastrophe in 1999 and, through the late 1980s, had instructed members to help fend off the event by transforming the evil energy of the world. But some time around 1990, the goal had switched from avoiding the apocalypse to surviving, and even hastening it. Asahara instructed his followers, who in 1995 numbered ten thousand in Japan and thirty thousand in Russia, to abandon their families and retreat to rural religious centers. At the same time, the core of the movement was becoming increasingly authoritarian and violent. During these years, at least thirty-three members were killed, and twenty-one were reported missing. Those inside the main compound were subjected to prolonged sleep deprivation and physical abuse, including a helmet that delivered painful electric shocks to the wearer.

But the most shocking events were yet to occur. Hidden away in their secret compounds, Aum members, some of whom had advanced degrees in chemistry, had been preparing large quantities of highly toxic sarin gas. On the morning of March 20, 1995, a handful of members carried containers of the gas to the Tokyo subway, choosing lines that they knew would be the most packed full of commuters. Working in teams, they left the gas containers concealed near the doors of the train, puncturing them with the tip of an umbrella as they left the carriage. Miraculously, only twelve people died, although thousands were made violently ill. Police attention finally turned to Asahara, who evaded arrest for two months before being captured in the Aum compound along with large amounts of cash and gold bars.

Since that time, Asahara has been convicted and sentenced to death (although the punishment has still not been carried out), and a few of the followers who had taken part in the attack remain at large. But the most interesting development has been the attempt by a few remaining members to reconstitute the sect. Religious groups can survive the discredit of apocalyptic predictions, but with blood on its hands, and the revelation of the horrific activities that took place inside the rural compounds, Aum Shinrkyō will have a much more difficult time of it than did the Millerites. They began by changing their name from *Aum* to the more hopeful sounding *Aleph* (first letter of the Hebrew alphabet). Their teaching, at least according to their Web site, is now a rather bland mixture of exercises and mild New Age self-affirmation, mixed with the same sort of absolute pacifism espoused by Sōka Gakkai or Japanese society more generally. The new Aleph takes as its logo a dove with an olive branch, written to resemble the letter aleph. The group continues to publish materials in English, Esperanto, and Russian, but it remains to be seen whether Japan will ever see fit to accept them.

Box 9.b. *Nakaya Yasuko v. Yasukuni Shrine*

The principled separation of church and state, originally inserted by American jurists into the postwar constitution, has taken root in Japanese society, giving rise to a number of well-known legal challenges. Some of these involve private citizens who object to the use of public money to pay for Shintō ritual. Others are matters of conscience.

In 1973, Nakaya Takafumi was killed in a traffic accident while on duty as a member of Japan's Special Defense Forces (SDF). Takafumi himself was not religious, but his wife, Yasuko, was a Christian. Soon after her husband's death, a veterans' group asked for permission to enshrine Takafumi in a local branch of the Yasukuni Shrine. When Yasuko refused, the group (with the cooperation of the SDF) went ahead with the ceremony over her objections.

Yasuko took her case to court, and was awarded a million yen for pain and suffering, a decision which was upheld on appeal to an intermediate court. In 1988, the case finally reached the Supreme Court of Japan, which reversed the verdict of the lower courts in a decision of fourteen to one. The basis for the decision was that although Yasuko had her right to religious freedom, so too did the SDF and Yasukuni shrine have a freedom to enshrine her husband's spirit, regardless of the wishes of the widow. As one analysis of the case expresses it, "by dying, Mr. Nakaya had become public property."

Winnifred Fallers Sullivan, *Paying the Words Extra: Religious Discourse in the Supreme Court of the United States* (Cambridge: Harvard University Center for the Study of World Religions, 1994), 94–109

The frequency with which Aleph Web pages are hacked (and diverted to some pretty unsavory locations) suggests that such an outcome is unlikely.

The rise of groups like Aum Shinrkyō was a painful blow to Japan's self-image as peaceful, modern society, and led people to reflect on the unintended price of Western-style religious freedoms. But these new freedoms have transformed Japanese religion in a number of ways. On the one hand, they have allowed the rise of unsavory religious groups and renewed debate around topics such as political visits to the Yasukuni Shrine. New freedoms have also accelerated the commercialization of religion. Temples had always been business entities, and they are even more so under the new laws. Beyond temples, the growing commercialization of religion has prompted the creation of a variety of ritual professions and services. Funeral and commemorative rituals, for centuries the exclusive purview of Buddhist temples, are now provided by agencies that arrange the entire process from beginning to end, including contracting the services of Buddhist monks. The business of funerals has not only added new rituals, but has in the process changed the way that people deal with and think about death, dying, and remembrance.[11] Such developments are only possible because the state has restricted its ability to interfere in private religious affairs.

[11] Hikaru Suzuki, *The Price of Death: The Funeral Industry in Contemporary Japan* (Stanford, CA: Stanford University Press, 2000), 203–21.

10   The globalization of Asian religion

> Let us especially cease calling the Emperor of China, and the souban of the Deccan idolaters.... I must repeat, the religion of their learned is admirable, and free from superstitions, from absurd legends, from dogmas insulting both to reason and to nature.
>
> Voltaire, *A Philosophical Dictionary*, 269–70

It would be hard to point to a precise moment when the world became "global." After all, people have been communicating on a global scale for tens of thousands of years – the fact that early humans managed to travel from Africa through Eurasia and settle the Americas and Australia represents globalization of a rather profound sort. Of course, the pace of communication started out very slow indeed. Even a very good idea, such as the domestication of the horse, probably took a thousand years to reach all corners of Europe and Asia. Political integration advanced the flow of ideas. When the Roman Empire connected much of Europe and the Mediterranean, it also created a cultural world that was linked by technologies, language, and eventually Christianity. The last great frontiers were the oceans: the New World did not have horses *or* Christianity (or smallpox, for that matter) until the Spanish introduced them in the late fifteenth century. Over the past century, however, the rate of global communication has advanced exponentially. New communications technologies are one obvious reason. To appreciate the pace of change, try taking the big innovations and working backward. Imagine life without a cell phone, satellite television, or the Internet; then imagine losing something even more basic: telephones, radio, or daily newspapers. This was the world of not so very long ago. And not all advances are technological – politics still plays a vital role. For much of the twentieth century, from the end of the Second World War to the fall of the Berlin Wall, one half of Europe could not communicate with the other. Barring a major political change, it is highly unlikely that you will ever have a pen pal in North Korea.

We could certainly point to a number of moments when the world got smaller, or, more specifically, when Asia got closer. The era of the Silk Road, the Age of Exploration, the advent of European imperialism, and the end of the Cold War each marked an advance in the contact between East Asia and the rest of world. We have seen some of the ways that these advances made their mark on Asian religion: how the Silk Road connected China to the Buddhism of South and Central Asia, how European trade ships also carried Jesuit missionaries, and how the cultural dominance that accompanied Western imperialism provoked people in China and Japan to seek new spiritual directions. But this was not a one-way exchange: each of these advances also conveyed Asian culture and religion to the world. Jesuit mission went in two directions – it took Christianity to China but also carried Confucianism back to Europe. Experience in Asia also changed the way the imperial powers thought about themselves. When British observers looked at places like India, some saw filth, superstition, and backwardness, but others saw spirituality that they felt was lacking in their own culture.[1] And as the world grows ever closer, the influence of Asia and Asian religions on global culture becomes easier and easier to see.

Asian immigrants carried their religions throughout the world, and in most countries, they still constitute the largest communities of believers. There has, of course, always been immigration, but its speed and scope have been accelerating since the nineteenth century, a time when overcrowding at home pushed Chinese, Korean, and Japanese peasants off the land. At the same time, new global networks and opportunities made it easy (relatively speaking) for them to settle in the Americas (both North and South), in Southeast Asia, Europe, and even Africa. When Asian immigrants reached new shores, they immediately built halls and temples as centers of their new community. Years and generations later, religion often remained a spiritual and practical tie to their old home, even as practices changed to suit their new one. In China, most people who visit a temple do so on the first or fifteenth of the lunar month. But many Chinese temples overseas are most crowded on Sunday mornings, a fact that is probably less a concession to Christianity than a simple question of when people have free time. Sometimes the merger of cultures even changes religious beliefs. Just as they would have at home, Chinese migrants to Southeast Asia established shrines

---

[1] Peter van der Veer, *Imperial Encounters: Religion and Modernity in India and Britain* (Princeton, NJ: Princeton University Press, 2001).

Figure 10.1 Chinese shrine to Malay datuk spirit. Shrines like this one near Malacca are a common sight throughout much of Malaysia and Indonesia. The clothes and facial features of the statues clearly identify the deities as Malay, rather than Chinese. Photo by Wendy Choo Liyun.

to the earth spirits known as tutelary deities (*tudi shen*). But those who settled in largely Muslim countries such as Malaysia or Indonesia often assumed that these local spirits would be Muslim, as well. They painted their shrines (see Figure 10.1) yellow, the color of Muslim *karamat*, and referred to the spirits as "datuk," an honorific title for a Malay elder. When they left offerings, they were only halal or vegetarian, never the traditional sacrifices of pork or alcohol.[2]

Along with immigrants, there are translators: those individuals who have found a way to act as a bridge between Asian and Western religions. Besides popularizers of Asian religions such as D. T. Suzuki, religious luminaries such as the current Dalai Lama and the Vietnamese monk

---

[2] Students at the National University of Singapore have conducted a number of very interesting field studies on these shrines. These and other studies of Chinese religion in Malaysia can be found on the Religion and Society in Malacca Web page. Available online at http://courses.nus.edu.sg/course/histdd/notes/Malaysia.html.

Venerable Thich Nhat Hanh (1926–) have worked tirelessly to adapt and explain their Buddhism to Western audiences. Approaching the same mission from the other direction was the American Zen master Philip Kapleau (1912–2000), who, like Thich Nhat Hanh, established his own retreat center, where devotees can immerse themselves in the Zen experience. Of particular note is the perspective of the Trappist monk Thomas Merton (1915–1968), who studied Asian religions from the perspective of his own Catholic faith and entered into fruitful dialogue with Buddhist contemporaries, including D. T. Suzuki and Thich Nhat Hanh.

In a variety of ways, Asian religions have spread through the region and the world. As we have seen throughout this study, ethics tend to travel better than theology. Even if people find it difficult to accept the divinity of the Buddha or the images of the afterlife developed in Asian religions, they might be willing to incorporate Asian ethical philosophies into their daily lives. This was, of course, the image of Confucianism that the Jesuits had once tried to offer the Vatican and the tactic adopted by Japanese Buddhists at the beginning of the twentieth century. It is one reason that the popular incarnation of Buddhism in the West has dropped much of its theological baggage and in some cases more closely resembles a bland self-help seminar than anything we might think of as a religion. Sometimes the divorce of theology and ethics is a natural evolution; sometimes it is a conscious decision. Governments are quick to separate out those elements of their religious tradition that are useful to them. Quite often, it seems, the preference is for ethics without theology.

When China began promoting its Confucian revival during the 1980s, it pointed to the role traditional ethics had played in the economic success of its neighbors, the so-called four Asian tigers of Taiwan, South Korea, Hong Kong, and Singapore. These countries do indeed take Confucianism seriously: South Korean companies such as Hyundai routinely send their management on Confucian retreats, and even multiracial Singapore taught Confucianism in schools well into the 1990s. For many observers, it became axiomatic that Confucianism was indeed the root of the industrial might of East Asia – at least it was so until 1997, when the Asian economic crisis revealed that much of this economic growth was built on unsustainable debt, forcing many of these countries to appeal to outside agencies, such as the International Monetary Fund, for help. A few political leaders, notably Prime Minister Mahathir bin Mohamad (1925–) of Malaysia, rejected both the funds and the criticism that accompanied it, calling the crisis a plot of Jewish financiers. Mahathir and Singapore's Lee Kwan Yew (1923–) both stood behind what they have termed "Asian values," to fend off criticisms of their own governments and as a counter to what they described as the cultural dominance of the West.

In other ways, the globalization of Asian religions is a piecemeal process, with different people picking and choosing elements that they find attractive or compelling. More often than not, attempts at interfaith dialogue succeed when they purposely restrict themselves to a very shallow level, dwelling on those characteristics that all religions have in common, such as the instruction to be mindful, sincere, and devout. Points of difference, such as injunctions not to marry outside the faith, or, most fundamentally, the question of which conception of the supernatural is actually *correct*, are tactfully glossed over. This is by no means evidence of insincerity, because theological questions are themselves not so much functions of empirical knowledge as they are of faith. This is why you cannot logically prove or disprove religion, nor settle matters of theological difference as you would matters of scientific fact.

Westerners who are attracted to Asian religions often find their own paths to engage these theological challenges. One way is by approaching them as metaphor. Scriptural stories such as the expulsion of man from the Garden of Eden or the escape of the young Śākyamuni from his golden palace could each be read in one of two ways: either as a literal account of historical fact or as a parable of a greater truth. In the case of these two stories, the similarities are striking: both describe the fall of mankind from a state of innocence. Theological truths can be treated in the same way. Karma, for example, is most frequently understood in a literal sense – of the good and bad deeds that determine the fate of the postmortem soul. But according to the Buddhist approach to existence, the past and future are themselves illusions, and true existence is only in the present moment. In this sense, we are in a state of constant rebirth every second of our lives. Our consciousness thus creates and recreates our existence not only at the moment of physical birth, but also from moment to moment. Think about the power of an unpleasant experience to destroy an entire day or a week. Think of how easy it is to be carried away remembering a rude encounter on the street or worrying about an unpaid bill, to the point that it becomes difficult to see the beauty of the world around us. Then imagine the descriptions of tortured demons and ghosts from Buddhist lore. Are they really so different? And might this explanation of karma be at least as meaningful to some people as the stories of devas and demons, heavens and hells, are to others?

In some cases, the attraction of Asian religions is grounded in Western social trends. The "beat poets" of the 1950s and 1960s gravitated to Zen, or at least one particular understanding of it, because it closely matched the countercultural drive of their generation. Novels like Jack Kerouac's 1958 *Dharma Bums* expounded an ethos of pure experience, albeit one that was frequently filtered through booze and drugs. The tumbling poetry of Philip Whalen expressed raw, immediate consciousness, the ideal of a generation striving to escape the confines of 1950s consumerism and conformity. In a letter to Allen Ginsburg, he described the goal of this search for pure, unvarnished consciousness: to "eat that old, imaginary self each one of us imagines we 'have'" in order to make way for the "Real self," "our true identity."[3]

At a more popular level, many people seek in Asian religions the simple attraction of the exotic. Entertainers seem particularly drawn to public avowal of Asian religions: the Beatles briefly followed Maharishi Mahesh Yogi. Richard Gere is an outspoken devotee of Tibetan Buddhism. To date, Madonna has experienced a number of well-publicized conversions. This is not in any way to doubt the sincerity of anyone's religious convictions, but it is notable that those with the greatest commercial success also seem to be the most spiritually restless. The sociologist Wade Clark Roof has referred to this as a "quest mentality," meaning that people tend to value things more when they have to go and look for them, and identifies this trait as particularly characteristic of the American baby boom generation.[4]

But by now, Asian religions have indeed sunk deep into Western soil – so much so that it may be difficult to recognize them as anything "foreign." Even if they are often misused, concepts such as karma and enlightenment are now firmly rooted in American consciousness. Perhaps the best evidence of all is how routinely themes and ideas from Asian religions make their way into movies and television. Films such as *Ghost Dog: The Way of the Samurai* (1999), in which an African American assassin for the mafia seeks comfort and direction in the *Hagakure*, take on Asian themes overtly. Others such as *The Matrix* (1999) present an obvious metaphor for Buddhist enlightenment without ever declaring it as such. Nevertheless, the film is loaded with Asia-lite symbolism – the guru-disciple relationship between Laurence Fishburne and Keanu Reeves, and of course the martial arts. In some cases, the themes are so accepted that they are never marked

---

[3] Jane Falk, "Finger Pointing at the Moon: Zen and the Poetry of Philip Whalen," in John Whalen-Bridge and Gary Storhoff, eds., *The Emergence of Buddhist American Literature* (Albany: SUNY Press, 2009), 104.

[4] Wade Clark Roof, *Spiritual Marketplace: Baby Boomers and the Remaking of American Religion* (Princeton, NJ: Princeton University Press, 1999); see also Richard N. Ostling, "The Church Search," *Time*, April 5, 1993.

as "Asian" at all. The spaghetti Westerns of the 1960s and 1970s were shot in the style of Japanese samurai films from a decade earlier. Many of these were direct copies: *The Magnificent Seven* (1960) was a remake of *Seven Samurai* (1954). But more fundamentally, the new cinematic image of the lone gunslinger was enhanced by that of the wandering samurai, which was, in turn, heavily influenced by an ethos promoted by Zen. One can see many of the same themes in more recent films such as *Fight Club* (1999), a film that few would associate with religion, at least at first glance.

The ability of these religions to take root outside Asia in a way brings us full circle. We began by asking whether the religions of Asia make their societies, and their history, unique. To some degree they did. Certain ideas of political authority, of divine kingship, and of the ideal society were unique to China or Japan and continue to mark a very distinct cultural divide between Asia and the West. But even if the ideas were different, much of the story should sound familiar to anyone who studies history, or, for that matter, pays attention to current events anywhere in the world.

Glossary

Amaterasu (Jp.)	female Sun deity considered as the progenitress of the Japanese imperial household
Amida (Jp.)	see Amitābha
Amitābha (Skt.)	a Buddha who has vowed to save any being who calls his name. Associated particularly with the practice of name recitation (Ch. *nian fo*, Jp. *nembutsu*)
Aum Shinrikyō (Jp.)	"Aum True Principle teaching," Japanese New Age teaching responsible for releasing sarin gas in Tokyo in 1995
Avalokiteśvara (Skt.)	bodhisattva who embodies the compassion of the Buddha. Devotion to Avalokiteśvara is particularly strong within the Vajrayāna and Mahāyāna traditions.
bailian jiao (Ch.)	see White Lotus Teaching
bodhisattva (Skt.)	a being who has reached the highest level of consciousness before entering nirvāna
Buddha (Skt.)	"enlightened one." Title given to Siddhārtha Gautama
cakravartin (Skt.)	"wheel turning monarch." Buddhist ideal of divine kingship
Chakhar Mongols	coalition of Mongol tribes in eastern Mongolia, and thus closer to Chinese influence, as opposed to Khalkha Mongols
Comintern	short for Communist International
daimyō (Jp.)	ruler of a feudal fief (Han) during the shogunal period
Dalai Lama (Mon.)	title given to a line of Tibetan lamas believed to be earthly incarnations of Avalokiteśvara
danka (Jp.)	households tied to a Buddhist temple through funerary registration

Dao (Ch.)	"the way," the all-encompassing whole. Central idea of Daoism
Daodejing (Ch.)	"The Way and Its Power." Central text of Daoism
dharma (Skt.)	the teaching of the Buddha, also called the law of the Buddha
Dragon Flower Assembly (Ch. *longhua hui*)	heavenly meeting that marks the end of the current epoch
Edo (Jp.)	name given to Tokyo during Tokugawa period; alternate name for the Tokugawa period
Eternal Venerable Mother (Ch. *wusheng laomu*)	female deity at the center of the White Lotus belief system in China
Falungong (Ch.)	Dharma Wheel Method, school of Chinese meditation practice, banned in the People's Republic of China
Greater Vehicle	see Mahāyāna
Guanyin	see Avalokiteśvara
Guomindang (Ch.)	National People's Party, political party that ruled China from late 1920s through 1949. Generally called the Nationalist Party
Hachiman (Jp.)	Shintō deity
Han (Jp.)	a fiefdom during the period of shogunal rule
Hīnayāna (Skt.)	see Theravāda
Honganji (Jp.)	"Temple of the Original Vow," name also used to signify two branches of the True Pure Land school
honji suijaku (Jp.)	theory of dual identity of Shintō and Buddhist deities
ikkō (Jp.)	"single-minded," name given to militarized devotees of True Pure Land Buddhism
Ise	Japanese shrine complex to the *kami* Amaterasu
kami (Jp.)	a spirit or divine presence in Japanese belief, often associated with nature
kamidana (Jp.)	"spirit shelf." A Shintō shrine kept in the home

kamikaze (Jp.)	the "divine wind" that destroyed two thirteenth-century Mongol invasion fleets. The term was later reused to refer to the suicide pilots of the late Pacific War
Kannon (Jp.)	see Avalokiteśvara
karma (Skt.)	belief common to many South Asian religions (such as Buddhism) that all actions produce effects. Commonly associated with cycle of reincarnation
khaghan (Mon.)	"great khan." Title invented for the leader of Mongol federations and used retroactively to refer to Chinggis
Khalkha Mongols	coalition of Mongol tribes in western Mongolia and Central Asia, as opposed to Chakhar Mongols
khan (Mon.)	title for ruler used throughout Central Asia. Slightly varied in different Turkic languages
kōan (Jp.)	stylized questions used by Zen monks in their training
Koguryŏ	ancient kingdom spanning modern North Korea and Manchuria
Kojiki (Jp.)	"record of ancient matters." Chronicle of Japanese myths and history
kokugaku (Jp.)	"national learning." Scholarly movement aimed broadly at restoring Japanese native traditions
kōminka (Jp.)	acculturation policy employed in Japanese colonies of Korea and Taiwan during early twentieth century
lamaism	form of Buddhism practiced in Tibet and Mongolia. Combines Mahāyāna and Vajrayāna elements
Laozi	mythical Chinese founder of Daoism
law of the Buddha (Ch. Fofa, Jp. Buppō)	the dharma
Lotus Sutra	Buddhist scripture of particular importance to Mahāyāna Buddhism
Mahākāla (Skt.)	Vajrayāna deity at the center of a cult encouraged by Hong Taiji

Mahāyāna (Skt.)	"Greater Vehicle" Buddhism, prevalent in East Asia
Maitreya (Ch. Mile fo, Jp. Miroku)	Buddha of the coming epoch
Mandate of Heaven (Ch. *tian ming*)	Chinese political concept of a moral right to rule that is granted and can be revoked by Heaven
Most Supreme Lord Lao (Ch. Taishang laojun)	deified incarnation of Laozi
nao (Port.)	deep-keeled ships of the Portuguese spice trade
national learning	see *kokugaku*
Nationalist Party	see Guomindang
nembutsu (Jp.)	see *nian fo*
New Life Movement (Ch. *xin shenghuo yundong*)	spiritual revivalist movement initiated by Chiang Kai-shek in 1934
nian fo (Ch.)	devotional practice of calling out the name of the Buddha, particularly Amitābha
Nihongi (Jp.)	"Chronicles of Japan." Ancient chronicle of Japanese myths and history. Alternately titled *Nihon shoki*.
nirvāna (Skt.)	the highest state of Buddhist consciousness, one that is neither existence nor nonexistence
padroado (Port.)	protectorate over Christian missions in Asia bestowed on Portugal by the Vatican. Succeeded in mid-nineteenth century by French Protectorate over Church in China
Paekche	kingdom in southwest of ancient Korea
Radiant King (Ch. *Ming wang*)	prophesied savior ruler, associated with arrival of Maitreya Buddha
Red Turbans (Ch. *Hong shizi*)	rebellion toward the end of the Yuan dynasty
ru (Ch.)	ancient Chinese scholarly tradition from which Confucius and Confucianism emerged
sakoku (Jp.)	sealed border policy enforced through most of the Tokugawa era

Sākyamuni (Skt.)	"Sage of the Śāykas." Alternate name for Siddhārtha Gautama, especially to distinguish him from other Buddhas, such as Maitreya
san jiao (Ch.)	the "three teachings" of Confucianism, Daoism, and Buddhism
sangha (Pali)	the community of Buddhist monks
SCAP	Supreme Command of Allies in the Pacific
shintō (Jp.)	"way of the *kami*." Name given to Japanese native worship, as distinguished from Buddhism
shōgun (Jp.)	military ruler of Japan from twelfth through nineteenth century
sōhei (Jp.)	Japanese warrior monks, often kept on retainer by wealthy temples
sutra (Skt.)	Buddhist scripture
taiji (Ch.)	the circular symbol of yin and yang in opposition
Taiping tianguo (Ch.)	"Heavenly Kingdom of Great Peace," a rebel state in mid-nineteenth-century China
tantra	see Vajrayāna
terauke (Jp.)	document given by Tokugawa-era Buddhist temples to certify that a household is not Christian; see also *danka*
Theravāda (Skt.)	"Way of the Elders" branch of Buddhism prevalent in South and Southeast Asia. Sometimes referred to as the "Smaller Vehicle" (Skt. Hīnayāna)
three teachings	see *san jiao*
tian ming	see Mandate of Heaven
Tōdaiji (Jp.)	"Great Eastern Temple." Temple complex at heart of Nara Buddhism
Vajrayāna (Skt.)	a third branch of Buddhism associated with mystical techniques, also called *tantra*. Although Vajrayāna schools spread through East and Southeast Asia, the teaching became most influential in Tibet and Mongolia as the foundation for Lamaism

vinaya (Skt.)	the code of behavior for a Buddhist monk.
Way of Penetrating Unity	see Yiguandao
White Lotus Teaching (Ch. *bailian jiao*)	name given to a banned tradition of lay teachings in China, often associated with millenarianism
Yasukuni	Japanese shrine chosen in 1879 to house the spirits of the war dead of the Meiji Restoration. Remains controversial for enshrining soldiers of Pacific War
Yiguandao (Ch.)	Way of Penetrating Unity, a lay teaching of the early twentieth century that was banned in People's Republic of China but has since prospered in Taiwan and Southeast Asia
Yihetuan (Ch.)	Society of Justice and Harmony, mass antiforeign movement that reached a peak in China in 1900. More commonly known as the Boxer Rebellion
yin-yang (Ch.)	a theory that all things arise from dual opposing forces. Associated with Daoism
Yuanming yuan (Ch.)	ornate temple complex designed by Jesuit architects for Chinese emperors. Damaged by French troops in 1860 and destroyed by Eight Nation Army in 1900

Timeline of dynasties and major events

China

Shang	1600–1046 BC
Western Zhou	1046–771 BC
Eastern Zhou	770–256 BC
	479 BC Death of Confucius
Qin	221–206 BC
Han	206 BC–220 AD

(Succession of short-lived dynasties)

Sui	581–618
Tang	618–907
	High point of court Buddhism
Song	960–1279
	1227 Death of Chinggis Khaghan
Yuan	1271–1368
Ming	1368–1644
	1610 Death of Matteo Ricci
Qing	1644–1911
	1742 *Ex quo singulari*
	1839–1842 First Opium War
	1862 Fall of Taiping capital
Republic of China	1911–1949
	1937 Japan invades north China
People's Republic of China	1949–
	1976 Death of Mao Zedong

Emperors of the Great Qing

Reign title	Reign dates
Chongde (personal name Hong Taiji)	1626–1643 (reign ended before fall of previous dynasty)
Shunzhi	1644–1662

Kangxi	1662–1723
Yongzheng	1723–1736
Qianlong	1736–1796
Jiaqing	1796–1821
Daoguang	1821–1851
Xianfeng	1851–1862
Tongzhi	1862–1875
Guangxu	1875–1908
Xuantong	1908–1911

Japan

Formative kingdoms	300–710
	538 Arrival of Buddhism
	622 Death of Prince Shotoku
Nara period	710–794
Heian period	794–1185
Kamakura shōgun	1185–1333
	1274, 1281 Mongol invasions
Ashikaga shōgun	1338–1573
	1549 Arrival of Francis Xavier
	1582 Death of Oda Nobunaga
Tokugawa shōgun	1603–1868
	1641 Most Westerners expelled
Meiji reign	1868–1912
	1868 Meiji Restoration
	1894–1895 Sino-Japanese War
	1904–1905 Russo-Japanese War
Taishō reign	1912–1926
Shōwa reign	1926–1989
	1945 End of Pacific War
Heisei reign	1989–

Suggestions for further reading

General

The best place to begin any historical research is arguably with the authoritative Cambridge histories. Many of the topics touched upon in this book are explored in far greater detail in the twelve-volume *Cambridge History of China* (*CHOC*) and six-volume *Cambridge History of Japan* (*CHOJ*).

Of particular use for the history of religion and ideas are the *Sources of Chinese Tradition* and *Sources of Japanese Tradition* published by Columbia University Press. These classic readers have been updated numerous times since their original printing a half-century ago. They consist primarily of original texts, translated and prefaced with careful scholarly commentary. A similar approach is taken by the Princeton Readings in Religion series, which includes the titles *Religions of China in Practice* and *Religions of Japan in Practice* (as well as similar volumes on Buddhism, Korea, and Tibet).

In addition, see:

Brian Bocking. *A Popular Dictionary of Shinto* (Richmond, UK: Curzon, 1996).
Richard John Bowring. *The Religious Traditions of Japan, 500–1600* (Cambridge: Cambridge University Press, 2005).
John Breen and Mark Teeuwen, eds. *Shinto in History: Ways of the Kami* (Richmond, UK: Curzon, 2000).
Joseph Mitsuo Kitagawa. *Religion in Japanese History* (New York: Columbia University Press, 1966).
Daniel L. Overmyer. *Religion in China Today* (Cambridge: Cambridge University Press, 2003).
Paul L. Swanson and Clark Chilson. *Nanzan Guide to Japanese Religions* (Honolulu: University of Hawaii Press, 2006).

Chapter 1. In the beginning: Religion and history

Talal Asad. *Genealogies of Religion: Discipline and Reasons of Power in Christianity and Islam* (Baltimore: Johns Hopkins University Press, 1993).

Thomas David DuBois (ed.). *Casting Faiths: Imperialism and the Transformation of Religion in East and Southeast Asia* (Basingstoke, UK: Palgrave Macmillan, 2009).

Donald S. Lopez. *Curators of the Buddha: The Study of Buddhism under Colonialism* (Chicago, University of Chicago Press, 1995).

Tomoko Masuzawa. *The Invention of World Religions, or, How European Universalism Was Preserved in the Language of Pluralism* (Chicago, University of Chicago Press, 2005).

Chapter 2. Ming China: The fourteenth century's new world order

Chang, Kwang-chih. *Shang Civilization* (New Haven, CT: Yale University Press, 1980).

Edward L. Farmer. *Zhu Yuanzhang and Early Ming Legislation: The Reordering of Chinese Society Following the Era of Mongol Rule* (Leiden: E. J. Brill, 1995).

Jacques Gernet. *Buddhism in Chinese Society: An Economic History from the Fifth to the Tenth Centuries* (New York: Columbia University Press, 1995).

David N. Keightley and Noel Barnard. The *Origins of Chinese Civilization* (Berkeley: University of California Press, 1983).

John Lagerwey. *China: A Religious State* (Hong Kong: Hong Kong University Press, 2010).

Frederick W. Mote. *Intellectual Foundations of China* (New York: Knopf, 1971).

Mu-chou Poo. *In Search of Personal Welfare: A View of Ancient Chinese Religion* (Albany: SUNY Press, 1998).

Arthur F. Wright. *Buddhism in Chinese History* (Stanford, CA: Stanford University Press, 1959).

Erik Zürcher. *The Buddhist Conquest of China: The Spread and Adaptation of Buddhism in Early Medieval China* (Leiden: E. J. Brill, 2007).

Chapter 3. The Buddha and the shōgun in sixteenth-century Japan

James C. Dobbins. *Jōdo Shinshū: Shin Buddhism in Medieval Japan* (Honolulu: University of Hawaii Press, 2002).

Neil McMullin. *Buddhism and the State in Sixteenth-Century Japan* (Princeton, NJ: Princeton University Press, 1984).

Kuroda Toshio. "The Imperial Law and the Buddhist Law," *Japanese Journal of Religious Studies* 23, no. 3–4 (1996), 271–85.

Carol Richmond Tsang. *War and Faith: Ikkō ikki in Late Muromachi Japan* (Cambridge: Harvard University Press, 2007).

Chapter 4. Opportunities lost: The failure of Christianity, 1550–1750

George Elison. *Deus Destroyed: The Image of Christianity in Early Modern Japan* (Cambridge: Harvard University Press, 1973).

George Minamiki. *The Chinese Rites Controversy: From Its Beginning to Modern Times* (Chicago: Loyola University Press, 1985).

J. F. Moran. *The Japanese and the Jesuits: Alessandro Valignano in Sixteenth-Century Japan* (London: Routledge, 1993).

Matteo Ricci. *The True Meaning of the Lord of Heaven: T'ien-Chu Shih-I*, trans. Douglas Lancashire and Guozhen Hu (St. Louis: Institute of Jesuit Sources, 1985).

Andrew Ross. *A Vision Betrayed: The Jesuits in Japan and China, 1542–1742* (Maryknoll, NY: Orbis Books, 1994).

Chapter 5. Buddhism: Incarnations and reincarnations

William M. Bodiford. *Sōtō Zen in Medieval Japan* (Honolulu: University of Hawaii Press, 1993).

Timothy Brook. *Praying for Power: Buddhism and the Formation of Gentry Society in Late-Ming China* (Cambridge: Harvard University Press, 1993).

Martin Collcutt. "The Zen Monastery in Kamakura Society" in Jeffrey P. Mass (ed.), *Court and Bakufu in Japan: Essays in Kamakura History* (New Haven, CT: Yale University Press, 1982).

Pamela Kyle Crossley. *A Translucent Mirror: History and Identity in Qing Imperial Ideology* (Berkeley: University of California Press, 1999).

Herbert Franke. *China under Mongol Rule* (Brookfield, VT: Variorum, 1994).

Allan Grapard. "The Shinto of Yoshida Kanetomo," *Monumenta Nipponica* 47, no. 4 (1992), 33–58.

Steven Heine and Dale S. Wright (eds.). *The Zen Canon: Understanding the Classic Texts* (New York: Oxford University Press, 2004).

Nam-lin Hur. *Death and Social Order in Tokugawa Japan: Buddhism, Anti-Christianity, and the Danka System* (Cambridge: Harvard University Asia Center, 2007).

Winston L. King. *Zen and the Way of the Sword: Arming the Samurai Psyche* (New York: Oxford University Press, 1993).

Miyazaki Fumiko. "Religious Life of Kamakura Bushi: Kumagai Naozane and His Descendants," *Monumenta Nipponica* 41, no. 4 (1992), 435–46.

Herman Ooms. *Tokugawa Ideology: Early Constructs, 1570–1680* (Princeton, NJ: Princeton University Press, 1985).

Chapter 6. Apocalypse now

Albert I. Baumgarten. *Apocalyptic Time* (Leiden: E. J. Brill, 2000).

Thomas David DuBois. *The Sacred Village: Social Change and Religious Life in Rural North China* (Honolulu: University of Hawaii Press, 2005).

David Ownby. "Chinese Millenarian Traditions: The Formative Age," *American Historical Review* 104, no. 5 (1999), 1513–30.

Jonathan D. Spence. *God's Chinese Son: The Taiping Heavenly Kingdom of Hong Xiuquan* (New York: W. W. Norton, 1996).

Alan Sponberg and Helen Hardacre (eds.). *Maitreya, the Future Buddha* (Cambridge: Cambridge University Press, 1988).

Barend J. ter Haar. *The White Lotus Teachings in Chinese Religious History* (Leiden: E. J. Brill, 1992).

Chapter 7. Out of the twilight: Religion and the late nineteenth century

Robert A. Bickers and R. G. Tiedemann. *The Boxers, China, and the World* (Totowa, NJ: Rowman & Littlefield, 2007).

Paul A. Cohen. *History in Three Keys: The Boxers as Event, Experience, and Myth* (New York: Columbia University Press, 1997).

Joseph Esherick. *The Origins of the Boxer Uprising* (Berkeley: University of California Press, 1987).

Helen Hardacre. *Shinto and the State, 1868–1988* (Princeton, NJ: Princeton University Press, 1989).

James Edward Ketelaar. *Of Heretics and Martyrs in Meiji Japan: Buddhism and Its Persecution* (Princeton, NJ: Princeton University Press, 1990).

Emily G. Ooms. *Women and Millenarian Protest in Meiji Japan: Deguchi Nao and Omotokyo* (Ithaca: Cornell University Press, 1993).

Judith Snodgrass. *Presenting Japanese Buddhism to the West* (Chapel Hill: University of North Carolina Press, 2003).

D. T. Suzuki. *Zen and Japanese Culture* (Princeton, NJ: Princeton University Press, 1993).

Chapter 8. Into the abyss: Religion and the road to disaster during the early twentieth century

Arif Dirlik. "The Ideological Foundations of the New Life Movement: A Study in Counterrevolution," *Journal of Asian Studies* 34, no. 4 (1975), 945–80.

Lloyd E. Eastman. "Fascism in Kuomintang China: The Blue Shirts," *China Quarterly*, no. 49 (1972), 1–31.

Sheldon M. Garon. "State and Religion in Imperial Japan, 1912–1945," *Journal of Japanese Studies* 12 (1986), 273–302.

Vincent Goossaert. *The Taoists of Peking, 1800–1949: A Social History of Urban Clerics* (Cambridge: Harvard University Press, 2007).

A. Hamish Ion. *The Cross and the Rising Sun*, Vol. 2, *The British Protestant Missionary Movement in Japan, Korea, and Taiwan, 1865–1945* (Waterloo, Ont.: Wilfrid Laurier, 1993).

Christopher Ives, *Imperial-Way Zen: Ichikawa Hakugen's Critique and Lingering Questions for Buddhist Ethics* (Honolulu: University of Hawaii Press, 2009).

Brian Daizen Victoria. *Zen at War* (Totowa, NJ: Rowman & Littlefield, 2006).

Holmes Welch. *The Practice of Chinese Buddhism* (Cambridge: Harvard University Press, 1967).

Chapter 9. Brave new world: Religion in the reinvention of postwar Asia

John Breen. *Yasukuni, the War Dead and the Struggle for Japan's Past* (New York: Columbia University Press, 2008).

William Husband. *"Godless Communists": Atheism and Society in Soviet Russia, 1917–1932* (Dekalb: Northern Illinois University Press, 2000).

Robert Kisala and Mark Mullins. *Religion and Social Crisis in Japan: Understanding Japanese Society through the Aum Affair* (Basingstoke, UK: Palgrave Macmillan, 2001).

Donald E. MacInnis. *Religion in China Today: Policy and Practice* (Maryknoll, NY: Orbis Books, 1989).

Mao Tse-tung (Mao Zedong). *Report on an Investigation of the Peasant Movement in Hunan,* at Marxists Internet Archive (http://www.marxists.org/reference/archive/mao/selected-works/volume-1/mswv1_2.htm).

Karl Marx. *A Contribution to the Critique of Hegel's Philosophy of Right* (http://www.marxists.org/archive/marx/works/1843/critique-hpr/intro.htm).

Daniel Alfred Metraux. *How Soka Gakkai Became a Global Buddhist Movement: The Internationalization of a Japanese Religion* (Lewiston, NY: Edwin Mellen, 2010).

David Ownby. *Falun Gong and the Future of China* (New York: Oxford University Press, 2008).

David A. Palmer. *Qigong Fever: Body, Science, and Utopia in China* (New York: Columbia University Press, 2007).

Hikaru Suzuki. *The Price of Death: The Funeral Industry in Contemporary Japan* (Stanford, CA: Stanford University Press, 2000).

Holmes Welch. *Buddhism under Mao* (Cambridge: Harvard University Press, 1972).

Chapter 10. The globalization of Asian religion

Jack Kerouac. *The Dharma Bums* (New York: Penguin, 1990).

Thomas Merton. *The Asian Journal of Thomas Merton* (New York: New Directions, 1973).

Helen Tworkov. *Zen in America: Five Teachers and the Search for an American Buddhism* (Tokyo: Kodansha International, 1994).

John Whalen-Bridge and Gary Storhoff. *The Emergence of Buddhist American Literature* (Albany: SUNY Press, 2009).

Index

Acheson, Dean, 216
Africa
  circumnavigation of, 73
  Portuguese outposts in, 74, 76
Ah Q, True Story of 阿Q正傳, 170–3
Altan Khaghan, 100
Amaterasu 天照
  identity as Guanyin, 61
  and imperial family, 60, 158
  veneration by Christians, 191
  veneration by royal clan, 55
Amida 阿弥陀
  identity as Hachiman, 61
  and *nembutsu*, 64, 154, 185
  vow of, 64
Anderson, Rufus, 145, 211, 212
apocalypse, 29, 36, 39, 72
  Aum Shinrikyō and, 220
  Buddhist conceptions, 34, 135
  Christian, 124, 126–7, 135
  Daoist conceptions, 132, 135
  Falungong and, 214
  immanence of, 130, 135, 204
  Maitreya and, 133, 135
  manmade, 127, 130
  religious cults and, 129
  significance of, 127, 131
  truth or falsity of, 124, 125, 131
  violence as means of hastening, 135, 137, 220, 221
  Way of Penetrating Unity and, 204, 205
Asahara Shoko 麻原彰晃, 220–1

Ashikaga 足利 shogunate, 63, 66, 77, 121
Ashikaga Yoshiteru 足利義輝, 78
Asian values debate, 228
Ašoka, 99
Aum Shinrikyō オウム真理教, 220–1
Avalokiteśvara. *See also* Guanyin
  in art, 102
  Chinese transformation of, 11–12
  in Tibet, 210

Ba Jin 巴金, 169, 170, 172
baptism
  Catholic preference for, 144, 145
  of new converts, 78, 89
  in Taiping Heavenly Kingdom, 139
Beijing 北京
  Boxer Uprising in, 148–9, 150, 151, 161
  Buddhism in, 133
  intellectual life in twentieth century, 167, 179
  Jesuits in, 81–3
  lamaism in, 102
  modernization of, 164
  Qing capture of, 101
  Taiping advance on, 141
  warlord politics, 168, 175
  Way of Penetrating Unity in, 204
  White Lotus in, 138
Benedict XIV, Pope, 91, 92, 192
Blue Shirts, 176
Bodhidharma, 114
bodhisattva, 61, 101, 112, 132, 156

Boxer Uprising, 148–51. *See also*
    Justice and Harmony Fist,
    Justice and Harmony
    Society
Buddha. *See* Siddhārtha Gautama,
    Śākyamuni
Buddhism
    enlightenment, 31, 114–19, 229
    existentialism, 32, 94, 115–16, 228
    in medieval Asian diplomacy, 57
    origins, 30–1
Buddhism in China
    arrival and spread, 33
    Ming dynasty, 95–7
    Qing dynasty, 101–5
    Tang dynasty, 34
    Yuan dynasty, 99
Buddhism in Japan. *See also* Shintō
    and Buddhism
    arrival and early years, 56–60
    formation of medieval schools,
        61–4
    Imperial-way Buddhism 皇道仏教,
        185
    Nara period, 58–9
    nineteenth-century opposition to,
        153, 156
    as protector of the Japanese state,
        58, 65
    relations between schools, 64
    support for Japanese imperialism,
        190
    Tokugawa, 71, 105–13
Buddhism, sects and schools.
    See Lamaism, Mahāyāna, Nara
    Buddhism, Nichiren, Rinzai
    Zen, Shingon, Sōka Gakkai,
    Sōtō Zen, Tendai, Theravāda,
    Zen

cakravartin, 99, 100, 103, 132, 191
    Chinggis Khagan as, 99–100, 101
Castiglione, Giuseppe, 81
Catholic Church. *See also*
    missionaries, Vatican

abuses within, 8
Chinese Catholic Patriotic
    Association 中國天主教愛國
    會, 212
    medieval, 6, 9, 65, 104, 115
    in People's Republic of China, 211
    response to Reformation, 74
    Second Vatican Council, 91
    in Soviet Union, 200
    and veneration of Confucius, 90,
        192
Central Asia. *See also* Silk Road
    Buddhism in, 11, 33, 103
    as cultural region, 100
    and Ming dynasty, 97
    and Qing dynasty, 104, 151
    Soviet Central Asia, 199, 200
    and Yuan dynasty, 98
Chengde 承德, 102, 104
Chiang Kai-shek 蔣介石, 173–9, 196,
    216
China Inland Mission, 145
Chinggis Khagan, 98
    as *cakravartin*, 99–100, 101
    Japanese Empire and, 191
    Qing dynasty and, 105
    reincarnations of, 100–1, 191
Christianity. *See also* Catholic Church,
    missionaries, Vatican
    anti-Christian sentiment, 88, 90,
        145–7, 181
    as a bulwark against communism,
        212, 219
    iconography, 9, 31, 90
    imperialism and, 144, 181, 212
    in Korea, 191
    liberation theology, 197
    as modern religion, 145,
        173, 211
    role in shaping Western history, 2,
        9, 68
    as standard for religion, 5, 6, 173,
        182
    translation of terms and texts, 17,
        77, 81, 90

Christianity in China
   Chinese variations of, 139, 211, 213
   late Ming and early Qing, 80–4,
      89–93
   nineteenth century. *See* Taiping
      Heavenly Kingdom, 143–51
   numbers of Chinese Christians, 84,
      211
   Tang dynasty, 80
   twentieth century, 173, 210–13
Christianity in Japan
   Empire of Japan, 191–2
   laws against, 85, 87, 89
   nineteenth century, 157, 180, 185
   numbers of Japanese Christians, 89
   postwar Japan, 219, 222
   sixteenth and seventeenth centuries,
      77–80, 84–9
civil service examinations, 44, 95,
      139, 161, 168
Cixi 慈禧, Empress Dowager, 34, 148,
      151, 162, 163
Clean Government Party 公明党, 220
Clement XI, Pope, 90, 91, 92
Coelho, Gaspar, 80, 84–7, 89
Cold War, 195, 216, 219, 225
Commissioner for Temples and
      Shrines 寺社奉行, 107
communism. *See also* Marxism
   Guomindang opposition to, 175,
      178, 179
   influence in Asia, 216
Communist International
      (Comintern), 195
Communist Party, Chinese, 50, 173,
      195, 200, 212, 214
Communist revolution
   in China, 194, 216
   as social ideal, 212
   Soviet influence and assistance, 195
Confucian elite
   charitable donations by, 144
   compared to samurai, 106, 121
   as keepers of orthodox tradition,
      94, 133

   in Ming, 41, 43, 46
   patronage of Buddhism, 95–7
   recruitment, 43, 44, 94, 95, 139,
      161
   role in late Qing reforms, 161
   social status, 4, 46, 81, 94, 165
   in Yuan, 41, 47
Confucianism
   attitude toward commerce, 46
   attitude toward law, 44
   Buddhism and, 34, 35, 83, 95
   Daoism and, 35, 83
   in early Ming, 40–1, 46–50
   family relations, 20–1, 29, 35,
      164
   Japan, 106, 157, 192
   Korea, 227
   moral suasion in, 21, 43, 47–9, 166,
      178
   origins and early history, 15–19,
      21–3
   Qin suppression of, 3, 23
   in Qing governance, 105
   twentieth century
      anti-Confucian movements, 169,
         172, 214
      contribution to political reforms,
         168, 176, 178
      resurgence since 1980s, 214–15,
         227
   women in, 21
Confucius (Kong Qiu 孔丘)
   Christian views of, 84, 90
   life of, 19, 21, 24, 25
   ru teaching and, 18–19, 22
   superior man, 21
   veneration of, 90–2, 173, 192
   views on human nature, 21
   views on the supernatural, 6, 21,
      90, 95
   in White Lotus eschatology, 135
Constitution
   China (People's Republic of China,
      1954), 202
   Japan (1947), 216, 217, 218, 222

Constitution *(cont.)*
  Japan (Empire of Japan, 1889),
    157, 160, 216
cults. *See* apocalypse, religious cults and
Cultural Revolution, 128, 214

daimyō 大名, 66, 105
  Christian, 78, 79, 84–6, 89
  competition for Portuguese trade,
    79
  relationship with Jesuits, 77, 78
  during Tokugawa, 105
Dainichi Nyorai 大日如来, 77
Dalai Lama, 210
  acceptance outside of Asia, 226
  conflict with People's Republic of
    China, 209–10
  Mongol support for, 100, 104
danka 檀家, 108–9, 133, 152
Dao 道, 25, 26, 54
Daodejing 道德經, 24, 25–6
Datuk gong, 226
dharma
  calls to defend, 69, 120
  decline of the dharma, 111, 132
  law of the Buddha, 58, 85, 99, 184
  revival of, 181
divination, 17, 28. *See also* spirit
    writing 16
Dōgen 道元, 116
Dominicans, 86, 90
Donation of Bartolemeu, 79
Dragon Flower Assembly 龍花會, 135
Dutch. *See also* Netherlands East
    India Company
  arrival in Asia, 73
  capture of Taiwan, 74
  confinement to Dejima, 89, 154
  Dutch learning, 154
  Japanese portrayals of, 153

Eastern Lightning Teaching 東方閃
    電, 213
Edo 江戸
  arrival of Commodore Perry, 154

Buddhism in, 111, 157
  economic conditions, 151
  Tokugawa governance, 105, 110
Eight Nation Army, 150
eight trigrams 八卦, 28
Eight Trigrams Teaching 八卦教, 133,
    136, 138
Eight-fold Path, 32
Engels, Friedrich, 123, 195, 197
Enlightenment, European, 5, 37
Enryakuji 延暦寺, 68, 69
Eternal Venerable Mother 無生老母,
    135
Ex illa die, 90, 192
Ex quo singulari, 91–2, 192

Falungong 法輪功, 205, 213–14
Family 家, 169
fascism, 36, 176–8
feng shui 風水, 26, 27
Fengtian 奉天, 186
Four Noble Truths, 31
Franciscans, 86, 87, 90
Funchal, 74
funerals. *See also* mourning
  Buddhist monopoly in Tokugawa
    Japan, 8, 109–10, 111–12, 152
  China, extravagence of, 163
  China, village, 134, 146
  postwar Japan, 218, 223
  regulation by Ming dynasty, 44
  Shintō, 109, 111, 159

García, Diego, 87
Gateless Gate 無門関, 119, 120
gentry. *See* Confucian elite
Goa, 73, 74–7, 81
Grand Pronouncements 御制大告, 47
Great Code of Ming Law 大明律, 43,
    45
Great Ming Commandment 大明令, 45
Great Peace. *See* Taiping Heavenly
    Kingdom, Way of Great Peace
Great Teaching Institute 大教院, 158
Great Unification 大同, 163, 166

Guangxi 廣西, 139
Guangxu 光緒 Emperor, 161, 162, 163, 176
Guanyin (Kannon) 觀音, 210. *See also* Avalokiteśvara
    identity as Amaterasu, 61
    in popular worship, 201
    transformation in China, 11–12
Guomindang 國民黨, 176

Hachiman 八幡, 60, 61
Hagakure 葉隱, 120, 229
Hakka 客家, 139
Han 漢
    dynasty, 23, 29, 34, 35, 44
    ethnicity, 23, 98, 138, 168, 209
    Han synthesis, 23, 44
Han Feizi 韓非子, 23
Han Lin'er 韓林兒, 39
Heaven and Earth Teaching 天地門教, 134
Heavenly Kingdom of Great Peace. *See* Taiping Heavenly Kingdom
Hebei 河北, 167
Heian 平安 period, 61, 63, 65
Henry the Navigator, 73
heresy, 5
    concept in Chinese religion, 35
    Japanese Buddhists accused of, 64
    in medieval Catholic Church, 9
    as Ming legal category, 50, 202
    surveillance of in Tokugawa, 8
    White Lotus teachings as, 133
Hiei, Mount 比叡山, 63, 64, 66, 68, 106
Hirata Atsutane 平田篤胤, 153–4, 155, 156
Hitler, Adolf, 128, 176, 178, 216
Hokkaido 北海道, 53, 180, 183
Hōnen 法然, 63, 64
Hong Xiuquan 洪秀全, 1, 139, 143, 161
Honganji 本願寺, 66, 69, 70, 86, 181, 182

Hongwu 洪武 Emperor. *See* Zhu Yuanzhang
honji suijaku 本地垂迹, 61, 112
House Churches, 213
Huanglao 黃老, 39
Hunan 湖南, 194, 201
Hundred Days of Reform, 163, 167

Ihara Saikaku 井原西鶴, 110
ikkō 一向, 66. *See also* True Pure Land
    compared with Christians, 86
    suppression of, 69, 70, 120
Incense Army 香軍, 39, 131
India
    flight of Dalai Lama, 209
    Japanese images of, 154
    Jesuit mission in, 1, 74, 76, 91
    Mongol conquest of, 98
    pilgrimage to, 114, 220
    as source of Buddhism, 11, 30, 34, 77, 114
    as symbol of Buddhist decadence, 112, 154, 181
    Western images of, 225
Indonesia, 214, 226
Inoue Enryō 井上円了, 181, 182, 184
Internet, 129, 214, 224
Iran, 7
Ise 伊勢 shrine, 158
    imperial visits to, 60, 158
    shrine network, 157, 160, 187
Ishin Sūden 以心崇伝, 106, 107
Islam
    in Central Asia, 98, 200
    in China, 89, 149, 208
    Chinese policy toward, 208, 209, 212
    in Chinese ritual, 226
    in Europe, 3
    in Russia/Soviet Union, 200
    in Southeast Asia, 226
Islamic Revolution, 7

Izumo 出雲 shrine, 158

Jests on Emerging from Meditation 出定
笑語, 153
Jesuits, 77, 79
  Ashikaga shogun and, 78
  Buddhist monks and, 77, 81, 84
  in Chinese court, 82, 84
  conflict with other missionary
    orders, 86, 90
  conflict with Vatican, 91
  construction of Yuanming Palace,
    150
  as cultural ambassadors, 225
  founding of order, 74, 76
  in India, 74, 76
  Japanese, 88
  mastery of Confucian scholarship,
    81
  in Nagasaki, 78–9
  origins of cultural policy, 76
  positive views of Confucianism, 90,
    227
  Toyotomi Hideyoshi and, 80, 84–6
Jesus
  in Christian eschatology, 124, 127
  as founder of Christianity, 21
  Hong Xiuquan and, 1, 139, 143
  iconography of, 90
  rebirth in China, 213
  Society of Jesus. *See* Jesuits
  in White Lotus eschatology, 135
Jiaqing 嘉慶 Emperor, 139
Judaism, 3, 198, 199, 211
Jurchen 女真, 100
Justice and Harmony
  Fist 義和拳, 147
  Society 義和團, 164, 211

kami 神
  imperial descent from, 55, 60, 112,
    153
  as patron deities, 55, 57
  relation to Buddhist deities, 112,
    153, 156. *See also honji suijaku*
    57, 60

worship in ancient Japan, 54
kamidana 神棚, 158, 187
kamikaze 神風, 2, 65
Kang Youwei 康有為, 161–7, 168,
    169, 176, 179
Kangxi 康熙 Emperor, 82, 84, 92, 93,
    101
Kannon 観音. *See* Avalokiteśvara,
    Guanyin
karma
  and cycle of rebirth, 32
  expression in Chinese
    religion, 35
  Mahayana conceptions of, 33
  metaphoric interpretations, 228
  in popular culture, 229
  and the taking of life, 184
Kennyo 顕如, 69
Kerouac, Jack, 229
Khubilai Khagan, 99
kingship
  Buddhist conceptions. *See also*
    cakravartin
  adoption by Manchus, 100–2
  adoption by Mongols, 99–100
  in formation of Japanese political
    institutions, 57–8
  in Qing diplomacy, 101
  Confucian conceptions
    origins, 17–18
    transformation during Han
      dynasty, 23
  Daoist conceptions, 29, 132
Kinmei 欽明, Emperor, 57
Kitabatake Chikafusa 北畠親房, 112,
    156
kōan 公案, 119
Koguryŏ 高句麗, 56, 57
Kojiki 古事記, 59, 152
kōminka 皇民化, 187
Korea, 3, 53
  ancient invasion of Japan, 55
  ancient kingdoms of, 56–7
  Buddhism in, 114
  Central Asia and, 100
  Christianity in, 191

Confucianism in, 47, 227
invasion by Toyotomi Hideyoshi, 70
Japanese Buddhists in, 181, 189
Japanese occupation, 183, 187, 192
Mongol occupation, 65
Korean War, 211
Kōtoku 孝徳, Emperor, 59
Kūkai 空海, 61, 109, 113
Kyōtō 京都, 1, 54, 63, 67–9, 71, 78,
    106, 122
Kyūshū 九州
    early communication with
        continent, 56
    Jesuits in, 74, 77–80, 84, 87
    persecution of Christians in, 89

Lamaism. *See also* Dalai Lama
    adoption by Manchus, 100
    adoption by Mongols, 99
    Ge-lugs, 100
    in Qing diplomacy, 101
Land Reform, 203, 209
Laozi 老子
    life of, 24–5
    as millenarian figure, 39, 132
    Most Supreme Lord Lao 太上老君,
        132
    in White Lotus eschatology, 135
law. *See also* Constitution
    Church law, 79
    jus primae noctis, 51
    Law of the Buddha. *See* dharma
    sacred, 88
law in China. *See also* Grand
        Pronouncements, *Great Code
        of Ming Law, Great Ming
        Commandment, Placard of
        People's Instructions,* Wine
        Drinking Ceremony
    anti-superstition legislation, 173
    Christian missionaries and, 147
    Confucian elites and, 96, 147
    dissemination of law to common
        people, 48
    enshrinement of Confucian
        orthodoxy, 43, 44, 92, 94

late Qing reforms, 167
legal status of religion in People's
    Republic of China, 212
legalism, 22
local custom under Qing law, 101
Manchu hairstyle, 140
Ming innovations, 37
persecution of heresy, 3, 50, 133,
    165, 202
Qing preservation of Ming laws, 105
law in Japan. *See also* Commissioner
        for Temples and Shrines,
        Ordinances Regarding the
        Various Sects and Temples
    expansion of codes in Nara period,
        58
    law of sovereign and law of the
        Buddha 王法仏法, 58
    legal authority of Jesuits in
        Nagasaki, 79
    legal foundations of early
        Buddhism, 57
    legal status of Meiji Emperor, 157
    Meiji legal reforms, 159
    Nara regulation of Buddhism, 58
    postwar Japan. *See also* Religious
        Organizations Law, Religious
        Persons Law
    regulation of Buddhism in postwar
        Japan, 222
    separation of church and state, 218,
        222
    separation of Sect and Shrine
        Shintō, 160
    separation of Shintō and Buddhism
        神仏分離, 156
    status of new religions during Meiji,
        190
    Tokugawa expansion of codes, 106
    Tokugawa regulation of Buddhism,
        106–8, 111
Lee Kwan Yew, 227
Lenin, V. I., 195
Life of an Amorous Woman 好色一代
    女, 110
Lighdan Khagan, 100–1, 104

Lisbon, 76, 80, 86
Lotus Sutra, 33, 61, 64
Loyola, Ignatius of, 74–6
Lu Xun 鲁迅, 170–3, 179, 201

Macao, 73, 80, 82, 87, 89
  nao trade from, 78, 79
MacArthur, Douglas, 216, 217, 219
Mahākāla, 100, 101
Mahathir bin Mohamad, 227
Mahāyāna, 32–3
  contingent truth, 61, 112, 135
  salvation, 132
  scriptures, 182, *See also Lotus Sutra*
Maitreya Buddha
  in Buddhist eschatology, 132
  in Chinese eschatology, 132, 135
  incarnations of, 34, 138, 204
  White Lotus Society of, 50, 133
Makiguchi Tsunesaburō 牧口常三郎, 219
Malabar Rites, 91
Malacca, 73, 76, 77
Malaya, 76
Malaysia, 226, 227
Manchukuo 滿洲國, 186, 191
Manchuria, 53
  Christian missionaries in, 144
  Japan in, 175, 183, 185–7, 192
  Japanese religion in, 187–90
  Koreans in, 191
  in Republic, 209
Mandate of Heaven 天命, 18, 131, 139
Manjušri, 102
Mao Zedong 毛澤東
  compared with Zhu Yuanzhang, 50
  conflict with Chinese Communists, 200, 201–2
  conflict with Soviet Union, 195–6, 200
  death, 215
  early life, 200
  and founding of People's Republic of China, 194
  as a millenarian figure, 128, 200

  and rural revolution, 200–1
  praise for Lu Xun, 170
  views on religion, 200–2
Marx, Karl, 123, 201
Marxism, 128
  core ideas, 196–7
  in China, 195, 200, 202, 205, 208
  influence on Chinese Christianity, 212
  opposition to religion, 197–8, 208
Matrix, The, 229
May Fourth Movement 五四運動, 169, 173, 174
Meiji 明治 Emperor, 163
  enthronement of, 154
  ritual observance by, 155, 158
  veneration of, 157
Mencius (Meng Ke 孟軻), 21, 22, 25
Merton, Thomas, 227
millenarianism, 126, 132
  political, 128
Miller, William, 123, 124
Millerites, 125, 130, 139, 221
Ming 明 dynasty
  administration, 43
  Buddhism in, 95–7, 105, 165
  charities in, 144
  compared with Qing, 105
  compared with Tokugawa, 72, 106, 107
  corruption in, 95
  diplomacy with Central Asia, 97
  enshrinement of Confucian orthodoxy, 43, 92, 94
  fall of, 89, 100
  founding, 37, 40, 52, 72
  heresy in, 50, 133
  institutions under Qing, 101
  Jesuits in, 83
  non-Han subjects, 53
  relations with Europe, 73
  significance of name, 37, 40
missionaries, Buddhist, 56, 180–1, 189
missionaries, Catholic. *See also* Dominicans, Franciscans,

Jesuits, Missions Étrangères de
  Paris
  arrival in Asia, 4, 72, 74
  arrival in China, 80
  arrival in Japan, 77
  charities, 145
  expulsion from China, 93
  expulsion from Japan, 89
  in Japanese Empire, 185
  in nineteenth-century China, 143
  in People's Republic of China, 211
  organization of, 144
  preference for baptism, 144
  schools, 144, 192
missionaries, Christian
  attitudes toward local culture, 76,
    78, 80, 90–1, 145, 192
  Buddhism and, 77, 90, 94
  charities, 144, 181
  church construction, 146
  commerce and, 74, 78, 225
  diplomacy and, 147
  during Boxer Uprising, 149
  images of Asian religion, 11, 17
  imperialism and, 211
  in nineteenth-century China, 143,
    144
  in People's Republic of China, 211,
    212
  in postwar Japan, 219
  relations between Catholic and
    Protestant missions, 144
  schools, 144, 168
  suspicion of, 145
  views of Taiping, 141
missionaries, Protestant
  control of Chinese church, 211
  in Japanese Empire, 191
  in nineteenth-century China, 143–5
  in People's Republic of China, 213
Missions Étrangères de Paris, 143,
  192
Mito 水戸, 155, 156
modernity
  compatability with Christianity,
    145, 173, 211
  compatability with Confucianism,
    169, 172, 178, 215
  idea of in Chinese Republic, 168
  idea of in Meiji reforms, 159
  as an obstacle to understanding
    religious belief, 124
  as understood by historians, 36
Mongols
  attempted invasion of Japan, 65
  Buddhism and Buddhist kingship,
    51, 99, 100, 104
  Chakhar, 100
  conquests of, 98, 121
  ethnicity, 98
  Khalkha, 100
  Mongol dynasty. See Yuan
  pre-Buddhist religion, 98
  unification and fragmentation, 98,
    100
Motoori Norinaga 本居宣長, 152–3
mourning, 44–6
Mozi 墨子, 22
Müller, Max, 182
Mussolini, Benito, 36, 176–8

Nagasaki 長崎, 89
  Catholic Church in nineteenth
    century, 185
  Jesuits in, 78–9, 86, 87
  nuclear destruction of, 205, 219
Nanjing 南京, 37, 38, 51, 175
  Nanjing Massacre, 215
  under Taiping rule, 139–41
Nara 奈良
  Buddhism in, 58, 59, 111, 156
  kingdom, 58
  schools of Nara Buddhism, 59, 61,
    115
  Shintō worship, 54
national learning 国学, 152
nembutsu 念仏/nian fo 念佛, 64, 154, 185
Netherlands. See Dutch
Netherlands East India Company,
  73
New Life Movement 新生活運動,
  178–9

Nichiren 日蓮, 219
  mission to Asian continent, 181,
    190
  Nichiren Buddhism, 220. *See also*
    Sōka Gakkai 63–4, 114,
    219
Nihongi 日本紀, 59
nirvāna, 32, 33
nuclear war, fears of, 127, 205
Nurgaci, 100

Oda Nobunaga 織田信長, 67–71,
    84–6, 106, 120
  tea ceremony, 122
Ogurusu Kōchō 小栗栖香頂, 181
Okinawa 沖縄, 183, 215
Ōmura Sumitada 大村純忠,
    78–9, 86
opium, 141, 142
Opium Wars, 142, 143, 154
oracle bone writing 甲骨文, 16
Ordinances Regarding the Various
    Sects and Temples 諸宗寺院法
    度, 107
Osaka 大阪, 70, 151
Ōtomo Sōrin 大友宗麟, 80, 84

padroado, 74, 76, 86
Paekche 百濟, 56, 57, 112
Panchen Lama, 210
People's Liberation Army, 209
People's Republic of China, 52
  Christianity in, 211–13
  conflict with Dalai Lama, 209–10
  Confucianism in, 214–15
  early years, 205, 208, 211
  founding, 194
  political purges, 203, 205
  religious tolerance in, 202
  suppression of Falungong, 213–14
Peter the Great, 163, 176
Philippines
  Catholic Church in, 87, 192, 197
  political change in, 214
  Spanish colonization, 73

Placard of People's Instructions 教民榜
    文, 48
Plane compertum, 192
Portugal. *See also* Union of the
    Crowns
  early expansion into Asia, 73
  expulsion from Japan, 89
  missionaries, 1, 74–7, 90
  nao trade, 78–9
Precious Scripture of the Five Sages 五聖
    寶卷, 28
Prime Shinto 唯一神道, 112
Promulgation Campaign, Great 大教
    宣布運動, 159–60, 180
Protestants. *See* Christianity,
    missionaries
  Chinese Protestant Patriotic
    Association 中國基督教愛國
    會, 212
Pu Yi 溥儀, 164, 176
Pure Land 淨土, 33, 120, 185
  Pure Land Buddhism, 63–4, 109,
    114, 122

Qianlong 乾隆 Emperor, 93, 101,
    104, 142, 143
Qin 秦 dynasty, 22, 80
Qin, Former 前秦, 56
Qin Shi Huang 秦始皇, 3, 16, 22, 23,
    29
Qing 清 dynasty
  administration, 109, 143
  as an alien regime, 138, 148
  Boxer Uprising and, 148
  Buddhism in, 101–5, 165, 191
  charities in, 144
  Dalai Lama and, 104
  decline of, 1, 139, 141, 142, 143,
    165, 181, 183
  fall of, 168, 194, 209
  founding, 89, 100
  Jesuits in, 81–2, 84
  lamaism and, 52, 102
  missionaries in, 143
  non-Han subjects, 101–5, 209

policy toward heresy, 50
rebellions against, 136–41
Western powers and, 142, 143
queue, 145

Radiant King 明王, 39, 40
rain, prayer for 求雨, 146
recitation. *See nembutsu/nian fo*
Red Turbans 紅巾, 38–40, 50, 51, 131
Reformation, Protestant, 1, 8, 9, 65,
    74
religion
    Asian terms for, 4, 159
    definition of, 4, 160, 182, 202
Religious Organizations Law 宗教団
    体法, 218
Religious Persons Law 宗教法人法,
    218
Report on an Investigation of the
    Peasant Movement in Hunan,
    201
Republic of China
    administration of Tibet, 209
    Christianity in, 211
    ethnic nationalism in, 209
    founding, 164
    liberal democracy, 173
    political disorganization, 168
Rescript on Education 教育勅語, 157
Revelation, Book of, 124, 126, 135
revere the *kami* and destroy the
    Buddha 敬神廃仏, 155
Ricci, Matteo, 82–4, 90, 93
Rinzai Zen 臨済禅, 119, 190
Ritual, Ministry of 禮部, 51
Roman Empire, 1, 12, 224
ru 儒, 18, 19, 22, 23
Russia
    Aum Shinrikyō in, 221
    Japanese images of, 184
    as model for Qing reforms, 163
    populist movements in, 166
    religious purges in, 198
Russian Orthodox Church, 198–200
Russo-Japanese War, 170, 183–6, 187

sakoku 鎖国, 89
Śākyamuni, 31, 84, 132, 135, 228
samurai
    anti-Buddhist activism, 155, 156
    Buddhist beliefs. 184. *See also*
        samurai, Zen and
    compared with Confucian elite, 4,
        106
    conversion to Christianity, 78
    economic conditions, 151
    in film, 230
    loss of rank, 155
    in popular culture, 2
    privileges under Tokugawa, 71
    role in Meiji Restoration, 154
    Zen and, 114, 120–1, 122
sangha, 95, 182
Satsuma 薩摩, 77, 154
SCAP (Supreme Command of Allies
    in the Pacific), 216–19
Schall von Bell, Johann Adam, 81, 89
secret dharma transmission 秘事法
    門, 111
Sen no Rikyū 千利休, 122
Sendai 仙台, 170
separation of Shintō and Buddhism
    神仏分離, 156
Shaku Sōen 釈宗演, 181, 182
Shang 商 kingdom, 15–18, 29
Shangdi 上帝, 17, 90, 91
Shanghai 上海, 175
    Buddhism in, 101
    foreign concessions, 143, 162,
        211
    Japanese missionaries in, 181
Shenyang 瀋陽. *See Fengtian*
Shimabara 島原 rebellion, 89
Shimazu 島津, 80, 84
Shingon 真言, 61–3, 65, 71, 77, 109,
    113, 114, 122
Shinran 親鸞, 64
Shintō 神道
    ancient, 54–5
    Buddhism and. *See also*
        honji suijaku

Shintō *(cont.)*
  Christianity and, 79, 192
  consolidation of shrines, 160
  emperor and, 60, 155, 190
  Heian period, 61
  and Japanese empire, 185–90, 191
  as Japanese spirit, 152, 160
  in Meiji government, 156, 160
  in Meiji period, 155–60
  names for, 54
  as national religion, 158–60, 179
  nativism and, 153, 155
  as nonreligion, 160, 182, 202
  reform of in postwar Japan, xi, 222
  ritual, 54, 158
    funerals, 108, 109, 111
  Sect Shintō 宗派神道, 158, 160
  Shrine Shintō 神社神道, 160
  and Soka Gakkai, 219
  State Shintō 国家神道, 160, 173,
    180, 218
Shintō and Buddhism
  Heian, 61
  Meiji, 155, 156, 159, 180, 181
  Nara, 59
  through Tokugawa, 8, 95, 112–13
Shintō Divinity, Department of 神祇
    官, 156
Shōmu 聖武 Emperor, 58, 60
Shōtoku 聖徳 Prince, 57, 60
Shunzhi 順治 Emperor, 81
Sichuan 四川, 132, 141, 169
Siddhārtha Gautama. *See also*
    Śākyamuni 30–1
Silk Road, 11, 34, 53, 80, 97, 225
Silla 新羅, 56
Singapore, 27
  Confucianism in, 227
Smash the Four Olds 破四舊, 214
social gospel, 212
Soga 蘇我, 57
sōhei 僧兵, 65
Sōka Gakkai 創価学会, 219–20, 221
Song 宋 dynasty, 23, 35, 39, 40
Song 宋 kingdom, 40
Sŏngmyŏng 聖明 King, 57

Songnam Gyamtso, 100
Sosurim 小獸林 King, 56
Sōtō Zen 曹洞禅, 107, 116, 118, 119,
    183, 190
Southeast Asia, 53, 54
  Buddhism in, 30, 33
  Chinese in, 215, 225
  Islam in, 226
  Way of Penetrating Unity, 204
Soviet Union. *See also* Cold War, 127
  and Communist revolution
    worldwide, 195, 216
  Chiang Kai-shek and, 173
  dissolution of, 215
  religion in, 198–200
  religious policy compared with
    China, 203, 208, 211
Spain. *See also* Union of the Crowns
  in Americas, 224
  colonization of Philippines, 73
  early trade with China, 73
  expulsion from Japan, 89
  loss of Taiwan, 74
  missionaries, 1, 73, 86, 87, 90
  Spanish Inquisition, 7
spirit writing, 50, 165, 204, 205
Stalin, Joseph, 195, 196, 198
Suiko 推古 Empress, 57, 112
Sun Yat-sen 孫逸仙, 164
Sunzi 孫子, 2, 19
Suzuki, D. T. 鈴木大拙, 183, 226, 227

taiji 太极, 25, 26, 28, 84
Taiping Heavenly Kingdom 太平天國,
    139–41
  foreign impressions of, 141
  legacy and memory, 166, 213
  suppression of, 141
Taiwan 臺灣, 20
  Confucianism in, 47, 227
  Dutch capture of, 74
  flight of Chiang Kai-shek, 179
  Japanese Buddhists in, 190
  Japanese occupation, 183
  as repository of Chinese culture,
    215

Spanish missionaries in, 73
Way of Penetrating Unity, 204
Tang 唐 dynasty, 7, 61, 65, 80
tantra, 63
taxation, 23, 162
　religious exemption from, 7, 34,
　　65, 95
Taylor, James Hudson, 145, 211
tea ceremony 茶道, 25, 54, 119, 122,
　142
　Toyotomi Hideyoshi and, 122
Teaching of the Divine Principle 天理
　教, 190
Teaching of the Great Source 大本教,
　190
Ten Ox Herding Pictures, 116
Tendai 天台, 61–6, 68, 106, 113, 114,
　119, 122
Tenzin Gyatso. See Dalai Lama
terauke 寺請, 108, 109, 111
Theravāda, 32–3
Thich Nhat Hanh, 227
Three Teachings, 15, 36
　in White Lotus eschatology, 135
Three-Self churches
　as missionary ideal, 145
　in People's Republic of China,
　　212
Three-Self Declaration 三自宣告, 212
Tian'anmen Massacre, 215
Tianjin 天津, 143, 205
　Boxer Uprising in, 148, 150
　Buddhism in, 133
　Christian mission in, 145, 146
　Empress of Heaven Temple 天后宮,
　　173–5
　Taiping advance on, 141
Tianjin, Treaty of, 144
Tianjing 天京, 141
Tiantai. See Tendai
Tibet, 53, 102
　1959 uprising, 210
　Buddhism in, 30
　Japanese views of, 181
　relations with China, twentieth
　　century, 209, 210

relations with Ming, 51, 52
relations with Qing, 104, 209
time, religious conceptions of, 124,
　126, 132
Toda Jōsei 戸田城聖, 219
Tōdaiji 東大寺, 58–61, 63
Tokugawa Ieyasu 徳川家康, 70, 88,
　89, 106, 109
Tokugawa Tsunayoshi 徳川綱吉,
　110
Tokugawa 徳川 shogunate, 8, 70, 72
　Buddhism under, 71, 105–13
　compared with Ming, 72
Tokyo 東京. See also Edo, Yasukuni
　shrine
　1960 Olympics, 219
　Aum Shinrikyō in, 220–1
　war trials, 217
Tordesillas, Treaty of, 74
Toyotomi Hideyoshi 豊臣秀吉, 88
　Buddhism and, 70–1, 86, 106
　Christianity and, 80, 84–8
　tea ceremony, 122
treaty ports, 162
True Meaning of the Lord of Heaven 天
　主實義, 83
True Pure Land Buddhism 浄土真宗,
　106, 114. See also ikkō
　mission to Asian continent, 181,
　　190
　rejection of clerical authority, 66,
　　69, 111
Truman, Harry, 179, 219
Tu Wei-ming, 215
Twenty Four Filial Examples 二十四孝,
　47, 49

Ultimate Book of Cause and Effect 太上
　感應篇, 32
Union of the Crowns, 86, 90
United States, 123
　Chinese in, 215
　missionaries, 145, 211
　occupation of Japan, 216. See also
　　SCAP
　opening of Japan, 154

United States *(cont.)*
    universities, 144
unity of ritual and government
    祭政一致, 155
universities
    Beijing University, 167, 168, 200
    International Christian University,
        219
    Tokyo Imperial University, 182

Valignano, Alessandro, 80, 87, 89
Vatican. *See also* Catholic Church
    74
    opposition to communism, 212
    relations with Japanese Empire, 91,
        192
    relations with People's Republic of
        China, 212
    role in coordinating Catholic
        mission, 74, 144
    Second Vatican Council, 91
    stance on Confucian veneration,
        91–2, 192
Verbiest, Ferdinand, 81
Vietnam, 3
Vilela, Gaspar, 78
vinaya, 107

Wang Lun 王倫, 136
Wanli 萬曆 Emperor, 83
Way of Great Peace 太平道, 39, 132
Way of Penetrating Unity 一貫道,
    204–5
White Lotus Teaching 白蓮教, 133–5
Wine Drinking Ceremony 飲酒禮,
    46, 49
World Parliament of Religions, 182
World War I, 1, 127
Wu Yaozong 吳耀宗, 211–12
Wu Zetian 武則天, 34
Wuzong 武宗 Emperor, 65

Xavier, Francis, 74–8, 80
Xinjiang 新疆, 209
Xunzi 荀子, 22

Yamato 大和, 55
Yasukuni 靖国 shrine, 185, 222
Yasutani Haku'un 安谷白雲, 190,
    219
Yellow Turbans 黃巾, 38
yin-yang 陰陽, 25–9, 84
Yongzheng 雍正 Emperor, 93, 101,
    143
Yoshida Kanetomo 吉田兼俱,
    112
Young Men's Buddhist Association,
    181
Yuan Shikai 袁世凱, 149, 168
Yuan 元 dynasty, 98
    Buddhist kingship in, 99–101
    Confucianism in, 23, 35, 47
    decline, 38
    fall of, 37, 40, 131
    as khanate, 98
    lamaism in, 51
    legacy of, 97, 100
    non-Han subjects, 101
    religion in, 99
    rule of non-Han subjects, 98
    vilification of, 47
Yuanming Palace 圓明園, 81, 150

zazen 座禅, 119, 120
Zen 禅. *See also* Rinzai Zen, Sōtō
    Zen
    as essence of Japan, 122,
        183
    as essence of religion, 183
    and Japanese arts, 121
    monastic organization, 81
    origins, 63, 64, 114
    in popular cuture, 113
    samurai and, 120–1, 122
    in West, 227, 228
*Zen and the Art of Motorcycle
    Maintenance*, 113
Zhang Guangbi 張光璧, 204
Zhenyan. *See* Shingon
Zhou Enlai 周恩來, 215
Zhou 周 kingdom, 17–19, 141

Zhu Yuanzhang 朱元璋, 37–52, 106,
    131, 133, 166, 178
  anti-Mongol rhetoric, 40, 47, 51
  Buddhism and, 38, 51, 94
  Confucianism and, 40, 41, 43, 46
  lamaism and, 51
  long-term influence of, 52
  military career, 38
  mistrust of scholarly class, 50
  policies of, 41–52
  proper name of, 37
  Red Turbans and, 38–40
  supernatural protection of, 37
Zongle 宗泐, 51